A CHAMPION

JOHN CLARE

A Champion for the Poor
Political Verse and Prose

EDITED BY

P.M.S. Dawson, Eric Robinson and David Powell

Mid Northumberland Arts Group

Carcanet Press

2000

This edition first published in 2000 by
Mid Northumberland Arts Group
Woodhorn Colliery Museum
Ashington
Northumberland NE63 9YS

in association with

Carcanet Press Limited
4th Floor, Conavon Court
12–16 Blackfriars Street
Manchester M3 5BQ

A CIP catalogue record for this book
is available from the British Library
ISBN 0 904790 91 6 (MidNAG)
ISBN 1 85754 423 4 (Carcanet)

The publishers acknowledge financial assistance
from the Arts Council of England and Northern Arts

Set in 10pt Palatino by XL Publishing Services, Tiverton
Printed and bound in England by SRP Ltd, Exeter

Contents

POEMS
Titles in square brackets are provided by the editors

PROSE

Acknowledgements

We would like to thank our publishers for their patience in waiting for this book. We also wish to thank the staffs of Peterborough Museum and Art Gallery, Northampton Central Library, Peterborough Central Library (particularly Mr Sayed Ashraf), the British Library, Cambridge University Library, the Bodleian Library, and the Pforzheimer and Berg Collections at the New York City Library. We are grateful to the scholars who have helped us, particularly Dr Robert Heyes, Dr James McKusick, Professor Anne Barton, Professor Christopher Ricks and Dr John Goodridge. Dr Stephen Colclough kindly provided a copy of his unpublished Ph. D. thesis, and Dr McKusick and Dr Alan Vardy supplied copies of their forthcoming articles. As always, the officers of the John Clare Society have been supportive and we urge those who are interested to join the Society. (The Secretary is Peter Moyse, 1A West Street, Helpston, Peterborough PE6 7DU.) Admirers of John Clare in North America should address enquiries for membership of the John Clare Society of North America to Dr James McKusick, English Dept., 1000 Hilltop Circle, University of Maryland, Baltimore, Maryland 21043 (tel. 410–455–2164; fax 410–455–1030).

Paul Dawson wishes to acknowledge assistance from the Department of English and American Studies and the Faculty of Arts of the University of Manchester.

Eric Robinson especially feels grateful to Noël Staples for his computer-assistance and wishes to thank both him and his wife, Lynn, for their hospitality. He wishes to thank Dr V. Gatrell for generous help with his research on the illustrations for this book. He thanks the National Endowment for the Humanities for its award to him of a Fellowship to assist his work. Daphne Faux has always rallied round when asked for help and so has Dr James McKusick. The Master and Fellows of Jesus College, Cambridge, have extended to him their usual generous hospitality and the Rev. Canon Jack Higham of Peterborough Cathedral has helped, in several ways, to shelter him from the 'pelting storm'. Above all, Eric wishes to thank his wife, Victoria.

Introduction

by Eric Robinson

I never meddle with politics in fact you would laugh at my idea of that branch of art for I consider it nothing more or less then a game at hide & seek for self interest & the terms wig & tory are nothing more in my mind then the left & right hand of that monster the only difference being that the latter lyes nearer the windfalls of wills for self interest then the other – that there are some & many who have the good of the people at heart is not to be doubted but with the others who have only the good of themselves in view when balloted I fear that they will always be as the few

(Pet. MS A46, p. R43, cancelled)

Selecting from over two thousand poems and several hundreds of passages of prose and letters for an anthology of Clare's political writings has been difficult, even contentious, not least because the poet is best known for his nature-poems, his love-poems and perhaps, to a much lesser extent, his satirical writings.[1] Yet it is important that we should do so, if we are to make it clear that Clare was a much more diverse poet in his subject-matter than is generally allowed. Of course, some of his poems on enclosure, such as 'The Mores' (see below, pp. 46–8) or on the loss of trees (see 'The Fallen Elm', below pp. 188–90) have become more widely appreciated because of the environmentalist movement and its impact on political life as well as on modern literary criticism, but Clare is still thought of differently from other great poets of his period – Coleridge, Wordsworth, Shelley and Byron – as though he were a non-political creature living in a social vacuum, uncaring about the great changes occurring in England during the first half of the nineteenth century. He did not, of course, like Coleridge, occupy himself with the great philosophical problems of his time; nor did he, like Wordsworth, compose vast spiritual autobiographies in verse explaining his experience of the French Revolution and of the reaction that followed it, though he did try his hand at political pamphleteering; nor, like Byron, become the darling of the Greeks and a member of Parliament commenting on the Luddite Riots. After all, would we expect such intellectual adventures from an agricultural labourer who spent much of his time round the market-cross or in the fields or in the local pub? And it is true that Tom Paine, or Napoleon, or the Slave Trade or the Bourbons, though he mentions all except the last, do not seem to have been major concerns in his life, and his native village, Helpston, never was the hub of the universe. We must, however, as always, be careful not to condescend to Clare, regarding him as a semi-literate whopstraw unaffected by the great issues of his time – even perhaps dead to them.

Clare himself thought that 'The Parish' (see below pp. 49–112), a political satire, was the best poem he had ever written, though it was never published in his lifetime and has had to wait until the late twentieth century for its first complete publication. Yet it is a political poem of some 2,200 lines and entirely occupied with the political life of Clare's region. It is not, however, for that reason, of limited parochial significance. Agriculture employed more people in Clare's day than any other industry and hundreds of provincial newspapers all over England printed column upon column of political discussion about agricultural matters. Cobbett was the prototypical English countryman as well as being the most widely read journalist of his age. When he attended a political meeting, the hall was jam-packed – and largely because he spoke of agriculture and his concerns for the people employed in it. Cobbett's words reached the ears of every agricultural worker – including those of John Clare. The issues of the Corn Laws and of agricultural unrest were discussed throughout the nation – in parliament, on the hustings, in pubs, in ballads and chapbooks, in vaudeville shows and in newspapers. Clare was an avid reader of newspapers and popular literature and, as a poor man, naturally much concerned about the price of bread on which his own family life as well as the Speenhamland System was based. Besides the problems of the labourer, he also knew the difficulties of the small farmer once the inflated demand for feeding the armed forces had subsided at the end of the Napoleonic wars. As the cost of the family loaf grew, his patrons, the Fitzwilliams, unlike many landowners, were strong protagonists for the repeal of the Corn Laws, but they encountered much opposition on that score in the East Midlands from other landowners. Clare was familiar with their views.

Industrialization was transforming much of England. Population was growing rapidly and much of that increase was absorbed in the textile industries and in light engineering. Such urban and semi-rural workers were more specialized than in the past and had to buy their food instead of growing it themselves. Even among agricultural workers, particularly after enclosure, many cottagers were unable to raise much in the way of food on their own garden-plots. They too had to wonder whether they might not be better off if England imported more of its basic food-stuffs. Yet, at the same time, they had to be cautious not to reduce the demand for their own labour. The Swing Riots were only the peak of an agricultural unrest that lasted for at least forty years. Food riots and other rural disturbances were common throughout the first half of the nineteenth century. Clare wrote early in his career about rural poverty and the conflicts between master and man (see 'Lobin Clouts Satirical Sollilouquy on the Times', pp. 15–16), highlighting what he saw as the greater rift that was developing between capital and labour.

Raymond Williams distinguishes between *political* and *social* criticism made by the Romantics in what he calls 'those first apprehensions of the essential significance of the Industrial Revolution'[2] but is such a distinction realistic? The Romantic poet saw himself as opposed to all that was mechanical rather than organic in society and recognized an opposition between the Market and himself. As Williams says, the Romantic as poet sees in his art an

embodiment . . . of certain human values, capacities, energies, which the development of society towards an industrial civilization was felt to be threatening or even destroying. The element of professional protest is undoubtedly there, but the larger issue is the opposition on general human grounds to the kind of civilization that was being inaugurated.[3]

Clare, like other Romantic poets, stresses the organic nature of a society that he sees as passing; he too mourns the loss of community values – the sociability between master and man, the unifying strengths of old feasts and customs, the consolidation of society arising from shared values and mutual obligations. It is therefore natural that he should draw a biological parallel when speaking of men and kingdoms.[4]

Clare would have agreed with Wordsworth that the Poet

> is a rock of defence for human nature; an upholder and preserver, carrying everywhere with him relationship and love. In spite of difference of soil and climate, of language and manners, of laws and customs: in spite of things silently gone out of mind, and things violently destroyed: the Poet binds together by passion and knowledge the vast empire of human society, as it is spread over the whole earth, and over all time.[5]

But Clare does not, to the same extent as Wordsworth, theorize about it. He embodies it in his poetry. He generalizes less and is more specific. He starts with the local and expands outwards or leaves the reader to do the generalizing for himself. But Wordsworth and Clare are both speaking of matters that can properly be called 'political' though they are also 'social' and 'cultural'.

At one point in his career, difficult to date, but possibly in the late 1820s or early 1830s, we find Clare apparently quoting from memory from David Hume's *Enquiry concerning the Principles of Morals* (1777)[6], a book which is not among Clare's collection of books at Northampton Library, but which he might have borrowed from his Scots friend Joseph Henderson, the head gardener at Milton, with whom Clare stayed for days at a time. There are several ideas expressed in Hume that would have appealed to Clare and that would have prompted him to take an interest in political matters. Hume found the source of moral sentiment in usefulness, but not always usefulness 'considered with a reference to self', and if this was so:

> it follows, that everything which contributes to the happiness of society, recommends itself directly to our approbation and

good-will. Here is a principle which accounts, in great part, for the origin of morality ...[7]

Moreover:

> if any man from a cold insensibility, or narrow selfishness of temper, is unaffected with the images of human happiness or misery, he must be equally indifferent to the images of vice and virtue: As, on the other hand, it is always found, that a warm concern for the interests of our species is attended with a delicate feeling of all moral distinctions; a strong resentment of injury done to men; a lively approbation of their welfare.[8]

Hume also stresses the importance of doing good within one's own community, a sentiment that would have appealed to Clare:

> while every man consults the good of his own community, we are sensible, that the general interest of mankind is better promoted, than by any loose indeterminate views to the good of a species, whence no beneficial action could ever result, for want of a duly limited object ...[9]

This last statement occurs just before the page from which Clare takes the quotation mentioned above. Hume's point about the importance of serving one's immediate community is reinforced by the conclusion:

> Thus a small benefit done to ourselves, or our near friends, excites more lively sentiments of love and approbation than a great benefit done to a distant commonwealth.[10]

Hume also stresses the kind of character which a man should develop and it is one to which Clare would have subscribed:

> The best character, indeed, were it not rather too perfect for human nature, is that which is not swayed by temper of any kind, but alternately employs enterprise and caution, as each is *useful* to the particular purpose intended.[11]

Finally, Hume brings to his philosophy a strong sense of the relevance of poetry and, in particular, of pastoral poetry:

It is the business of poetry to bring every affection near to us by lively imagery and representation, and make it look like truth and reality: A certain proof, that, wherever that reality is found, our minds are disposed to be strongly affected by it.[12]

Few species of poetry are more entertaining than *pastoral;* and every one is sensible, that the chief source of its pleasure arises from those images of a gentle and tender tranquillity, which it represents in its personages, and of which it communicates a like sentiment to the reader. Sannazarius, who transferred the scene to the sea-shore, though he presented the most magnificent object in nature, is confessed to have erred in his choice. The idea of toil, labour, and danger suffered by the fishermen, is painful; by an unavoidable sympathy, which attends every conception of human happiness or misery.[13]

If Hume did not provide a programme for Clare's poetry, it must be admitted that he would have strongly appealed to the poet, for his philosophy is akin to that of the Romantics whose political poetry contains a strong social element.

For this reason some of the poems printed in this book may not at first sight appear to be political – they may be about a lost greyhound, a felled tree, or an old halfpenny, they may be about obstructions to Clare's wanderings in the fens, they may concern the social pretension and posturing of small farmers or the farmer's daughter's loss of housekeeping skills, or may be a protest against rigid sabbatarianism, rather than about extending the franchise or reducing political censorship, but they are none-the-less political in the way in which the nineteenth-century rural population viewed politics, and the agricultural labourer recognized the necessity for protest against the loss of traditional privileges and customs. Clare will be found objecting to national taxes on malt and beer, to national fasts in wartime, and to national financial corruption in high places, but essentially he presents the same outlook through all his work – the local reactions of a poor man in Helpston to the rigours and the joys of his experience. His politics are local, or at most regional, rather than national; conservative rather than radical; monarchical rather than revolutionary and republican. Enclosures are therefore a problem he has experienced at first hand in his neighbourhood, as he has the Game Laws. He is less concerned with the tithe as a general economic problem, than with his parson's transformation into a hunting, shooting, carriage-riding member of the gentry as a consequence of the commutation of the tithe.

There is for Clare, as there was for most members of the rural working-class, no hard and fast division between religion and politics. If the Speenhamland system involved subsidizing the farmer's wage-bill out of the poor rates, it was both inefficient and immoral. Traditionally the Church preached a doctrine of social responsibility, of charity towards the poor and sick, of not muzzling 'the ox that treadeth out the corn' and of not allowing funds destined for the poor to be redirected into the pockets of those who controlled the distribution of that money. The Speenhamland system, however, went against the spirit of all these principles. If the parish church became the scene of trespasses on the rights of the poor, the parson was simply not doing his job. The clergy should be servants of Christ not of Mammon. What Clare, like many another member of the 'respectable' poor, wanted was stability and for that stability he looked to Church and King. In society, as in the home, there was a place for everything (and everyone), and everything in its place. For that reason he objects to the parish bell-ringers pealing out their support for Queen Caroline or the farmers swaggering about in the coats of soldiers. He had no quarrel with the great, only with the avaricious and the pretentious.

Clare's opinions about religion and politics were, moreover, closely interwoven. Among the essays he projected and partly wrote was one on 'Political Religion' (see below, pp. 281–2):

> When religion is made to espouse politics for the advancement or support of power the excuse is never worthy of commendation for on one side it commends oppression & on the other encourages contention where the basest actions are always supported by the creeds of each party as justifiable & tho both profess kindness to all men yet they act with the bitterest enmity

towards each other & tho the weaker party in the case may be said to have triumphed as the race is not always to the swift nor the battle to the strong yet when in power they displayed more insolence & oppression then those of whom they so bitterly & loudly complained & so it is always that the remedy is worse then the disease & thus it ever is that a government tho imperfect is better then a new one forced upon its ruins – for force is the foundation of power & as the structure rises the weight & oppression increases so that at last it becomes like other new structures raised too high for its strength & too hastily for durability that it at last shrinks beneath its weight & becomes a heap of rubbish when the old building is seen again towering above its ruins with all its old imperfections about it & less inclination to correct them for having another authority added for severity & oppression it takes that for sanction which ought to have been an example to mend & thus becomes more oppressive & more powerful for oppression[14]

This account of cyclical fluctuation introduced into religion by a struggle for political power may reflect Clare's opinion not only of his own period but also of earlier times, particularly the seventeenth century.

Thus Clare's sympathies seem generally to have been with Charles I and against Cromwell. At least this appears to be so in his account, in *The Village Minstrel*, of the Parliamentarians' murder of the King's chaplain, Dr Michael Hudson, at Woodcroft Hall, a story which had clearly captured his imagination.[15] As James McKusick has pointed out, the Royalists are associated in Clare's poem with right-handedness and therefore with truth and honesty, while the opposing force is characterized by brutality and dishonesty.[16] Religious principles are sacrificed by the Parliamentarians in the interests of power, but, says Clare,

The religion of power is never the religion of common sense texts are perverted to purposes for which they were never intended & the odd combinations are so easily discovered that instead of forcing conviction they excite ridicule[17]

Yet the excesses of the Parliamentary party were also brought on by Charles I. Of him, Clare wrote:

> The royal martyr as he was called however he might extol himself or be extolled as a christain by others never forgot he was a king which was nothing at all to do with the merits of christianity . . .[18]

In turn, the Parliamentarians, who objected to 'his oppressive taxation', rejoiced when he was made a captive.[19] Neither one nor the other can be justified on religious grounds. That Charles I wrote some good prayers while in captivity was no defence of his absolutism. Neither can Cromwell's actions be justified on religious grounds. Both men were making religion the servant of politics, while Charles II displayed *his* tyranny by removing the bones of Admiral Blake from Westminster Abbey.

In such circumstances, the remedy is worse than the disease. Religion may neither be used to justify oppression nor to support rebellion. Moreover, when moral precepts are forced down the throats of the people in defence of an oppressive government and to persuade the people to patience, 'such precepts of religion turn pretexts of oppression in the eyes of the oppressed & instead of reconciling the subject to his lot make him stubborn for his right'.[20] But these remarks were also applicable to Clare's own lifetime, when religion was brought in to support the government's objectives both in peace and war. The Church called upon the nation to participate in a series of Fasts and Thanksgivings, as the defeats and victories of the Revolutionary and Napoleonic wars seemed, to the government, to demand them, but the sufferings inflicted upon the people by these events were not weighed in the balance.

Nevertheless Clare recognized that 'Religion is not only nessesary for the interests of the individual but useful for the better order & government of the comunity at large'.[21] He is pragmatic enough to acknowledge that the individual's opinion is not likely to prevail where the government judges the interests of the nation to be opposed:

> The government religion of a state or empire is properly speaking a political religion – framed to suit the demands or

nessesitys of governments as well as the conversion of souls
where the church like a standing army seems ready at any time
to maintain her opinions & join her banners with their voices if
not their conscience – self convenience & not honest opinions
weigh most in these matters.[22]

Accordingly he seems to approve of the Church's support for law
and order, the establishment of the Church in England, and the
relationship, in times of war, between Church and government.
We must remember, however, that Clare is not notable for the
consistency of his views and that literary critics in this century
have met with difficulties when they have tried to ascertain what
Clare's views on political and religious matters really were. The
suggestion has been made that one needs to assess what the audi-
ence was for some of his remarks. Would Clare, for example, say
the same thing to Lord Radstock as he might to Harry Stoe Van
Dyk? The problem is a difficult one, and perhaps we should not
ask for greater consistency in Clare's remarks than we can deter-
mine in our own *ad hoc* pronouncements. Take the issue of tithes,
which most Anglican clergymen took to represent a necessary
source of funding for the Church of England's establishment,
though it should be recalled that the tithes sometimes went into
the hands of lay impropriators rather than the parson's. Tithes,
taken in kind, whether by the parson or the lay impropriator, seem
to have aroused most resentment, in an era of rising prices, since
the actual goods represented a higher value than a fixed cash tithe
would have done. The description in 'July', in Clare's *Shepherd's
Calendar*, of the tithemen marking the shocks of hay:

> Sticking their green boughs where they go
> The parsons yearly claims to know
> Which farmers view wi grudging eye
> And grumbling drive their waggons bye
> (lines 15–18)[23]

expresses the farmer's discontent, but does it reflect Clare's
opinion? Was the labourer's view the same as the farmer's? The
lines above are not clear on that point. But elsewhere, Clare is
openly critical: 'Perhaps if manna was to fall from heaven as it did

in the time of Moses & Aaron it would soon have a tyth & tax on it'.[24] When agricultural depression set in after the end of the Napoleonic Wars, and especially in the late eighteen-twenties, the farmers petitioned the landowners for a reduction in rents, and sometimes the parson for a reduction in tithes. Ten years later, in 1830, Joseph Savill, a rope-braider from Bedfordshire, was caught distributing threatening messages from 'Captain Swing'. One read:

> You Clergy, ye Vipers, you love Tithes, Cummin and Mint; ye are men-eaters and not soul-savers, but Blind leaders of the Blind, twice dead, plucked up by the Roots.[25]

(Savill's activities coincided with the arson-attack on James Clark's farm at Deeping Fen which greatly disturbed Clare.[26]) When Anglican clergymen were asked by farmers for a reduction in the tithe, they often replied that it would do the farmers no good, first because the landowners would only increase their rents, and because the farmers' poor-rates would also increase. For example, the account of Joseph Savill, in the *Cambridge Chronicle* for 24 December 1830 (see Appendix), was immediately followed by a piece about Herbert Marsh, Bishop of Peterborough, who was also rector of Terrington St Clements and Terrington St Johns, near [Kings] Lynn, and who had been asked by occupiers of land in those parishes for a reduction of 20% in their tithes. He agreed to a reduction of 10%, but told the occupiers that the landowners would probably put up their rents. Would Clare have been aware of the Bishop of Peterborough's stance on tithes since he was friendly with him and his wife, and if so would it have caused Clare to be cautious in the expression of a critical opinion?

Clare, however, often expressed his view that no man's legal rights to property, including the parson's claims to the tithe, should ever be tinkered with. It was the Mob, in his opinion, that made such unfair claims:

> Common sense would never covet the property that belongs to another
> I could not feel happy with the wealth that I had no right too,

& therefore feel a greater happiness in peace & poverty then I should do in the riches of lawless force & unchecked rebellion –[27]

But he did criticize 'church-taxes' when they were 'forced down the throats of the people to teach them patience only to bear unjust burthens. . . for the sole benefit of luxury & extravagance'[28] and wrote to John Taylor, on 1 February 1830, that though he would 'want not a farthing of that which belongs to another', 'yet I feel as common sense dictates & I think that a universal reduction of tythes – clerical livings – placemens pensions – & taxes – & all renovated & placed upon a reasonable equality suitable to the present decreased value of money & property is the only way to bring salvation to the country'.[29]

In his descriptions of the Bone and Cleaver Club, he is clearly critical of the 'little spruce fellow in a shovel hat' who gives the toast, 'Heres to the destruction of the black locusts that eat up a tenth part of our land'.[30] Clare was no radical, no hater of the clergy, and he was, despite a short flirtation with the Ranters, a loyal member of the Church of England, the church of his father. He would not willingly take the tithe away from the local parson, though he sometimes disapproved of commutations of tithes that led to a huntin', shootin' and fishin' parson replacing a more modest clergyman who lived among his flock in a cottage very similar to those of the villagers.[31]

There is, however, one change in the political, economic and social standing of the Anglican clergyman that caused Clare as much concern as it did the radicals, and that was the increasing number of clergymen on the benches of the local magistracy. The 'black-coated brigade', as they were called, were the subject of almost universal dislike among the working-people who saw them as united in enforcing laws against gambling, drunkenness and Sunday drinking; they refused licences to publicans who took in radical newspapers, denied settlement in their parishes to anyone who might fall on the poor rates, and then, owning more land themselves as the result of compensation for the loss of the tithe, enforced laws of trespass even more rigorously than local landowners and farmers. These clergy now rode to the hunt, joined in local shoots, protected game on their own land and suspected every poor man of being a poacher. They were anathema to William Cobbett, to William Hone, and to John Drakard, as well as to Clare. We may imagine such a person as the Rev. Samuel Hopkinson a fit representative for 'Pride' in 'The Mole Catcher' confronting the poor old man in the fields:

> From whom his turnip thefts he will conseal
> Who as a tyrant wakes his humble fears[32]

The increasing evangelicalism of many clergy made them more enthusiastic in the enforcement of Sabbatarian laws; their growing economic status encouraged them to apply the laws of trespass and the Game Laws more rigorously. Boys and men were set in the stocks and/or fined for playing marbles during Sunday church or for gambling on the results[33]; women were fined for selling fruits and vegetables on Sunday, though it had long been the common practice[34]; innkeepers were in danger of losing their licences if they allowed drinking during Sunday service.[35] The magistrates' bench, sometimes composed of a majority of clerical magistrates or, at least, of attending magistrates, prosecuted villagers for collecting firewood, 'sticking', as it was called (though the 'sticks' sometimes included whole branches of trees), or for harvesting nuts, berries or mushrooms; and, of course, for poaching. These activities, in common with gleaning, were generally regarded by the rural poor, however, as customary rights.[36] The radical newspapers often stressed this common belief in customary rights in their denunciation of 'the black brigade'. Clare's clerical magistrate in 'The Parish', Justice Terror, though he has many virtues in defending and helping the poor, still 'lecture[s] drunkards & drive[s] boys from play'[37] and preserves the stocks for offenders. A living acquaintance of Clare, the Rev. Samuel Hopkinson of Morton, Lincolnshire, 'mistrusted every stranger for thieves or vagabonds' and was constantly on the look-out for poachers.[38] The Rev. James Plumptre, who tried to patronize Clare, searched the wares of passing pedlars for 'offensive' books and ballads, bullied the local innkeeper about Sunday drinking, and complained to the local magistrates about the miller working on Sunday and builders carrying out repair work, since he was not himself a J.P. and could himself not impose legal sanctions.[39]

The magistrates themselves were often under pressure from their middle-class parishioners to be vigilant in their duties to keep down poor-rates, to limit the holding of fairs and to restrict the conditions under which they were held, to prevent football-matches or other sports that might be the occasion of riot, to prosecute drunkenness and prostitution, and, in general, to create an atmosphere of 'respectability'.[40] Pedlars, especially those selling chapbooks; ballad-sellers; players of games of chance for money; fortune-tellers; and beggars (including crippled veterans of the Revolutionary and Napoleonic wars), all came under the magistrates' supervision. 'Helpstone Statute' shows how the local fair often was indeed the occasion for drunkenness and riot, but was also a crucial part of rural sociability[41]; 'Dollys Mistake' describes the seduction of a country-girl on her way home from the fair and *The Village Minstrel* gives an account of a poor sailor and 'civil will', an actual historical local character, both begging at the fair.[42] But where the magistrate saw disorder, Clare saw good fun, a relaxation from hard labour, and an occasion that knitted together the different classes in celebration of ancient custom. He did not favour over-regulation of the poor and, in particular, he lamented the loss of customary celebrations and freedoms.

The crime of trespass was a real threat to Clare's liberties.[43] His encounter with one of Sir John Trollope's gamekeepers is a case in point[44], and 'The Mores' shows that one of his main objections to enclosure was the obstacle presented by fences and trespass notices to persons who had always had the freedom to roam on the common lands of the Fens – 'All sighed when lawless laws enclosure came'.[45] The point is that the 'law' enforced by government is regarded by poor countryfolk as 'lawless'. The same is true of the Game Laws, regarded by many members of the middle class – such as Vicesimus Knox and the Rev. Sidney Smith – as well as working people as essentially unlawful and irrational.[46]

> The game they are a lawless breed
> That keep no bounds to feed upon

> They tresspass upon all to feed
> & are for all as well as one ...

So wrote Clare in his 'Robin Hood & the Gamekeepers' (lines 73–6; see below, p. 126). If deer can commit trespass at will it is illogical for the men who hunt them to be subject to arbitrary laws. E.P. Thompson speaks of the diminution of face-to-face relationships between landowners and people as a result of game-laws and a stronger sense of property.

> The rage for deer parks and the threat of poachers led to the closure of rights-of-way across their [the gentry's] parks and their encirclement with high palings or walls; landscape gardening, with ornamental waters and fishponds, menageries and valuable statuary, accentuated their seclusion and the defence of their grounds, which might be entered only through the high wrought-iron gates, watched over by the lodge.[47]

Clare's local newspapers, *Drakard's Stamford News* and the *Stamford Mercury* are filled with dire warnings to people trespassing on the estates of local landowners, organizing nutting or sticking expeditions, etc., or, of course, poaching. On some occasions, the conflict between gamekeepers and poachers might amount almost to a local war.[48] The stakes were high on both sides. Clare himself is usually careful to say that he was never a poacher, yet on one occasion, in the company of the Billings brothers, he was himself clearly part of a poaching expedition.[49]

Clare was critical of the penalties imposed upon poachers by the Game Laws, the refusal of the courts to recognise the aggressive behaviour of gamekeepers, and the consequences of a criminal record for poaching upon otherwise law-abiding citizens:

> how often do we hear the 'hue & cry'[50] made after its [the Game law's] transgressors as loud & as vehement as if like another flood they had stolen the crown of England[51] tho it comes out at last that shocking thing the horrible deed & so forth was the robbing the plantations of the Honb[e] M[r] [*blank*] of its hares & pheasants & a contest with some game keepers who began the agresion yet the characters of the intruders are eternally sacri-

ficed tho they are honest of all other matters but that of poaching if they wish a reccomendation from a magistrate for years after he searches his black book & hints that 'they have walked the carpet for poaching' tho every thing else speaks in their favour[52]

He contrasts the savage treatment of petty offenders with the indulgence shown towards fraudulent tradesmen who cheat their creditors and retire to live off their spoils. On the one hand, there is:

the poor outcast who robs for hunger [&] is sent to botany bay for stealing an hankerchief from a pocket & is described by the papers as the 'execrable villain [who] was overtaken by justice in the morning of his infamy' but which is the most infamous he who suffers the law or he who escapes it[53]

Of course there were some people who tended to be particularly open to suspicion from the magistrates. The gypsies, in particular, tended to keep to their customary migratory paths for travel and to their customary sites for setting up their tents, no matter how many new 'No Trespassing' signs were posted. A hare, a rabbit, or a pheasant was often popped into their pot and, no doubt, they might help themselves to a few turnips or potatoes to eke out their stew. For their fires they needed wood but they were unlikely to have been among the 'wanton fellows' who took it from the remnants of Langley Bush[54], which, in pre-Norman times, had been the site of an Anglo-Saxon *gemot* and was therefore symbolic of the ancient rights of Englishmen:

> . . . thus much I know is true
> That thou art reverencd even the rude clan
> Of lawless gypseys drove from stage to stage
> Pilfering the hedges of the husband man
> Leave thee as sacred in thy withering age
> ('Langley Bush', lines 8–12; see below, p. 46)

As John Bridges recorded, the court-leet held by the Marquis of Exeter's steward, 'corruptly called *Langley*-court, was formerly held at *Langdyke*-bush'.[55] Thus the 'lawless' became the guardians of the 'law'.

The gypsies were not observant Christians, though they could be moved to tears by itinerant Methodist preachers.[56] Their sexual customs were repugnant to evangelicals: they knew all about handfasting, jumping over the broom, and similar methods for cementing an illegal union.[57] They therefore brought down the wrath of the clerical magistracy on themselves for such offences, as well as for self-mutilation to avoid military service, fortune-telling[58] (sometimes used as a method of intimidation), petty theft, and especially for poaching and trespass.[59] The language of the magistrates in dealing with gypsies was sometimes offensive in the extreme:

> an ignorant iron hearted Justice of the Peace at ——— Sessions whose name may perish with his cruelty once sitting as a judge in the absence of a wise and kinder hearted assosiate mixd up this malicious sentence in his condemnation of 2 Gipseys for horse-stealing 'this atrosious tribe of wandering vagabonds ought to be made outlaws in every civilized kingdom and exter-minated from the face of the earth' and this persecuting unfeeling man was a cler[g]yman[60]

Clare's 'The Gipseys Song' has a political subtext that is partic-ularly close to the surface and before being submitted for publica-tion in the *European Magazine* it was subject to censorship by Mrs Emmerson and Harry Stoe Van Dyk. (We print the uncensored version.[61]) The published version retains, as does ours, the state-ment of gypsy habits in mating:

> False hearts hide in a lily skin
> But ours are coarse & fond
> No parsons fetters link us in
> Our hearts a stronger bond
> (Lines 45–8; see below, p. 119)

In his madness, Clare took this idea a stage further:

> Love worse then debt or drink or fate
> It is the damnest smart of matrimony
> A hell incarnate is a woman-mate

> The knot is tied – & then we loose the honey
> A wife is just the protetype to hate
> Commons for stock & warrens for the cony
> Are not more trespassed over in rights plan
> Then this incumberance on the rights of man
> ('Don Juan', lines 33–40; see below, p. 231)

Property-rights in land, in game, and in women may all, therefore, be restrictions on the free man. Marriage may be a kind of imprisonment, such as one might suffer for debt (an offence against another's property), drink (an offence against some else's social conventions) or fate (just general bad luck). In this discussion of property-rights, the seizing of common-lands in order to pasture one man's cattle on them is as wrong as making private property out of a rabbit-warren. And all property-rights are equally an encumbrance on the Rights of Man. Any of the offences against the law of property may bring the offender before the magistrate who is a symbol of tyranny.

> Go were we will may kindred fate
> Our friendly partners be
> Protect us from the magistrate
> & keep our dwellings free
>
> & we will sing & dance around
> With a heart that never fails
> Tho magistrates like hungry hounds
> Still threaten us with jails
> ('The Gipseys Song', lines 77–84; see below, p. 120)

These were the lines that Mrs Emmerson conspired to have removed from the poem before submitting it to the editor of the *European Magazine*, while using a specious excuse for what she and Van Dyk were doing.[62] Gypsies were a challenge to the Laws of Settlement, game laws, enclosure laws, marriage-law, laws of trespass, as well as being anathema to the magistracy, particularly the clerical magistracy.[63] When Clare approves of the gypsies – for their music, for the beauty of their women, for the freedom of their habits – he makes a political statement against the rural establishment, so that even a statement like the following has its political implications:

> I thought the gipseys camp by the green wood side a picturesque and an adorning object to nature and I lovd the gipseys for the beautys which they added to the landscape.[64]

Such then were some of the political issues that confronted Clare in his own backyard. His political feelings and views, as we have said, are deepest about local matters or at least about such national issues as have strong local ramifications. Sabbatarian laws, game laws, laws of trespass, all these, had direct consequences for Clare's way of life. They also had moral implications of a sort that appealed to the evangelical clergy and their middle-class supporters. Moreover they had effects upon property rights. Even the Sabbatarian laws, for example, protected the shopkeeper from competition from the huckster and street-trader who sold their goods at the market-cross while the respectable shopkeeper was at church or chapel. Only the innkeeper lost out, and he was closest in his interests to the rural poor. Besides, as Clare realized, the more prosperous classes could get round the Sabbatarian laws where the poor man could not.[65] There is a print showing a working man freezing in his kitchen, on Sunday, complaining that he could not get his wages on Saturday night until after the shops were shut.[66] The fact that he had no fire, perhaps because he was prevented from picking up firewood, meant that he could not get his hot Sunday meal, since the Sabbatarian laws made it illegal for the baker to accept the poor man's victuals for heating in the bakery oven.[67] One instance where the Vicar would openly condone Sunday work was when the harvest had to be brought in,[68] but in fact Clare's poetry shows that farm-life *always* made it necessary for some part of the work-force to undertake Sunday work. The kitchen-maid only got to church because the farm-boy collected the eggs or assembled the firewood for the stove and kept it going. What was the vicar going to say about that? And who had to feed the stock and water them on Sundays? The shepherd, too, had to guard his flock.

Of course, international events such as the Revolutionary and

Napoleonic wars also had important consequences at the local level. Clare himself was recruited as a soldier though he never served overseas. He and his like in the local militia were a second line of defence in the event of an invasion. On the first occasion when he volunteered for the Nottinghamshire Militia he was turned down as being too short. When he was later accepted and went to Oundle for training, it was simply because he could get two guineas for volunteering but would have got nothing if he had been conscripted.[69] He was no sort of a soldier and knew it, and he found some of his officers to be ridiculous. On the third occasion there was a further bounty for those who would enlist for extended service, and Clare once more accepted it.[70] He was a patriot but hardly a bloodthirsty one. Nevertheless war left its mark on his poetry. His ballads celebrating Collingwood, Benbow, Levison and Nelson as great naval leaders and Wellington as a soldier were the stock stuff of his time.[71] There are also several poems about working-men being pressed for the navy or running away to join the army, but none of them are Clare at his best.[72] Yet, like most of his contemporaries he thought of himself as a patriotic and loyal Englishman. This, of course, went along with his monarchism. He wrote poems to George IV, William IV and Queen Victoria.[73] Unlike the Radicals he was never a supporter of Queen Caroline, even though most of the villagers around Helpston favoured Caroline rather than her consort.[74] His political poem 'The Summons' (below, pp. 142–50) is almost medieval in the way in which Clare appeals to the monarch as a defence against the King's ministers and servants. In 'The Parish', Clare is quick to denounce those who regularly attend church on Sundays but omit to pray for the King when that prayer was read (lines 471–2; see below, p. 62). Church and King go together for Clare, as they did for William Cobbett and many of their contemporaries. The King's image on the national currency is almost sacrosanct in Clare's eyes[75] and to cast doubt upon either Church or King is simply unEnglish. He finds that ants and bees have a form of monarchy and he argues from that that it is the best form of government for man.[76] To Hessey, his publisher, during the Queen Caroline scandal, he wrote that he had 'bluntly' told Lord Radstock: 'if the

King of England was a madman, I should love him as a brother of the soil', though the statement seems more appropriate to George III than to George IV.[77] Clare seems to agree with one of his favourite authors, Tusser:

> Great kings I do succour, else wrong it would go,
> The KING of all Kings hath appointed it so[78]

Like a medieval rioting peasant of the times of Ball and Ket, Clare saw the King as the ultimate source of justice who might be appealed to against those who committed injustice in his name, so that in 'The Hue & Cry' he says:

> . . . the King on his throne was a true honest man
> So the world it went on very well
> (Lines 531–2; see below, p. 188)

On 4 October 1825, Henry Stoe Van Dyk wrote to Clare denouncing an article in the *European Magazine* entitled 'A Plea for Passive Obedience':[79]

> The politics appear to me disgusting & detestable . . . it has the double demerit of being false & damned stupid at the same time[80]

Unfortunately Clare's reply appears not to have survived. But, as we have seen, with regard to Clare's attitudes to Charles I and Charles II,[81] the poet's attitude to monarchy was neither totally submissive nor entirely consistent. He was familiar, for example, with the seventeenth-century doctrine of 'The Norman Yoke'[82] which claimed that the monarchy, and the aristocracy, of England derived from the Conquest and were therefore the usurpers of the rights of Anglo-Saxons.

> Men make a boast of pedigree – as well might the decendants of Richard Turpin boast of their's for both honours spring from robbery & spoilation – what was William the Conquerer but a robber by wholesale & what were his followers but high way men by his authority recieving titles by their expertness at plunder for which Turpin (a more noble plunderer if absence

from fear or dareing achievements make one) recieved a halter
because he dared to rob & could show only his courage for the
liscence – the ancestors of a Newton have somthing to boast of
– but pedigree belongs to a race horse & confers nothing to the
mind or the man[83]

Thus the monarchy was descended from Norman plunderers, as
were the great landowners, such as his patrons, the Fitzwilliams
and the Cecils, yet Clare was always grateful for their patronage
and regarded them as superior landlords. The longer established
the great landowners were, the better Clare liked them and he was
also critical of recent additions to the peerage.[84]

Yet how far was Clare deceiving himself? G. E. Mingay provides
a careful analysis of the 'landed interest' in the eighteenth
century,[85] 'a body of propertied men who tended to hold broadly
compatible views on social and political questions' and who
tended to hold together sharing the same interests but not always
the same party allegiance in the first decades of the nineteenth
century. The principal threat to the great landowners came from
the 'commercial interests', the captains of industry, the bankers,
and large merchants, who established their wealth in the towns
rather than in the countryside. But in Clare's district, the
Fitzwilliams and the Cecils were so long established that they
remained largely unchallenged. These very large landowners,
members of the House of Lords, were at the pinnacle of society.
They did, in fact, do a great deal to help the poor of the villages
that they controlled, sometimes providing food, sometimes
creating work in the maintenance of their properties, and some-
times showing individual acts of kindness to their tenants. Clare's
father, for example, had been sent to the Sea-bathing Infirmary at
Scarborough by Lord Milton in an attempt to alleviate his rheuma-
tism.[86] And Clare himself was allowed by the same family to rent
a larger cottage in Northborough. Clare was employed for a time
as a gardener by the Marquis of Exeter at Burghley and provided
with a small allowance when he published his first book. He was
always respectful towards these families and grateful for their
kindnesses. The Fitzwilliams actually helped to maintain him as
an inmate of the Northampton General Lunatic Asylum.

Nevertheless, the Fitzwilliams and the Exeters both made large increases in revenue from their estates during the war years at the beginning of the century.[87] Though both families maintained home farms, they were landlords rather than farmers, like other members of their class, and they well knew how to protect their own interests.[88]

At the other end of rural society were the labouring poor – 'the labourers, cottagers, seamen and soldiers, paupers and vagrants, with no property or special skill to shield them from the pressures of the daily struggle for existence'.[89] They amounted to over a third of the population in 1803, when 'over a million people, one in nine of the population, were said to be in receipt of poor relief, to the tune of £5,348,205'.[90]

While Clare admired the Fitzwilliams and the Exeters, his antagonism was directed against the farmers who were strung along a hierarchical descent of social and economic standing between the great landowners and the labouring poor, and against the small traders who sold inferior goods at high prices to the poor. In this he was following the time-honoured pattern in which each class vents its anger against that immediately superior to it. The farmers, for the most part, reduced the wages of their labourers in the post-war years and resorted to hiring seasonal or part-time labourers in order to keep down their wage-bills. They were often the local administrators of the poor rates which they juggled to their own advantage. At the same time, they sought reductions in their rents and the reduction or abolition of tithes from their land-lords and from the clergy. Clare himself suffered from the change to day-labour from long-term employment:

> it is very irksome to be obliged to beg of people to get work of them which is actually the case for there is so many that they are forced to employ that those they are not forced to take not being paupers they will not have therefore if labour will not bring a man independance it is worse then nothing & he may as well sell himself for an india slave as belong to such places[91]

As for poor relief, the reduction of commoning was particularly severe on the fen-lands, throwing small occupiers into destitution, and creating tension with those who had to pay the poor-rate. Neeson cites a telling anonymous threatening letter addressed 'To the Gentlemen of Ashill, Norfolk':

> This is to inform you that you have by this time brought us under the heaviest burden and into the hardest Yoke we ever knowed; it is too hard for us to bear . . . You do as you like, you rob the poor of their Commons right, plough the grass up that God send to grow, that a poor man may feed neither a Cow, Pig, Horse, nor Ass; lay muck and stones in the road to prevent the grass growing. If a poor man is out of work and wants a day or two's work you will give him 6d. per week, and then a little man that does not employ a labourer at all, must help pay for your work doing, which will bring him, chargeable to the parish. There is a 5 or 6 of you have gotten all the whole of the land in this parish in your own hands and you would wish to be rich and starve all the other part of the poor of the parish. If any poor man wanted anything, then you will call a Town meeting about it, to hear which could contrive to hiss him the most . . .
>
> Gentlemen, these few lines are to inform you that God Almighty have brought our blood to a proper circulation, that have been in a very bad state a long time, and now without alteration of the foresaid, we mean to circulate your blood with the leave of God.[92]

Apart from the threat of blood-letting, Clare would have had every sympathy with this statement. It is this situation which inspires Clare's anger in 'The Parish'. These are the small farmers Clare trounces in that work, but the Fitzwilliams come out smelling of roses. This is not to say that the Fitzwilliams did not try to help the labouring population. In 1822, for example, they lowered rents on the Milton estate and recommended that the labourer should be paid a fair wage.

Throughout his work Clare demonstrates his sympathy with the poor – the widow and the orphan, the sick and elderly, the mentally disturbed, the crippled, and the unemployed – often castigating those who turned the poor from the door or praising those, like the old couple in 'Dobson and Judie' and Robin in 'The

Welcome Stranger',[93] who are concerned for the homeless and do their best to help them. These categories of poor, however, were augmented during the days of agricultural depression by the able-bodied who were simply unable to find work at a living wage.

Ian Dyck claims that Clare's nostalgia for an earlier period was historically justified: 'There was little abstract or ill-defined about the primary golden age of Cobbett and the rural workers: it dated from 1720 to 1785'; and he argues that 'the golden age of the farmers, 1793 to 1815, began where that of the labourers left off'.[94] However that may be, Clare, like Cobbett, certainly believed that an older, better order of things had been replaced by a degraded present. It enabled him to denounce those who had destroyed the old order as both tyrants and rebels, as in his reference to the 'rebel schemes' of the enclosers ('The Mores', line 79). Clare's conservative social values rest on a natural hostility to progressive, modernising economic trends, which promoted enclosure, the replacement of small farmers by large tenants, and the gentrification of the farmers; all trends which he rightly considered hostile to the interests of labourers. Thus, in 'The Cottager', he celebrates the kind of small owner-occupier who was regarded as hopelessly backward and benighted by progressives like Arthur Young.[95]

Yet it should always be remembered that Clare's experience of these events is essentially local. What mattered first to him was not so much the general problem of enclosure but the local enclosures in the fens; not the Game Laws so much as the fate of local men caught poaching, a fate of which he himself always seems to have been in mortal fear; not acts against the adulteration of foods or for the better observance of weights and measures so much as the cheating Helpston baker or fruiterer; not how the laws for Sabbath observance were observed in the nation at large so much as the manner in which the Rev. Charles Mossop or the Rev. Samuel Hopkinson interpreted them. 'The Parish' demonstrates this in some detail. Most of the characters there probably have a local identity: 'Old Ralph' is certainly R. B. Henson, Clare's bookseller, who became minister to a Ranting congregation in the Deepings; 'Old Saveall' is probably Farmer Gee who lived across the road from Clare; 'Bailiff Bum-tagg' is the officer who branded Parker

Clare's goods and perhaps 'Proud Farmer Cheetum' or 'Farmer Thrifty' is Harry Ryde, steward to Lord Cecil. Clare's denunciation of 'Bragg' is of a farmer who has copied his Whiggism from Lord Fitzwilliam but would actually like to own his farm rather than be tenant of it. He talks radical rhetoric but:

> To sink the many & exalt the few
> Is still his creed in an extended view
> Reform thus leveld to brags selfish will
> Want still might toil & be contented still
> ('The Parish', lines 961–64; below, p. 76)

It is particularly interesting too to see Clare's attention to language and its misuse. Thus he exposes the real motives of radical rhetoric and savagely denounces, in 'The Fallen Elm', the 'knaves that brawl for better laws' (line 71) and who mean by 'freedom', freedom to pursue their own interests. In 'Apology for the Poor', Clare speaks with all the vigour engendered by personal suffering. He accuses the tenant farmers of entering into a combination to keep down the labourers' wages and describes them as 'the lords and tyrants of every village', treating the rights of the poor with contempt, raising up mobs by their own crimes against the poor and then 'metamorphos[ing] into special constables and parad[ing] the dirty streets with shouldered muskets in all the swaggering awkwardness of the raw lobsters that now infest the metropolis'.[96] True he talks here of London but one feels that he has Stamford in mind. As always in Clare, we see politics from the bottom up.

One occasion on which Clare placed himself firmly in the anti-radical camp was during the Queen Caroline riots of 1820. Though by no means an anti-feminist, since he always showed himself to be extremely sympathetic towards women who suffered from sexual oppression, he was yet determined to take a cudgel to any mob of Caroline's supporters who threw a stone at his house.[97] Recent historical research has shown the Queen Caroline affair to be far more important than was supposed, since it created a watershed in public opinion.[98] Artisanal opinion seems, on the whole, to have strongly supported the Queen against her husband. Local newspapers in Clare's neighbourhood reported many incidents similar to those in Helpston where the bell-ringers of a parish church rang the bells in defiance of the local vicar or rector to display their sympathy for the Queen. Another section of pro-Caroline opinion was middle-class, especially among Methodists and Evangelical Anglicans who deplored George IV's sexual conduct and were also deeply suspicious of his previous marriage to a Catholic. Clare's monarchism may have been reinforced by several factors, including his friendship with the Bishop of Peterborough and his wife and with Charles Mossop, the rector of Helpston, as well as his distaste for those who used politics to impose their own sexual morality upon others. The whole censorious movement helped to create the atmosphere of respectability that was to control the Victorian court. Moreover the impact of respectable middle-class opinion stemming from both Anglican and Nonconformist attitudes towards sexual conduct, together with the threat of unrest in Ireland emanating from the Catholic population, allowed Wellington and Peel to force through Catholic Emancipation in the face of royal reluctance and Anglican trepidation. What astonished many opponents of Catholic Emancipation a few years later was how little disturbance had been, in fact, created by the repeal.

The issues raised in 'The Parish', however, are much closer to Clare's personal concerns about the ways in which rural society in the Helpston area had changed and was still in the process of changing. Clare's earliest memories of Helpston predate the enclosure of 1809, itself notable for being a comparatively late enclosure, and mention the ceremonies associated with beating the parish bounds under a common-field system, as well as the opening up of the fen commons to the village stock.[99] We know from W.E. Tate that 'Between 1750 and 1815 two-thirds of Northamptonshire's agricultural land was turned from open fields and commons to enclosed farmland'.[100] Clare described some of the consequences in 'The Lamentations of Round-Oak Waters':

> 'But now alas my charms are done
> 'For shepherds & for thee

'The Cow boy with his Green is gone
'And every Bush & tree
'Dire nakedness oer all prevails
'Yon fallows bare and brown
'Is all beset wi' posts & rails
'And turned upside down'
(Lines 93–100; see below, p. 21)

The loss of pasture-rights, involved not only the loss of stock for the small farmer but also the loss of wood-pasture on which so many poor men depended. In consequence of enclosure, too, much sociability was lost to the work-system:

That good old fame the farmers earnd of yore
That made as equals not as slaves the poor
That good old fame did in two sparks expire
A shooting coxcomb & a hunting Squire
('The Parish', lines 105–8; see below, p. 52)

The numbers of poor falling on the parish increased, bankruptcies among small tradesmen who served the labouring class became more common, and many labourers lost small amounts of land on which they had been able to raise subsistence crops. Neeson tells us that over half the original landholders disappeared or lost some of their land between 1774 and 1814.[101] They could not grow barley for their own malt and they could no longer rely upon steady employment. Fence-breaking and hedge-wood stealing became offences created by new necessities for wood and also developed into symbolic attacks upon the enclosure-system.[102] Hence Clare's hatred of fences and his pity for poor persons looking for fire-wood.

What comes through most strongly in 'The Parish' is the lack of independence among the poor and the greater pressure upon them to become subservient to 'parish kings & queens' (line 5; see below, p. 49). Clare is preoccupied with the consequencies of enclosure for human rights and relationships. The poor man becomes a 'slave' when he has lost his 'rights'. He no longer mixes on equal terms with the farmers. We should remember here how Clare suddenly lost his first love, Mary Joyce, probably because her family put pressure upon her to stop consorting with a labouring boy whom she had known first as a school-friend in Glinton vestry-school.[103] Like Cobbett, Clare saw the way in which the farmer's wife and daughters put on new airs and lost old graces. He seems to have had little expectation that much relief would come from legislation and, of course, the First Reform Act of 1832 left him as much without a vote in the nation's affairs as he had been before. While the 'Apology for the Poor' sees him claiming a position as 'Champion for the poor', his statements are indicative of utter frustration in the face of Mr Manners' presumption and of a natural concern with the basic subsistence-costs of bread and beer. Unlike Cobbett, Clare had no proposals of a specific nature for wider reform but he had the advantage, as a commentator, of being less doctrinaire. But for all his scepticism about politics and his deliberate distancing of himself from political parties, the continuing debates about public issues and the existence of a popular radical movement initially served to politicize an intelligent observer of the world and to provoke him to express his own views. The crisis of the unreformed system came in the years 1825 to 1832, which coincided with the years of Clare's greatest self-confidence and maturity as a writer, and prompted him to become, both in print and in other writings that were never published, 'the representative of an increasing number of constituents who look up to me to represent their wants & protect their interests & welfare because they are unable to do it themselves'.[104]

We have a good deal yet to discover about Clare's political journalism. We are not certain that 'Apology for the Poor' was published, but it may well have been written, at least in part, as a response to John Drakard's letter to him of 21 December 1829 inviting him to send forward for publication in a new paper, the *Stamford Champion*, any 'politically inspired thought' he might have.[105] Drakard thus was not only soliciting poetical contributions from Clare but also explicitly inviting him to express views on politics. The poet replied by modestly denying that he was 'a Scott or a Cobbett'.[106] Within a year Clare was invited to become a contributor to another Stamford newspaper, the *Bee*.[107] The

Champion supported the cause of Reform: the *Bee* opposed it. Mrs Emmerson advised Clare to be '*friendly* on the score of *poesy*, & have nothing to say on *Polotics* for you have *patrons*, & friends on each side of the question'.[108] Clare, however, chose to send his political poems, 'The Summons' and 'The Hue and Cry', to Drakard's paper. Clare's words that he wanted to become 'the advocate and Champion for the poor'[109] suggest that he may have intended to send his 'Apology' to Drakard's paper. Unfortunately we have not been able to find copies of the *Champion* for 30 March, 11 May and 27 July 1830 in which the 'Apology' might have appeared. Nor have we been able to identify the article that was the immediate occasion of the 'Apology'.[110]

In the 'Apology' Clare refers to the campaign for the abolition of the tax on malt, a duty that hit the beer-drinking population. He took part some time at the end of 1829 and during the first two months of 1830 in pouring scorn on William Thorpe, who wrote a letter in the *Stamford Mercury* of 18 December 1829 against John Bedford of Sleaford who wanted to abolish the malt tax. Eventually, (in the *Stamford Mercury* of 5 February 1830), Thorpe retired from the fray and was mocked in Clare's poem, 'Just like the lion in alarms' (see below, pp. 157–8). That poem, which was intended for publication, never appeared. It is clear, however, that in these months Clare was politically active and favouring the more radical view.

'The Reformers Hymn'[111] celebrates William IV's supposed support for reform. The 'sailor-king' also gets Clare's support because the navy, unlike the army, could not be used for internal policing. The main drive, however, is:

> Our freedom is our birth right & shall each pleading knave
> Blind our enlightened reason that freedom to enslave
> No – firesides shall be parliments our cottages be towers
> Ere wrong shall cheat us of the rights our king declares as ours
> (Lines 27–30; see below, p. 192)

This, and 'A scene in the Election' with a song, 'The Blues & the Sailors' (see below, pp. 162–4), a satirical squib directed against the Whig party in Stamford, are all pretty poor stuff, not surprisingly, since Clare had no taste for party politics and party rhetoric. What they do show is Clare alternating his attacks on Whigs and Tories, and offering his writing to papers on either side.

John Drakard printed five of Clare's poems in this period – '1830' (under the title 'St Stephens', *Drakard's Stamford News*, 5 March 1830); 'The Summons' (*Drakard's Stamford News*, 25 September 1829, and reprinted in the *Champion*, 30 November 1830); 'The Triumphs of Time' (*Champion*, 1, 8, 15 June 1830); 'Familliar Epistle to a Friend' (*Champion*, 14 December 1830); and 'The Hue & Cry' (*Champion*, 11 January 1831).[112] Only 'The Triumphs of Time', the least obviously political of these poems, was published in Clare's name. Though none of these poems was party-political, 'The Hue & Cry' managed to alarm Mrs Emmerson who thought that 'The Summons' might be regarded as a satire on the Law, 'a "*radical" invention*!!' and though the 'Hue and Cry' was '*very clever*', some of Clare's patrons might take offence at it.[113] Clare was trying to publish both poems in a book illustrated by Cruikshank and Mrs Emmerson was trying to dissuade him from this. The fact is, as he says in his 'Familiar Epistle':

> Im neither wig nor tory clean
> To swear knaves act uprightly
> But just a water mark between
> That skims opinions lightly
> (Lines 25–8; see below, p. 165)

or, as he says in a letter to Mrs Emmerson, December 1830–January 1831 'between such matter[s] I am as a blank leaf between two pages of letter press ready to receive all impressions that coincide with my opinions or refute them'.[114]

'The Summons' and 'The Hue and Cry' are perhaps the two most powerful political poems that Clare ever wrote and it is interesting that Clare wanted them both to be published with illustrations by George Cruikshank, the greatest political cartoonist and caricaturist of his age. Cruikshank had illustrated the months in William Hone's *Every-Day Book* which were introduced by excerpts from Clare's *The Shepherds Calendar*. Clare and his friend, Henry Behnes Burlowe, were known to Cruikshank, therefore, and they may have met. Unfortunately, by the time Clare wrote these poems, Cruikshank had moved away from political caricatures into the illustration of novels, folk-tales and comic anthologies. 'The Summons' was first published in *Drakard's Stamford News* 25 September 1829, with lines 149–72 omitted, and then in *The Stamford Champion* with lines 117–40 omitted. John Drakard, the owner and editor of those papers, had been imprisoned in Lincoln Gaol because he had been found guilty of seditious libel merely for *reprinting* Cobbett's article attacking the authorities for permitting flogging in the British army. Clare, a close friend of Drakard, was, of course, familiar with the circumstances. Even while in prison, Drakard created trouble for the Gaoler at Lincoln by bringing charges of corruption against him and the publisher was eventually released to be greeted with a celebratory banquet and a gift of money to help him meet some of his expenses. He had invited Clare to send him some political verse and he will go down to history for this invitation, if not for his political bravery, though that was considerable. The following stanza may represent Drakard's personal experience:

> Then the old man passed a prison
> & in passing made a call
> He thought the folks in such a place
> Were knaves & robbers all
> Yet he found to his supprise
> What he knew not all his time
> That those sent there for speaking truth
> Exceeded those for crime
> (Lines 149–56; see below, p. 146)

By commenting on such matters Clare was exposing himself to the danger of prosecution and must have known that he was doing so.

The 'meddlesome old man' who is the protagonist of this poem visits many different kinds of persons and places – a small village with a drunken and neglectful parson, a magistrate who makes the law his own servant, a rich lady preparing for a ball, a mansion, the Houses of Parliament, and even the royal palace. In every place he exposes injustice and silences the perpetrator of it. In the last lines of the poem the old man's identity is revealed:

> For the strangers mask fell from his face
> & that old mans name was death
> (Lines 243–4; see below, p. 150)

The summons is therefore an 'invite to eternity'. Everyone he visits tries to put him off by rebuking him for his abrupt manners, threatens him with the stocks, abuses him as a vagrant or laughs at his mission. Only the poor widow and the prisoners in gaol are treated by the old man with respect. The social hierarchy is turned topsy-turvy. What is particularly noticeable is the scant respect that the old man uses towards monarchy:

> Tho the king was on his throne
> Decked in his robes of state
> He seemed no more to that old man
> Then the porter at the gate
> (Lines 233–6)

Etiquette is thrown out of the window. The old man does not touch his hat to the parson (we may recall that earlier in his career Clare approved of the parson who did not demand these outward forms of respect from his parishioners); nor does he remove his hat before the magistrate but, Quaker-like, metes out justice to the Justice. In parliament, the old man 'cared not for the houses rules' and in the royal palace 'ettiquette with all its pomp / Fell like a rotten stone' (lines 191, 223–4). Death thus exposes the futility of all ceremony and all pretence. He is a Lord of Misrule.

In 'The Hue & Cry', the old man has become a Captain Swing or Ned Ludd sort of character. Gossip spreads along just as the rumour of Napoleon's landings had swept like wildfire through the countryside. This gives greater scope to Clare's fantasy than 'The Summons'. His pictures of the local volunteers assembling to repel the enemy is farce at its best, with the farmers falling off their horses, turning right instead of left, and scouring the countryside absolutely to no purpose. The effects of rumour, to which Clare himself had contributed during the Swing Riots, make it impossible to identify the old man who is thought to appear in many disguises and many places simultaneously. 'Fasts and Thanksgivings' are mocked for their hypocrisy. Bonaparte, Cobbett, Paine, Hunt, O'Connell, and Voltaire are all identified with the old man. Handbills, newspapers, petitions and prophecies – the whole gamut of popular publicity with which Clare was so familiar – are all in action in this poem and truth is to be found among none of them:

> & trades & professions turned round with the news
> Like a 'second edition' of men
> (Lines 279–80)

which, considering the world described in the poem, needs to be taken with a pinch of salt. The energy, the range of reference, the good-humoured cynicism of this poem are outstanding and totally different from almost all of Clare's previous poems.

Yet much as these poems are based in their own time and the corruptions of it, they transcend contemporaneity to address issues for all times. It is important to recognise that neither 'The Summons' nor 'The Hue & Cry' bear the author's name but are signed by an anonymous N. (Could it stand for 'Nobody'?). Stephen Colclough declares:

> The political poems, like 'Apology for the Poor' were designed to be anonymous. This anonymity gave the author free range to explore this radical voice,[115]

and argues that when Clare was assembling *The Midsummer Cushion* under his own name in the following year, 1830, he disregarded 'material that appeared especially radical after the Swing Riots'. It is true that 'The Summons' and 'The Hue & Cry' made Mrs Emmerson nervous,[116] but Clare had already taken the greatest risk by publishing the poems in radical newspapers. His identity would have been easy for government spies to ascertain. 'The Summons' is certainly radical in its denunciation of parliament, declaring that the members 'by wishing well their country / They only meant themselves'; by reminding the monarch of his vulnerability to Death; and by the dismissal of 'lawyers courtiers gentlemen' for their betrayal of the poor and by its attack upon the clerical magistrate.[117] 'The Hue & Cry' might be regarded as even more dangerously threatening to Clare's own peace and safety, because it employs ridicule so effectively, as for example, that of the local elected officials:

> & the mob fell alaughing & hissing at last
> & their jokes they grew bitter & many
> For they knew that to make a poor alderman fast
> Was the cruelest torture of any
> (Lines 149–52)

To make such people his targets in a poem published in a local newspaper whose editor had just come out of gaol was really to put himself on the firing line. And if Cruikshank had actually illustrated it the danger would have been worse.

A third poem ('Good morning to ye honest swain') is an eclogue, taking the form of a dialogue between Toil and Honesty, in which the former serves as a mouthpiece for the poet. This poem seems to take up its direction from four earlier poems by Clare: 'Lobin Clouts satirical Sollilouquy on the times' (below, pp. 15–16), a poem rendered in heavy dialect, the purpose of which may be to distance Clare from the radicalism of his protagonist; 'Chubs Reply',[118] the account of a confrontation between Chub, a yokel, and a 'tom thumkin' midget; a single stanza beginning 'One monday morning sour & loath' (below, p. 17), in which a labourer complains about his hard life, comparing it to a slave's; and especially another fragment beginning 'Thy eye can witness more then others' (below, pp. 14–15) in which once again the protagonist complains of the hardships imposed by Luxury on Labour. The last is referred to in an autobiographical fragment, where Clare describes the loss of 'a sort of Pastoral' which is clearly this poem.[119] Stephen Colclough links all four pieces together under the theme of Labour and Luxury and shows how this theme was central to Clare's early poems about rural distress.[120] Clare may have felt that he could not afford, in the face of the views of Lord Radstock, to pursue the theme at the time, but it surfaced again in the 1830s. Not only is this important in establishing a continuity in Clare's political outlook but also in making it clear that it was not only enclo-sure that concerned him. It is 'Wealth' that is:

> ... the bar that keeps from being fed
> & thine our loss of labour & of bread
> Thou art the cause that levels every tree
> & woods bow down to clear a way for thee
> ('Helpstone', lines 131–4)

Radstock was right, from his point of view, in objecting to the famous lines about 'Accursed wealth' because Clare does refer to the direct agency of the wealthy in not giving Labour its fair reward. As Colclough makes clear, it is Clare's claim to speak for Labour that rattles the cages of the rich. When this message was expressed in a dialect voice it seems to have been doubly threat-ening.

John Barrell rightly brings together an earlier poem 'The Lamentations of Round-Oak Waters' and 'The Lament of Swordy Well', in which two streams speak for themselves about the suffer-ings they have endured as a result of enclosure.[121] Though the style of the first is less eighteenth-century in tone than many of his early poems, there is still an artificiality about the 'Genius of the brook' complaining to the poor man on her brink that she is

> 'By Naiads and by all forsook
> 'Unheeded and alone
> (Lines 47–8)

The poor man's own lament is much more direct and non-literary:

> (For when my wretched state appears
> Hurt friendless poor and starv'd
> I never can withold my tears
> To think how I am sarv'd
> (Lines 17–20)

The dialect-word, 'sarv'd', gives immediacy to the poor man's distress. Not until lines 97–100 does the stream begin to strike the same tone as its observer:

> 'Dire nakedness oer all prevails
> 'Yon fallows bare and brown
> 'Is all beset wi' posts & rails
> 'And turned upside down'

As in 'The Mores', the shepherd can no longer cross the field by the baulks between the furrows in wet weather because the plough has churned everything into mush. Since every patch of land has been used, there are no 'eddings' (headings) left on which the ploughman can clean his shoes and the blade of his plough. Worse still:

> 'The greens the Meadows & the moors
> 'Are all cut up & done
> 'There's scarce a greensward spot remains
> 'And scarce a single tree
> (Lines 119–22)

Gradually the poem's language gathers strength until it echoes that of 'Labour and Luxury', 'Lobin Clouts Satirical Sollilouquy', and the fragmentary 'One Monday morning sour & loath' and 'O thrice lucky town'. The dialect speech introduces a roughness and force which create the solid nature of the injured labourer. The spring, regretting the loss of the willows on its bank cut down by 'senceless wretches' or 'sweating slaves', sees the labourers who despoiled it as only 'poor moilers', who are not themselves responsible for the desecration, but only the tools of the owners of the land. Some eighteenth-century poetic diction survives – 'days of yore', 'musing swains', the 'injur'd brook' – but the strength of feeling in the poem overcomes these limitations. The 'Lament of Swordy Well', while dealing in general with the same theme is much stronger. Swordy Well speaks for itself, not through the mediation of the Genius of the spring. Indeed the spring says:

> I'm swordy well a piece of land
> Thats fell upon the town
> (Lines 21–2),

and in falling upon the parish, the spring is not a beggar with a 'limping leg', a list of his troubles pinned on his coat, nor does it

xlv

> carry round some names to win
> More money from the rest
> (Lines 19–20)

We are grasped by the injured pride in which it declares its loss of independence, despite the fact of the plough's 'yearly gain', and the sense of assault and rape upon its own body:

> & me they turned me inside out
> For sand & grit & stones
> & turned my old green hills about
> & pickt my very bones
> (Lines 61–4)

Pride in its past, before enclosure, in the 'horses cows & sheep' (line 69) that it supported, its great age and life of extended usefulness have all been taken from it, though it is still prepared to leave a place for profit and allow 'pedigrees' to retain their 'honours' (line 55), so long as honest toil can get its due. The pleas of Swordy Well for a minimum of fair treatment, to be allowed a modicum of peace and the bare possibility of survival, become a protest against human injustice and greed.

A note of irony runs through the poem. The spring reminds us that it is 'no man to whine & beg' (line 121) and yet it also says:

> I couldnt keep a dust of grit
> Nor scarce a grain of sand
> But bags & carts claimed every bit
> & now theyve got the land
> (Lines 105–8),

so that it is both man and spring and neither – an entity that defies its own limits. More powerfully than in 'Lamentations of Round-Oak Waters' we see what the *system* has produced – a waste that cannot even support a rabbit, a man reduced to beggary but too proud to beg, and a condition in which the poor are obliged to exploit the poor.

While Clare was at his best in writing about Helpston, he was always conscious of his Scots heritage that came to him through his grandfather, John Donald Parker.[122] Poems inspired by the

Scottish struggles for liberty stretch from a very early poem, 'Alpins Harp New Strung from A Piece of "Ancient" Scottish "Poetry"'[123] to later poems like 'Scotland':

> So here's health to auld Scotland the brave and the free
> Her mountains and Glens are the dwellings for me
> (*LP*, I. 635–6),

'Heres a health to Scotland' (see below, p. 246), 'Heres to auld Scotland' (*LP*, II. 691–2) and several others of the same type. Scotland was the symbol of political freedom for Clare as Israel was for his escape from Egyptian bondage. The broadside ballads circulating in Clare's neighbourhood must have refreshed his memory with similar songs such as those published by John Pitts – 'My Native Highland Home', 'The Scotchman'[124] or by Jemmy Catnach[125] who described himself as 'King Catnach – King of the Picts – descended in a right straight line from the Picts' or several others. Though these songs seem remote from Helpston, they are not so to Clare's cultural heritage with his keen reading of Burns, Ramsay, and Tannahill. In a similar folk-tradition, ballads about bravery at sea, either in battle or in storms, contributed to Clare's imaginative life and to his political vision of liberty, as did the Robin Hood ballads. Perhaps Clare's father and mother, in their kitchen-concerts, had sung many such songs, overheard by their son. While not the best of Clare's poetry, some of these ballads were important in the formation of Clare's outlook on the world.

There are two important *national* and *international* movements in the eighteen-twenties and eighteen-thirties that Clare certainly read about in the national and the local press – Catholic Emancipation and Slavery. His friend, Joseph Henderson, the gardener at Milton, informed him, in a letter dated 11 March 1829:

> I have not seen the debates on the Catholic Cause, I have only seen an outline of the proceedings of thursday night in one of the Provincial papers, Mr Peel made a speech of *four hours length* & was followed by Mr Banks & others finishing with Lord Milton at the end of whose speech the house adjourned I have not heard if they got through it on Friday or till monday – I feel

equally anxious with yourself to see the debates on the question, you must know that I am a catholic emancipator of sixteen years standing & therefore must feel anxious *to get the matter off my hands*

I can assure you however that throughout that time I have never felt so sincere & anxious a wish that the question should be carried as I do now hitherto indeed it has been but a hopeless cause but now it seems almost a certainty & I sincerely hope that the expectations that have been excited may not be dissapointed to be sure it must come sooner or later, but the longer it is protracted the deeper will be those wounds which it is intended to heal – [126]

Henry Behnes sent Clare copies of *The Examiner* and *The Times* dealing with the Catholic question.[127] Four years earlier, in May 1825, Clare had mocked a London bookseller who announced that he was 'printing the Duke of Yorks Speech against the Catholics in *letters of gold*,' but a few days later declared:

The Catholics have lost their bill once more and its nothing but right they shoud when one beholds the following Sacred humbugs which their religion hurds up and sanctifys . . . [128]

There then follows a list of miracles performed through relics. Clare was evidently transfixed by such stories as he reverts to them on several occasions.[129]

He was, however, sympathetic to Irish immigrants, such as those who came over to labour in the harvests in the late summer months:

When the poor Irish from their country rove
& like scotch cattle throng the road in droves[130]

The image is a striking one and must have been more so in Clare's day when huge herds of cattle were driven down from Scotland to fatten in the Essex marshes. Occasionally there were fights between gangs of Irish and English harvesters but, in the Great Famine, there was a good deal of spontaneous East Anglian charity to help the starving Irish. Clare also wrote a comic song, 'Och by Jasus hes a Irish lad', poking fun at the Duke of

Wellington, an Irishman, for abolishing the beer tax[131] and a senti-
mental song, 'The Irish Emigrant', whose speaker yearns for his
hut, his pigs, and his girl.[132] As always Clare was sympathetic to
the homeless.

Clare believed, with Montesquieu, 'that the basis of all religions
ought to be humanity & was as nessesary to be a benefit to the
body in its present existance as its hopes was to the soul in its here-
after'.[133] In his sketch, 'For Vicar's Sermon—Novel', he makes that
clergyman say:

> O that people should quarrel oer their creeds Catholics why
> there are thousands of what men call Heretics who are better
> men then I who have done more good to their countrys then I
> can ever do for my cure & who have done more charitys in a day
> then I could in a life time[134]

But despite this, Clare was a dedicated Anglican and the defence
of the Church of England was posited upon it as the basis of the
Protestant Constitution. Opponents of the Catholic Relief Act of
1829 stressed the threat of a Catholic monarchy, a Catholic system
of education, a Catholic-dominated parliament and a Catholic
government, if the measure were once passed. It was strongly
resisted by George IV. We reproduce, facing p. li an election bill
addressed to 'the Electors of Stamford', which appears in the Clare
archives at Peterborough. It is directed against Charles Tennyson
who supported the Catholic Relief Bill and makes it clear that the
measure was opposed on religious grounds. Clare himself was not
in favour of disestablishment nor of the abolition of the tithes, and
it may be that this election bill came into his possession because his
views were known. It might well be that in Heaven, 'there will be
no methodists no {dissenters} Independants no church folks or
Chatholics',[135] but down below Clare adhered to his pro-Anglican
position.

If Catholic Emancipation was a major political issue based upon
religious opinion, so was the Slavery issue. Clare tells a story in his
journal about encountering a black man begging at St Paul's,
London, giving him his last few pence, conversing with him, and
returning the next day with a shilling only to find him gone.[136] His

ELECTORS

OF

Stamford.

YOU have been called upon to lay aside all regard for *Interest*, all *Worldly Considerations*, and to *follow the dictates* of an *Enlightened Conscience*, in returning Members who will promote the *Interest of True Religion*! Do so, my Friends! Let *this* be your *motive*! Let *this* be your *principle of action*! and the cause of true Religion *will abundantly triumph*! It is the *present* form of our Constitution alone which *encourages the spread of Religion*; it is the *present* form of our Constitution alone which provides for the *Instruction of the Poor*. It is the *present* form of our Constitution which has been the Temporal Instrument used in making England what she now is—*The Fountain of Gospel Light*. It is to *maintain that Constitution inviolate*, and to secure to you a *continuance* of those *mighty blessings*, that you are now called upon to come forward, and aid the sacred cause. It is to *Destroy* that Constitution, to *rob* you of those blessings, to *obscure* that light, that the *Bill* is to prepare the way. What else, think you, would have silenced the factious voice of the Agitator of Ireland? What else would have induced *him* to support the measure. He has pledged himself to bring about the *Repeal of the Union*, and the *overthrow of the Protestant Establishment*! and he *advocates the Bill*, because he knows that it will prepare the way for both.

Friends of Religion!! Join not with those who, in Hypocrisy and Deceit, have used Religion's Name to beguile you into an act, which, they well know, will tend to *destroy Religion's Power*, and *obscure its present brightness*.

Are *they* guided by Religion? Listen to their Speeches!! Shudder at their profane usage of the Sacred Volume!! Look at the lives and weekly writings of their Champions!! *Mark their threat* to induce one conscientious man to join their cause: They would *forsake the House where* THEY *believe their God to dwell*!— They would *forsake the place where they have been accustomed to offer prayer to him*— Listen!—IF THAT MAN REFUSED TO VOTE FOR TENNYSON.

These are the Men who have taken Religion for their Banner. These the Men who have pressed the sacred and powerful name of Religion into their service! Forsake them, my Friends; Forsake the Cause to which they are united!

Vote for *those* who will promote the *Interests* of *True Religion*, and you will vote for CECIL and for CHAPLIN.

study of 'The Vicar' is quite explicit about the religious basis of the treatment of Africans:

> Talk not of distinction – look at the poor Affrican does the color of his skin forbid us to treat him with mercy is his complextion the liscence for our inhumanity – is it a discont[in]uance of that link that enacts us to be humane to our fellow creatures in what ever grade or station we find them is color & complextion any insult to our {creeds} feelings no the blood of that poor emaciated black creature which I have in my minds eye is as crimson as that which flowed down the temples of our divine master when like the affrican he was injured & scourged & crowned with thorns & what for brethren why he suffered himself to be bound that that poor bleeding african might be free he suffered his own blood to flow that that poor affricans blood might be spared he suffered himself to die that the affrican might live & be happy in escaping the sufferings that he himself underwent for the very purpose that they might be free – & our only way to be happy is to be kind to all for he who sees so much difference between the negro & himself as to think a black man {is not so} cannot be human like a white one or that a black mans soul cannot be of so much consequence in the registery of heaven as his own or that he stands not on the same footing in the favour of god as him self – that man . . . I say be what he may in his own estimation is no christian[137]

Elsewhere Clare draws a direct connection between slavery (though he is talking of slavery in general and not black slavery) and 'the luxury of tyranny', and suggests that because tyranny has the seeds of its own decadence within it, it will eventually itself become the subject of tyranny from those that it has oppressed.[138]

In a letter to Clare, on 8 February 1832, the poet, Thomas Pringle, told him that an agent of the Anti-Slavery Society, of which Pringle was then Secretary, had been giving a talk in Market Deeping.[139] Clare replied that he had not heard about the talk or he would have been glad to see Pringle's friend, and added:

> lectures on slavery have been given in the neighbourhood but I

thought it was by Mr Buckingham the Traveller – I have very little interest in the slavedealing arguments but I have a feeling on the broad principle of common humanity that slavery is not only impiety but disgracful to {humanity} a country professing religion – but then I have an idea that war is as excessive a wrong [as] where mens attributes are founded on the basis of religious right – 'do unto others as we would be done unto' – & surely slavery & war must be two very great & very black contradictions to such principles – & yet people argue that blacks were made for bondage & that war was nessesary to keep peace – & so ones qualms are forced to be satisfied – Messrs Smith & Elder sent me a large book for what reason I know not on west Indian slavery – & I fancied to be sure it was against it but I found that it was in commendation of slavery – written by an ungenerous man & capable of better things[140]

Pringle sent Clare tracts on the subject of slavery occasionally[141] and Clare had read some of Pringle's South African poems. In addition there is a letter from Mary Anne Read, 16 May 1826, telling Clare that she is preparing a volume of poems about slavery, with contributions from Montgomery, Bowring, Bernard Barton, Wiffen, Allan Cunningham, Jane Taylor and others, and soliciting a contribution from Clare.[142] Clare replied on 10 July 1826:

I am sure Slavery is an abominable traffic & a disgrace to Mahomedism much more Christianity & they who sanction it cannot be Christians for it is utterly at variance with religion & nature . . . [143]

He would be prepared to write 'a few verse in the shape of a song on the "Negroe Boy"'. A further letter from Mary Anne Rawson, as she had become, on 13 February 1833, told Clare that she was at last about to publish her anthology and asked for his poem.[144] The book, entitled *The Bow in the Cloud,* was published 1834 but does not appear to include a Clare poem. The correspondence, however, demonstrates how deeply Clare felt about slavery. Thus Clare's positions over Catholic Emancipation and Slavery were clearly dictated by his religious feelings.

It is worthwhile perhaps noting here that William Cobbett felt less concern about slavery in Africa than did Clare, considering that attention paid to it was a diversion from the problem of 'slavery' among the English agricultural labourers.[145] At first it might be thought strange that Clare, while appreciating Cobbett's greatness as a writer and admiring his even greater potential, was very critical of him as a politician.[146] He considered Cobbett rash and unmeasured. There is a notable difference between the two men both in style and substance. Clare is often more balanced and considered, even to the point where he occasionally flounders in trying to get a moderate view across to his reader. He is not constantly 'on the thump' like Cobbett, and is certainly much less egotistical. He does not claim to have the answers to so many political problems as Cobbett does. He does not condemn the whole of the Anglican clergy for the misdemeanours of some of them[147] and his religious beliefs are far more integral to him than they are to Cobbett. He is generally very sympathetic to Quakerism while Cobbett holds Quakers and Jews alike responsible for the whole speculative 'Thing', or system, which he felt ought to be swept away.[148] To him Quakers are parasites and he never hesitates to condemn them. Cobbett has no good word to say of the great landowners, even denouncing Lord Milton on one occasion[149], but Clare had experienced kindnesses from the Fitzwilliams and Cecils and was not about to bite the hand that fed him. Clare rode fewer hobby-horses than Cobbett and had more trust in the innate goodness of man. He shared with Cobbett a distaste for the increasing gentrification of country parsons and tenant-farmers and rivalled Cobbett in his admiration of many domestic virtues. Both men valued 'independence', but Cobbett had gained much more in life than Clare was ever able to manage. Both of them loved nature but Clare's respect for, and knowledge of, natural life is much greater than Cobbett's. Perhaps the essential difference is that Cobbett always has a point to make and is not too particular how he makes it. Clare is more conservative than Cobbett. While both men were familiar with the concept of the Norman Yoke, Clare referred to it less frequently. He also accepts, at least on one occasion, the Great Chain of Being which posited that every part of creation was in that position in which God had placed it, so that the social hierarchy was part of the divine plan,[150] and should be accepted as such. Cobbett had more sweeping views of what reforms were desirable.

Alan Vardy, in a recently published article, says:

> For late twentieth-century critics, there is still much to be explored in the chaotic details of Clare's life, and that potential knowledge makes attempts to label Clare's politics as 'radical' or 'conservative' premature and thus difficult to assess.[151]

In an examination of the writings of John Lucas and P. M. S. Dawson on this subject he shows how Clare's reactions to the Swing Riots, for example, may demonstrate Clare's ambivalence and examines the poet's reactions to the arson at Clark's Deeping Fen farm in some detail. He contrasts Clare's first reactions to the incident, described in Clare's letter to Frank Simpson,[152] and his later satirical description of the locality's panic about such rural uprisings in 'The Hue & Cry'. He concludes this section by saying that Clare's analysis of the crisis in 'The Hue & Cry' is nearer to Cobbett's defence of rural violence in the 13 November 1830 and 11 December 1830 numbers of *The Political Register* than it is to the editorial comments of the conservative newspaper *The Stamford Bee*. Cobbett had written on 11 December:

> Without entering at present into the *motives* of the working people, it is unquestionable that their acts have produced good, and great good too.

I do not believe that this helps us to understand Clare much better. While he is necessarily interested in the implications of politics for the life of the agricultural poor and even anxious to become a champion for the poor, he is not a politician and therefore is under no obligation to follow a consistent party line whether it be 'radical' or 'conservative', Whig or Tory. He is free to react to particular crises such as the Queen Caroline affair or Catholic Emancipation or the Swing Riots, without seeking to establish a consistency in his attitudes to these events. No one political line is right for all situations. Thus it is as unnecessary for Clare to make a choice between Cobbett and the *Stamford Bee* as between Cobbett and Marianne Marsh, the wife of the Bishop of Peterborough. Clare detested the violence of the Swing Riots and was critical of Cobbett for his intemperate attitudes. He also had a very real sympathy with the agricultural poor, with their failure to secure a living wage, and their consequent exploitation by many farmers. He also would have been well informed of Herbert Marsh's position on tithes, but may have been reluctant to quarrel with it openly. It would not have affected his opinion that the Anglican Church should not be weakened. With Vardy's final sentence I am in complete agreement: 'We should celebrate Clare's 'contradictions' as evidence of his independence and strength of mind in a particularly complex, violent and dangerous time.'[153] But there is more consistency in Clare's outlook than he allows.

Finally, a word should be said about the political implications of Clare's use of language. Olivia Smith has shown how far-reaching such implications could be for those involved in political trials, such as seditious libel, in the first four decades of the nineteenth century, where even the use of plain English instead of legal diction might be interpreted by the courts as a form of contempt.[154] The vernacular as used by common men was threatening to the whole English cultural establishment. It has long remained so. The finest celebration of Clare's use of 'acoustic pattern, dialect, oral culture, the indwellingness of spoken language' is in Tom Paulin's essay, 'Strinkling Dropples: John Clare'.[155] In this essay Paulin analyzes the extraordinary resources of Clare's language – not just its country terms, its dialect, its sexual explicitness, but also its 'visionary quality', its 'elaborate sensitivity', its 'slippery liquid happenings'. There were also its lines of defence, its cyphers, its asterisked absences and the whole language of suppressed identity. Only recently has much of this been revealed to readers and critics. Many of his poems in which these qualities were most acutely expressed never saw the light of day. The standardizing forces of the press and the educational system, the dictionary-makers and the review-editors, the evangelical movement and the antipathy to regional identity made sure that it would be so. In his early years Clare bowed to their exterior influences so that his voice could be heard at all. As he grew more confident he began to express his opinion on political issues in his own words but, as we have said, poems like 'The Summons', 'The Hue & Cry' and the unpublished poems in Peterborough MS A59 were not included by Clare in his *Midsummer Cushion* collection presumably because he did not see them as the kind of work he could publish in his 'official' collections.[156] The newspapers offered him a unique opportunity in this respect, with their less restricted view of popular forms and language and their receptivity to polemic and satire, along with the shelter of anonymous publication. There he could oppose the repressive nature of the political and social climate of his age by becoming more intensely individual and creative in his own characteristic idiom. To a deep sense of respect for his local and traditional speech he added a new flair for expressing himself in a language that was specific to his own experience, and he did this at a time when he was becoming more outspoken on political matters.

Notes

1   I wish to thank my co-editors for their helpful suggestions and criticisms in the writing of this introduction.
2   Raymond Williams, *Culture and Society 1780–1950* (1958; Harmonsworth: Penguin Books, 1968), p. 49.
3   *Ibid*, p. 53.
4   Peterborough MS A43, p. 35 (see below, pp. 295–6). Cf. Peterborough MS A20, p. R76, cancelled.
5   *Wordsworth's Poetical Works*, ed. Thomas Hutchinson (Oxford, 1908), pp. 938–9; cited in Williams, p. 58.
6   See below, p. 301, note 4.
7   David Hume, *Enquiries concerning Human Understanding and concerning the Principles of Morals* (1777), ed. L.A. Selby-Bigge, third ed. with text revised and notes by P.H. Nidditch (Oxford: Clarendon Press, 1975), p. 219.
8   Ibid., p. 223.
9   Ibid., p. 223, note 1.
10   Ibid., p. 229, note 1.
11   Ibid., p. 237.
12   Ibid., pp. 222–3.

13   Ibid., p. 222. Jacopo Sannazaro (c. 1456–1530), Italian author of
      Arcadia (1504). One of Clare's first poems was 'Epigram on Rome
      Occasioned by Reading Mr Rolts Translation of Sannazarios
      (Famous!) Epigram on Venice':

> Sannazar'o makes Neptune to exclaim
> 'That men built Rome, but Gods did venice frame!'
> Here he must flatter – for if thats the odds
> Rome shows that men had better skill than Gods (*EP* I. 34)

14   Peterborough MS A46, p. 79–80.
15   'The Village Minstrel', lines 951–1047 (below, pp. 32–5). Clare had
      worked as a boy at Woodcroft Castle near Helpston (*JCBH*, pp. 65–6,
      69 and 232–3).
16   James McKusick, 'William Cobbett, John Clare, and the Agrarian
      Politics of the English Revolution', in Timothy Martin and Nigel
      Smith (eds.), *British Literary Radicalism, 1650–1830: from Revolution to
      Revolution* (Cambridge: Cambridge University Press, forthcoming).
17   See below, p. 303, note 45.
18   Peterborough MS A46, p. 78.
19   Peterborough MS A46, pp. 78–9.
20   Peterborough MS A18, p. R253 (see below, p. 281).
21   Peterborough MS A46, p. 74 (see below, p. 298).
22   Pforzheimer MS Misc.198, p. 48 (see below, p. 281).
23   Eric Robinson, Geoffrey Summerfield and David Powell (eds.), *John
      Clare: The Shepherd's Calendar* (Oxford University Press, 1993), p. 71.
24   Peterborough MS A46, p. 74 (see below, p. 303, note 31).
25   *Cambridge Chronicle*, 24 December 1830 (see Appendix, below, p.
      328).
26   *Ibid*; see *Letters*, pp. 522–3 (below, pp. 318–19).
27   Peterborough MS B5, p. 74 (see below, p. 295). Cf. Vicesimus Knox,
      Essays Moral and Literary (1786; 3 vols., London: G. Offer and T. Tegg,
      1819), vol. 1, essay X, 'The Respectableness of the Clergy', pp. 58–61,
      a defence of tithes by an author known to Clare (the 1819 edition is
      item 274 in his library). See David Powell, *Catalogue of the John Clare
      Collection in Northampton Public Library* (Northampton, 1964), pp.
      23–34 (hereafter referred to as Powell).
28   Peterborough MS A18, p. R253.
29   See below, p. 317.
30   Peterborough MS A17, p. 20 (see below, p. 285).
31   'The Parish', lines 355–380, 1583–1787 (see below, pp. 58–9, 94–101).
32   'The Molecatcher', lines 138–9 (*MP*, II. 128).
33   *Drakard's Stamford News*, 13 April 1821.
34   Ibid., 3 August 1821: 'A CAUTION AGAINST THE PROFANA-
      TION OF THE SABBATH'.
35   See Eric Robinson, 'John Clare (1793–1864) and James Plumptre

(1771–1832) "A Methodistical Parson"', *Transactions of the Cambridge Bibliographical Society*, 11 (1996), 59–88.

36 See Christopher Hill, *Liberty Against the Law: Some Sevententh-Century Controversies* (London: Allen Lane, 1996), pp. 31–34, 42–43, 88, 97–100, 102–3, 201–5, 234–6, 256–64, and 312–24; and E.P. Thompson, *Customs in Common* (London: The Merlin Press, 1991), pp. 99, 103–4 and 132.

37 'The Parish', line 1511 (see below, p. 92).

38 *JCBH*, p. 127.

39 See article cited in note 35 above.

40 *Drakard's Stamford News* and *Stamford Mercury*, *passim*.

41 See *MP*, III. 163–74.

42 See *EP*, I. 532–5 and II. 153–5.

43 See John Goodridge and Kelsey Thornton, 'John Clare: the trespasser', in Hugh Haughton, Adam Phillips and Geoffrey Summerfield (eds.), *John Clare in Context* (Cambridge: Cambridge University Press, 1994), pp. 87–129.

44 *JCBH*, p. 127.

45 Line 78 (see below, p. 48).

46 See, for example, William Cobbett, *Rural Rides* (Penguin, 1967), pp. 426–28.

47 E.P. Thompson, *Customs in Common*, p. 45.

48 The *Huntingdon. Bedford and Peterborough Gazette* for 3 March 1927 1827 under 'Peterborough', describes a 'Desperate Affray with Poachers' in the Earl of Winchilsea's lands in Rockingham Forest with gamekeepers and members of the Earl's family. The same paper, on 7 April 1827, describes the capital conviction of twelve poachers.

49 *JCBH*, p. 52.

50 Note the use of this phrase, later used as the title of one of Clare's political satires.

51 Presumably a reference to King John's loss of the crown jewels in the Wash.

52 Pet. MS A42, p. 73, cancelled.

53 Pet. MS A42, p. 66, cancelled.

54 *JCBH*, p. 42.

55 [John Bridges] Peter Whalley, *The History and Antiquities of Northamptonshire. Compiled from the Manuscript Collections of the late Learned Antiquary John Bridges, Esq.* (2 vols., Oxford: Sold by T. Payne, London; D. Prince and J. Cooke, Oxford; and Mr. Lacy, Northampton, 1791), II, p. 489.

56 *JCBH*, pp. 83–4.

57 See Christopher Hill, *Liberty Against the Law*, pp. 131–41.

58 *Stamford Mercury*, 24 June 1831, reports on an itinerant gypsy fortune-teller whose predictions led to a servant-maid attempting

suicide.

59 Clare's attitude to and treatment of gypsies in matters of trespass is discussed by John Goodridge and Kelsey Thornton in 'John Clare; the trespasser' (see above, note 43). See also *JCBH*, p. 84.

60 *JCBH*, p.83

61 See below pp. 118–20.

62 Mrs Emmerson to Clare, 30 September 1825, B.L. Egerton MS 2247, fol.79v: 'I forgot to tell you, that I have presumed to shorten yr Gipsey Song – of one Stanza – by bringing down the 4 first lines, of the last verse but one, and joining them to the 4 last lines of the concluding verse – *by such means we avoid repetitions of words – V D approved* [our italics] of my doing this'.

63 For the political significance of gypsies and other 'marginal' figures, see Christopher Hill, *Liberty Against the Law*, pp. 47–141.

64 *JCBH*, p. 37.

65 We have previously published the poem 'Rich and Poor', which deals with this subject, as being by Clare (see *EP*, II. 518–19). It is in fact by Thomas Love Peacock and was acknowledged as his by being included in his *Paper Money Lyrics* (1837), having been first published in the *Traveller* for 9 July 1821 over the signature 'DIVES' and reprinted frequently in national and local newspapers, including *Drakard's Stamford News*. It was evidently from one such republication that Clare copied lines 1–20 and 26–30, on paper watermarked 1828 and probably in use in 1830. He evidently approved of the sentiments of Peacock's poem, and may have intended to quote it, possibly in his 'Apology for the Poor'.

66 See Roy Palmer, *A Ballad History of England* (London: Batsford, 1979), p. 109.

67 Clare's character, Barnaby, says: ' . . . our baker who has turned methodist will not heat his oven on sundays at no consideration yet he has been detected on mondays of using light weights in weighing his flour & his bread' (Peterborough MS A42, p. 22). In his 'Letter to Allan Cunningham', Clare says that Cunningham will be unable to get hot bread for his Sunday breakfast without paying extra for it (Peterborough MS A42, p. 83).

68 See Eric Robinson and Geoffrey Summerfield, *Selected Poems and Prose of John Clare* (Oxford University Press, 1967), p. 30.

69 *JCBH*, p. 95.

70 *JCBH*, pp. 97–8.

71 See 'Nelson & the Nile' and 'Waterloo' (below, pp. 135–7 and 8–10); for Benbow and Levison, see 'Sea Song', *MP*, IV. 90–99; 'Lines on Wellington', *EP*, I. 54–5.

72 E.g. 'Wars Alarms', *MP*, II, p. 275.

73 See 'The Reformers Hymn' (below, pp. 191–2); 'Address to an Old Halfpenny' (below, pp. 225–7); 'George IV Death' (below, pp.

161–2); and 'On the Occasion of the Queen's Visit to Northampton', *LP*, I. 260–1.

74   See *The Stamford Mercury*, 24 January 1820 and *Drakard's Stamford News* 2 and 4 December 1820.

75   See 'Address to an old Halfpenny' and 'Thou king of half a score dominions' (see below, pp. 224–7).

76   See 'The Ants', *EP*, II. 56 and 'Monarchy of Nature' (below, p. 140).

77   Clare to Hessey, 1 December 1820 (below, p. 310).

78   Thomas Tusser, *Five Hundred Points of Good Husbandry* (1812), p. XVI, lines 15–16. See also p. XXIX, lines 10–13. This is the edition in Clare's library at Northampton, item 380 (Powell, p. 33).

79   *European Magazine*, New Series, I, ii, October 1825, pp. 115–19.

80   Van Dyk to Clare, 4 October 1825 (Peterborough MS F1, pp. 69–72).

81   See above, p. xvi–xvii.

82   See Christopher Hill, *Liberty Against the Law*, Chap. 6, pp. 83–90. Clare's acquaintance with the Norman Yoke may have derived from his reading of Drayton's *Polyolbion*, Pope's *Windsor Forest*, Joseph Ritson's *Robin Hood*, John Gay and even Winstanley.

83   Pforzheimer Misc. MS 198, p. 44. Clare may have derived this idea in part from chapbook histories of Turpin.

84   See Pforzheimer Misc MS 198, p. 41 (below, pp. 296–7).

85   G.E. Mingay, *Land and Society in England 1750–1980* (London and New York: Longman, 1994), pp. 259–88.

86   See J.W. and Anne Tibble, *John Clare: A Life* (London: Cobden-Sanderson, 1932), p. 83 and note 4 to Chap. IV, and also *JCBH*, p.167, '[Lord Milton's] long enduring kindness to my father'.

87   The Fitzwilliams' revenues from Northamptonshire nearly tripled from £7,639 in 1792 to £21,000 by the end of the Napoleon Wars. See F.M.L. Thompson, *English Landed Society in the Nineteenth Century* (London: Routledge & Kegan Paul, 1963), p.228. The author calculates (p.223), that 'on the enclosure after 1809 of Maxey and Helpstone on the edge of the fen country a return of 30 per cent was obtained on the outlay of £10,364'.

88   See N. Harte and R. Quinault, *Land and Society in Britain, 1700–1914* (Manchester, 1996), p. 213.

89   Harold Perkin, *The Origins of Modern English Society 1780–1880* (London: Routledge and Kegan Paul, 1969), p.19.

90   Ibid., p.22.

91   Clare to J.A. Hessey, 21 January 1827 (*Letters*, pp. 390–1). See *MP*, III. xx-xxi.

92   J.M. Neeson, *Commoners: common right, enclosure and social change in England, 1700–1820* (Cambridge: Cambridge University Press, 1993), *op. cit.*, pp. 256–7.

93   See *EP*, I. 172–80, 186–93.

94   Ian Dyck, *William Cobbett and Rural Popular Culture* (Cambridge:

Cambridge University Press, 1992), pp. 135, 138.

95 See below, pp. 137–40.

96 See below, p. 275.

97 To J.A. Hessey, 1 Dec. 1820; *Letters*, pp. 109–10 (see below, pp. 309–10).

98 See Rohan McWilliam, *Popular Politics in Nineteenth-Century England* (London: Routledge, 1998), pp. 7–13, *et passim*.

99 *JCBH*, p. 224.

100 W.E. Tate, 'Inclosure Movements in Northamptonshire', *Northamptonshire Past and Present*, 1 (1949), p.30, cited in J.M. Neeson, *Commoners*, p. 262.

101 Neeson, *op. cit.*, p. 242, cited in Stephen Michael Colclough, *Voicing loss: versions of pastoral in the poetry of John Clare, 1817–1832* (Ph. D. thesis, Open University, 1996), p. 104.

102 Neeson, *op. cit.*, p.280.

103 *JCBH*, p. 29.

104 Deleted passage in Peterborough MS A53, fol. 17r (below, p. 280).

105 BL MS Egerton 2248, fol. 198r.

106 Clare to Drakard, [after 21 December 1829], *Letters*, p. 490. I believe that the Scott here is Jonathan Scott who kept the *Stamford News* in publication when Drakard was imprisoned in Lincoln gaol, but it is just possible that it is Sir Walter Scott.

107 Henry Ryde to Clare, 19 October 1830 (B.L. Egerton MS 2248, fol. 276v).

108 Mrs Emmerson to Clare, 9 November 1831 (B.L. Egerton MS 2248, fols. 400r-v). Earl Fitzwilliam and Lord Milton were Whigs; the Marquis of Exeter, a Tory.

109 See below, p. 269.

110 It is possible that the writer of that article may have been Lord Charles Manners of Ufford Hall near Helpston since Clare describes the author as 'emerging from under a coronet'. See *JCBH*, pp. 2, 210 and 330, n. 209.

111 Given too early a date in *EP*, II. 593.

112 Clare's two great satirical poems, 'The Summons' and 'The Hue & Cry' have been made available in limited editions, edited by Eric Robinson and published by the Tern Press, Market Drayton (1989, 1990).

113 Mrs Emmerson to Clare, 7 February 1831 (B.L. Egerton, MS 2248, fol.328r), and 17 October 1831 (B.L. Egerton MS 2248, fols.395v-396r).

114 *Letters*, p. 527.

115 Colclough, *op. cit.*, p.175.

116 See above, note 113.

117 Colclough, *op. cit.*, p.175.

118 See *EP*, I. 111–12.

119   *JCBH*, p. 64.
120   In a paper delivered at Nottingham Trent University, 18 July 1998, entitled '"Labour and Luxury": Clare's Lost Pastoral and the Importance of the Voice of Labour in the Early Poems'.
121   John Barrell, *The Idea of Landscape and the Sense of Place* (Cambridge: Cambridge University Press, 1972), pp.116–18.
122   As stressed in Ronald Blythe's Annual Presidential Address to the John Clare Society at Helpston, July 1999.
123   *EP*, I. 235–9.
124   L. Shepard, *John Pitts: Ballad Printer of Seven Dials, London 1765–1844* (London: Private Libraries Association, 1969), pp. 128, 137.
125   See Charles Hindley, *The Life and Times of James Catnach (late of Seven Dials), Ballad Monger* (London, 1878), *passim*.
126   B.L. Egerton MS 2248, fols. 126r-v.
127   Henry Behnes to Clare, 2 June 1829 (B.L. Egerton MS 2247, fol. 296r).
128   Journal, 22 , 24 and 25May 1825 (*JCBH*, p. 229). See *Stamford Mercury,* 20 May 1825.
129   See Clare's 'Letter to Allan Cunningham', Peterborough MS A42, p. 81; also MS A18, p. 25r, and MS A45, p. 7. Some of this material on Catholic miracles is taken from Charles Colton's *Lacon,* item CXXIII. See also *The European Magazine* 'Monks and Monkery', N.S., vol. I, no. IV, to which Clare also contributed.
130   'Valentine Eve', lines 27–8 (*MP*, III. 72).
131   See pp. 159–60.
132   *EP*, II. 433.
133   Peterborough MS A42, pp. 54–5. Cf. *JCBH,* p. 132: 'My creed may be different to other creeds . . .'
134   Peterborough MS A42, p. 35.
135   Peterborough MS A42, p. 36.
136   *JCBH*, p. 149.
137   Peterborough MS A42, pp. 39–40.
138   Peterborough MS A49, p. 1.
139   BL Egerton MS 2249, fols. 14–15. See *Letters*, pp. 571–3.
140   Clare to Pringle, c.8 February 1832, *ibid.*, p. 572 (see below, p. 323). The book sent to Clare was Alexander Barclay, *A Practical View of the Present State of Slavery in the West Indies* (1828), item no. 109 in Clare's library (Powell, p. 24).
141   'I write at present in great haste & have only leisure to recommend the two or three Anti-Slavery tracts sent herewith to your perusal. I will send you more if you feel interested in the question' (Thomas Pringle to Clare, 19 June 1832; BL MS Egerton 2249, fol. 34v).
142   BL Egerton MS 2250, fols. 289r-290v. We owe this reference to the kindness of Robert Heyes.
143   John Rylands Library, English MS 415/158. We thank John Goodridge for his generosity in bringing this letter to our attention.

144 BL Egerton MS 2249, fols. 130r-131v.
145 *Rural Rides, ed. cit.,* pp. 261–62.
146 See below, pp. 299–300, 322-3.
147 It should be recalled, however, that, in June 1822, Mrs Emmerson was worried lest Clare should have offended the Rev. Henry Cary 'by saying you wished the churches were all in ashes and the parsons sent to beg their bread' (*Letters,* p. 245, n. 2.).
148 *Rural Rides,* pp. 109, 127, 156–57, 209, 225, 288, 343, and 345.
149 *Rural Rides,* p. 396: 'Of all the mean, all the cowardly, reptiles, that ever crawled on the face of the earth, the *English land-owners* are the most mean and the most cowardly . . .'. See p. 219, for his criticism of Lord Milton.
150 See below p. 11, and note to lines 117 and 127 of 'The Hue & Cry'.
151 Alan Vardy, 'Clare and Political Equivocation', *John Clare Society Journal,* 18 (July 1999), pp. 37–48.
152 See below, pp. 318–19.
153 Vardy, p. 47.
154 Olivia Smith, *The Politics of Language 1791–1819* (Oxford, 1984).
155 Tom Paulin, *Writing to the Moment: Selected Critical Essays, 1980–1996* (1996), pp.161–71.
156 Stephen Colclough, *op. cit.,* p.175.

Note on the text

Selection has been difficult and no doubt every reader would wish something to be included that we have omitted. We have included some poems that are available in convenient paperback editions because we consider them to be essential to a balanced representation of Clare's political views. All poems, except for a few, have already been published in the Oxford English Text of Clare's poems in eight volumes. In the list of Contents we indicate in which of those volumes the poems have been printed, thus:

> *EP* = *Early Poems of John Clare 1804–1822* (2 vols., Oxford: Clarendon Press, 1989)
>
> *MP* = *John Clare: Poems of the Middle-Period 1822–1837* (vols. 1–4, Oxford: Clarendon Press, 1996–98)
>
> *LP* = *Later Poems of John Clare* (2 vols., Oxford: Clarendon Press, 1984)

For poems not yet published in the *O.E.T. Clare,* we give references thus:

> Peterborough MS A18, p. 20; Northampton MS 17, p. 20; BL MS (for British Library MSS); Pforzheimer MS etc., followed by the page number.

References to prose passages are given in the same form. The prose selections represent our latest readings, and we have added passages not to be found in any of our earlier publications as well as corrections to passages previously published. We have inserted sentence-spaces into the text in order to help the reader, though we agree with Mark Storey that 'This is inevitably something of a compromise: some sentences clearly yearn to go on and on in an uninterrupted flow, whilst others can seem merely confusing' (*Letters*, p. xxxiii). We use curly brackets to indicate Clare's deletions and square brackets for our own insertions, but we have only retained those of Clare's deletions that seem to have potential significance and have kept our own insertions to a minimum.

Though this book is intended for the general reader, we have preserved Clare's spelling and punctuation in the belief that they are no real problem to an intelligent reader. Readers should be alert to Clare's confusion between 'where' and 'were', 'their' and 'there', 'near' and 'ne'er', and his omission of apostrophes in 'I'll', 'we'll', etc. and in possessives, but should soon become used to them.

We have occasionally excluded a short prose passage for one of the following reasons:

1. it has so many missing or indecipherable words that the great majority of readers would not profit from it,
2. it is garbled and does not make sense,
3. it repeats something already clearly said in a passage that we have included.

We have, however, provided references for those passages that come in category 3.

As with the verse, the selection of prose passages was sometimes difficult, depending on how one defined 'political'. Naturally, if a prose passage seemed to make a comment relating to one or more of our verse-selections, we have included it. We anticipate a full critical edition of Clare's prose writings in the future.

We publish selections from Clare's letters where they show Clare's participation in public events and it would be difficult for the reader to locate the passages in Mark Storey's *Letters of John Clare*. Occasionally we have been able to make corrections to Storey's edition.

The list of books and articles includes most of the publications found useful by any one of us, whether or not they are quoted in our text. If we had more space, we could have extended our Notes, especially from newspapers.

List of illustrations

Cover, 'The Freeborn Englishman' by George Cruikshank, from William Hone, *A Slap at Slop and the Bridge-Street Gang* (1822) Reproduced by kind permission of the John Rylands University Library, Manchester

p. l, 'Electors of Stamford', election poster (1830) Reproduced by kind permission of Peterborough Museum and Art Gallery

p. 23, vignette by George Cruikshank, from Anon., *Sunday in London* (1833)

p. 71, 'An Election Squib' by George Cruikshank, from *The Cruikshank Omnibus* (1842)

p. 89, 'The Clerical Magistrate' by George Cruikshank, from William Hone, *The Political House that Jack Built* (49th ed., 1820) Reproduced by kind permission of the John Rylands University Library, Manchester

p. 95, 'This is a Priest', artist unknown, from *The Real or Constitutional House that Jack Built* (1819)

p. 117, 'Liberty', by George Cruikshank, from William Hone, *The Political House that Jack Built* (49th ed., 1820) Reproduced by kind permission of the John Rylands University Library, Manchester

p. 147, 'To Check the Circulation of Little Books', by George Cruikshank, from William Hone, *The Man in the Moon* (7th ed., 1820) Reproduced by kind permission of the John Rylands University Library, Manchester

Note on George Cruikshank
(1792–1878)

When Clare failed to secure the services of Cruikshank as the illustrator to 'The Summons' and 'The Hue & Cry', because Cruikshank was beginning to turn from political caricature to book-illustration, it was a great loss to the worlds of literature and art. As the illustrator of the political pamphlets of William Hone, with whom Clare corresponded and who published work by Clare, Cruikshank had established himself as a preeminent caricaturist and an obvious choice to illustrate Clare's irreverent satires. Though Cruikshank was a Londoner and Clare a rural provincial, they had much in common. When Clare visited London, he, too, stood outside the windows of the print-shops to view their displays. He was alive to the wood-cuts in spelling-books, broadside ballads, story-books, bibles and political pamphlets, and may well have seen examples of Cruikshank's early work. He certainly revelled in Pierce Egan's *Life in London* (1820), and its heroes Tom and Jerry were part of his vocabulary. As boys, both men read many of the same books and played the same games. As men they were both Volunteers, though Cruikshank was clearly the keener soldier. Still they could both laugh at 'the awkward squad'. Though they were on opposite sides in the Queen Caroline affair, they both poked fun at evangelical sabbatarianism. Accordingly we have chosen Cruikshank as the main illustrator to this volume and so we hope, in part, to assuage Clare's disappointment.

POEMS

HELPSTONE

Hail humble Helpstone where thy valies spread
& thy mean Village lifts its lowly head
Unknown to grandeur & unknown to fame
No minstrel boasting to advance thy name
Unletterd spot unheard in poets song   5
Where bustling labour drives the hours along
Where dawning genius never met the day
Where usless ign'rance slumbers life away
Unknown nor heeded where low genius trys
Above the vulgar & the vain to rise   10
Whose low opinions rising thoughts subdues
Whose railing envy damps each humble view
Oh where can friendships cheering smiles abode
To guide young wanderers on a doubtful road
The trembling hand to lead, the steps to guide   15
& each vain wish (as reason proves) to chide –
Mysterious fate who can on thee depend
Thou opes the hour but hides its doubtful end
In fancys view the joys have long appear'd
Where the glad heart by laughing plentys cheer'd   20
& fancys eyes as oft as vainly fill
At first but doubtful & as doubtful still

So little birds in winters frost & snow
Doom'd (like to me) wants keener frost to know
Searching for food & 'better life' in vain   25
(Each hopeful track the yielding snows retain)
First on the ground each fairy dream pursues
Tho sought in vain – yet bent on higher views
Still chirps & hopes & wipes each glossy bill
Nor undiscourag'd nor dishartn'd still   30
Hops on the snow cloth'd bough & chirps again
Heedless of naked shade & f[r]ozen plain
With fruitles hopes each little bosom warms
Springs budding promise – summers plentious charms

A universal hope the whole prevades   35
& chirping plaudits fill the chilling shades
Till warn'd at once the vain deluded flies
& twitatwit their visions as they rise
Visions like mine that vanish as they flye
In each keen blast that fills the higher skye   40
Who find like me along their weary way
Each prospect lessen & each hope decay
& like to me these victims of the blast
(Each foolish fruitless wish resign'd at last)
Are glad to seek the place from whence they went   45
& put up with distress & be content –

Hail scenes obscure so near & dear to me
The church the brook the cottage & the tree
Still shall obscurity reherse the song
& hum your beauties as I stroll along   50
Dear native spot which length of time endears
The sweet retreat of twenty lingering years
& oh those years of infancy the scene
Those dear delights where once they all have been
Those golden days long vanish'd from the plain   55
Those sports those pastimes now belovd in vain
When happy youth in pleasures circle ran
Nor thought what pains awaited future man
No other thought employing or employ'd
But how to add to happiness enjoy'd   60
Each morning wak'd with hopes before unknown
& eve possesing made each wish their own
The day gone bye left no pursuit undone
Nor one vain wish save that they went too soon
Each sport each pastime ready at their call   65
As soon as wanted they posses'd em all
These joys all known in happy infancy
& all I ever knew where spent on thee
& who but loves to view where these where past
& who that views but loves em to the last   70

4

Feels his heart warm to view his native place
A fondness still those past delights to trace
The vanish'd green to mourn the spot to see
Where flourish'd many a bush & many a tree
Where once the brook (for now the brook is gone)   75
Oer pebbles dimpling sweet went wimpering on
Oft on whose oaken plank I've wondering stood
(That led a pathway o'er its gentle flood)
To see the beetles their wild mazes run
With getty jackets glittering in the sun   80
So apt & ready at their reels they seem
So true the dance is figur'd on the stream
Such justness such correctness they impart
They seem as ready as if taught by art
In those past days (for then I lov'd the shade)   85
How oft I've sighd at alterations made
To see the woodmans cruel axe employ'd
A tree beheaded or a bush destroy'd
Nay e'en a post (old standards) or a stone
Moss'd o'er by age & branded as her own   90
Would in my mind a strong attachment gain
A fond desire that there they might remain
& all old favourites fond taste approves
Griev'd me at heart to witness their remove[s]

Thou far fled pasture long evanish'd scene   95
Where nature's freedom spread the flowry green
Where golden kingcups open'd in to view
Where silver dazies charm'd the 'raptur'd view
& tottering hid amidst those brighter gems
Where silver grasses bent their tiny stems   100
Where the pale lilac mean & lowly grew
Courting in vain each gazer[s] heedless view
While Cows laps sweetest flowers upon the plain
Seeminly bow'd to shun the hand in vain
Where lowing oxen roamd to feed at large   105
& bleeting there the shepherds woolly charge

5

Whose constant calls thy echoing vallies cheer'd
Thy scenes adornd & rural life endeard
No calls of hunger pitys feelings wound
Twas wanton plenty rais'd the joyful sound   110
Thy grass in plenty gave the wish'd supply
Ere sultry sun's had wak'd the troubling flye
Then blest retiring by thy bounty fed
They sought thy shades & found an easy bed

But now alas those scenes exist no more   115
The pride of Life with thee (like mine) is oer
Thy pleasing spots to which fond memory clings
Sweet cooling shades & soft refreshing springs
& tho fates pleas'd to lay their beauties bye
In a dark corner of obscurity   120
As fair & sweet they blo[o]m'd thy plains among
As blooms those Edens by the poets sung
Now all laid waste by desolations hand
Whose cursed weapons levels half the land
Oh who could see my dear green willows fall   125
What feeling heart but dropt a tear for all
Accursed wealth oer bounding human laws
Of every evil thou remains the cause
Victims of want those wretches such as me
Too truly lay their wretchedness to thee   130
Thou art the bar that keeps from being fed
& thine our loss of labour & of bread
Thou art the cause that levels every tree
& woods bow down to clear a way for thee

Sweet rest & peace ye dear departed Charms   135
Which once Industry cherish'd in her arms
When peace & plenty known but now to few
Where known to all & labour had his due
When mirth & toil companions thro' the day
Made labour light & pass'd the hours away   140
When nature made the fields so dear to me
Thin scattering many a bush & many a tree

Where the wood minstrels sweetly join'd among
& cheer'd my needy toilings with a song
Ye perishd spots adieu ye ruind scenes   145
Ye well known pastures oft frequented greens
Tho now no more – fond memory's pleasing pains
Within her breast your every scene retains
Scarce did a bush spread its romantic bower
To shield the lazy shepherd from the shower   150
Scarce did a tree befriend the chattering pye
By lifting up its head so proud & high
(Whose nest stuck on the topmost bough sublime
Mocking the efforts of each boy to climb
Oft as they've fill'd my vain desiring eye   155
As oft in vain my skill essay'd to try)
Nor bush nor tree within thy vallies grew
When a mischevious boy but what I knew
No not a secret spot did then remain
Through out each spreading wood & winding plain   160
But in those days my presence once posest
The snail horn searching or the mossy nest

Oh happy Eden of those golden years
Which memory cherishes & use endears
Thou dear beloved spot may it be thine   165
To add a comfort to my life[s] decline
When this vain world & I have nearly done
& times drain'd glass has little left to run
When all the hopes that charm'd me once are oer
To warm my soul in extacys no more   170
By dissapointments prov'd a foolish cheat
Each ending bitter & beginning sweet
When weary age the grave a r[e]scue seeks
& prints its image on my wrinkl'd cheeks
Those charms of youth that I again may see   175
May it be mine to meet my end in thee
& as reward for all my troubles past
Find one hope true to die at home at last

So when the Traveller uncertain roams
On lost roads leading every where but home   180
Each vain desire that leaves his heart in pain
Each fruitless hope to cherish it in vain
Each hated track so slowly left behind
Makes for the home which night denies to find
& every wish that leaves the aching breast   185
Flies to the spot where all its wishes rest

WATERLOO

Ye tip-top Southeys first in fame
Ye poets worthy of the name
Arise arise great Bards arise
And sound your harps beyond the skies
Ye finest songsters of the plains   5
Ye Bloomfields sing your sweetest strains
Touch your top notes and highest strings
While England round with musick rings
To Britton's sons the praise is due
Her Sons who faught at Waterloo   10

Ye lowliest of the lowly plain
Ye meanest of the tunefull train
With me (your lowly brother) play
A tune to cellebrate the day
The lucky day when Brittons sons   15
Had chance to prove with swords and Guns
Their british courage british breed
How they could fight how they could bleed
For their own right and others too
So Nobly prov'd at Waterloo   20

Then all ye brother britons round
Still left behind on british ground
Who love to hear your Countreys fame
The glorious victorey proclaim
Let steeples bear the streaming blue   25
As Emblemn of her sons so true
While the bonfires blaze away
And the Guns and Cannons they
In thunders volly forth their praise
'Mid bursting cheers of loud Huzza's   30
Their fame demands all ye can do
To crown her sons at Waterloo

I from my labour will away
And twirl my beaver to Huzza
Now triumphing victories voice   35
Bids me for her sons rejoice
True bred sons of Britons isle
Boastfull thought creates a smile
Now it comes adieu to toil
And my rural strains awhile   40
Englands Victory now prevails
Over loves unfinish'd tales
Yes yes my bosom's fir'd from you
Ye British flowers at Waterloo

The Cannons roar in fancys ear   45
And long extended lines appear
All in motion ! all in arms !
Drums still beating to alarms
Guns their vollies pour again
Smoak decends to hide the slain   50
Britons wounded – glorious sight !
With redoubl'd fury fight
Prolong it fancy – let me view
How Britons faught at Waterloo
Whats Commanded now the cry   55

'Charge like Britons' rend the sky
O ! the savage blade is drawn
Now the bloody work comes on
Off they start Huzza's the noise
O ! your Courage british boys   60
Now the soldier's valour's try'd
Soldiers Hail on Englands side
Fancy rest – the trumpet blew
Victorys gain'd at Waterloo

Now my Country's glory come   65
Sheath your swords and march for home
Welcome to your native Isle
Here in triumph from your toil
March near deaf'n'd with Huzza's
Which we for your valour raise   70
For your valours glorious deeds
Englands Highest hope exceeds
All her boast and all her pride
True-blue britons prov'd and try'd
Come away your foes have flew   75
Thunder struck from Waterloo

Hero's all alike in Fame
None more worthy of the name
By his fellow none out brav'd
All as one in fight behav'd   80
British courage bold & true
Fir'd the noble army through
Gen'rals Privates all as one
Each at heart a Wellin[g]ton
Heroes hail – accept your due   85
Glory – fame, – & Waterloo

ON SEEING A LOST GREYHOUND IN WINTER
LYING UPON THE SNOW IN THE FIELDS

Ah thou poor neglected hound
Now thou'rt done wi' catching hares
Thou mayst lye upon the ground
Lost for what thy master cares
To see thee lye it makes me sigh   5
A proud hard hearted man
But men we know like dogs may go
When they've done all they can

And thus from witnesing thy fate
Thoughtfull reflection wakes   10
Tho thou'rt a dog (with grief I say't)
Poor men thy fare partakes
Like thee lost whelp the poor mans help
Ere while so much desir'd
Now harvests got is wanted not   15
Or little is requir'd

So now the over plus will be
As useles negros all
Turn'd in the bitter blast like thee
Meer cumber grounds to fall   20
But this reward for toil so hard
Is sure to meet return
From him whose ear is always near
When the oppressed mourn

For dogs as men are equally   25
A link in natures chain
Form'd by the hand that formed me
Which formeth naught in vain
All life contains as't were by chains
From him still perfect are   30
Nor does he think the meanest link
Unworthy of his Care

So let us both on him relye
And he'll for us provide
Find us a shelter warm and drye   35
With every thing beside
And while fools void of sense deride
My tenderness to thee
I'll take thee home from whence I've come
So rise and gang wi' me   40

Poor patient thing he seems to hear
And know what I have said
He wags his tale and ventures near
And bows his mournful head
Thou'rt welcome – come and tho' thou'rt dumb   45
Thy silence tells thy pains
So wi' me start to share a part
While I have aught remains

ELEGY HASTILY COMPOSED & WRITTEN WITH A PENCIL ON THE SPOT IN THE RUINS OF PICKWORTH RUTLAND

These buried Ruins now in dust forgot
These heaps of stone the only remnants seen
The 'Old Foundations' still they call the spot
Which plainly tells Enqu[i]rey what has been

A time was once – tho now the nettle grows   5
In triumph oer each heap that swells the ground
When they in buildings pil'd a village rose
With here a Cot & there a Garden crownd

& here while Grandeur with unequal share
Perhaps maintaind its idleness & pride   10
Industrys cottage rose contented there
With scarce as much as wants of life supplyd

12

Mysterious cause ! Still more mysterious pland
(– Altho undoubtedly the will of heaven)
To think what carless & unequal hand   15
Met[e]s out each portion that to man is given

While vain extravagance for one alone
Claims half the land their grandeur to mentain
What thousands – not a Rood to call their own
Like me but labour for support in vain   20

Here we see Luxury surfeit with excess
There want behol[d]ing beg from door to door
Still meeting sorrow where he meets sucess
By lengthening life that livd in vain before

Almighty power – but why should I repine   25
Or vainly live thy goodness to distrust
Since reason rules what providence designs
What ever is must certainly be just

Ye scenes of desolation spread around
Prosperity to you did once belong   30
& doubtless where these brambles claim the ground
The glass once flowd to hail the ranting song

The ale house here might stand – each hamlets boast
& here where elders rich from ruin grows
The tempting sign – but what was once is lost   35
Who would be proud of what this world bestows ?

How contemplation mourns your lost decay
To view thy pride laid level with the ground
To see where labour clears the soil away
What fragments of mortality abound   40

Theres not a Rood of Land demands our toil
Theres not a foot of ground we daily tread
But gains increase from times devouring spoil
& holds some fragment of the human dead

The very food thats to support us gave   45
Claims for its share an equal portion too
The dust of many a long forgotten grave
Serves to manure the soil from whence it grew

– Since first these ruins fell – how chang'd the scene
What busy bustling mortals now unknown   50
Have com'd & gone as tho there nought had been
Since first oblivion call'd the spot her own

Ye busy bustling mortals known before
Of what you've done – where went – or what you see
Of what your hopes attaind too (now no more)   55
For everlasting lyes a mystery

Like yours awaits for me that 'common lot'
Tis mine to be of every hope bereft
– A few more years & I shall be forgot
& not a Vestige of my memory left   60

[LABOUR AND LUXURY]

Thy eye can witness more then others
Thy feelings are thy own
& labours anguish & her sorrows
To thee has long been known
Luxurys wealth & pride upholding   5
Poor labours slav'd to dead
While they die gorg'd like beast in clover
We die for wants of bread

14

& what is worse – our little earnings
For which we toil & sweat   10
To uphold em [a]nd urge their coaches
They tax back half we get
We wear no rags but they ha part ont
They tax yer sho & shoetye
Yer barly bannock – theyle ha share   15
Like robber oer a booty

They run so eager arter wealth
Such upstarts & contrivers
Im made a very slave among em
Curst witling negroe drivers   20
Our p——s talk of hardships bless em
Well hells doom they unravel
But labour here in luxury proves
The devils very devil

& thou thought right their ans[we]rs matey   25
Tho plain to all thy kind
Thy feelings only coud disern it
Poor ignorance is blind
Im Labour friend & thats what I am
& that fat podgy knave   30
Is Luxury ye know 'nough on him
& I am Luxurys slave

LOBIN CLOUTS SATIRICAL SOLLILOUQUY ON THE TIMES

A Lab'rour journeying to his work betimes
Thus reak'd his vengance on the awkard times
'O cou'd I think as I wos doom'd to see
Sich shoking times as these ar' got to be
Poor men hod now be batter nokt o' t' head   5
Thon ha' to wok fo' nothin' else but bred

Ney ar' old ma'stur nosty fleerin' to'k
Say's I've no time for 'atins wen I wok
D—n his old c—r—s (g—d forgive my s—l)
Now I shud like a bruzzer at his joul   10
But tak' my wod he wil be f[i]tted fo't
When wonce the d—v—l hes his carcos got
No all his fleerin's oer all wul be dun
When he hes got his w—d—n j—k—t on
When swarms of m—g—ts at his h—m—r s—k   15
And turn thot p—dg—y s—ll—ng t—b to muk
Then whon he sees th' place he must be in
He'll wont to pray fur all his wiked sin
But he'all wont whot never must be had
His crimes will be so meny an' so bad   20
An' then he'll cos I wonty fo't the day
He ever chet poor labourers o' their pay
Ah he'all wish he'd pey'd um fo' their wok
An' never plag'd um wi' sich fleering tauk
So I mun wait an' I shal' see him sarv'd   25
Just os I wish'd an' just os he d[e]sarv'd
But his mak gamely touk meks me so mad
And if I leave him uthers ar' os bad
Aye Aye they'r all a like poor-pekt-up hogs
They treat the poor os if they wo' but dogs   30
An' if ther' is sum better on's fo' sooth
That wou'd hear reason when we spok' th' truth
Sich d—m—d deep r—g—s os ar old be—g—r is
Soon smells it out on tutors em a mis
For like a scab'd-a—sd-ship on rogue's enouf   35
To foul a very nation throf an' throf
Then if are goes to then an wines about
(Tho they'd be sorry ot their hart no doubt)
Yet 'fear o'fruntin' th' d—m—d r—g—sh set
They'll em an' aye an that is all yah'll get   40
Be os it will they'r sure to mek excuse
So beggin' prayin' nothink's a' no use

[ONE MONDAY MORNING SOUR & LOATH]

One monday morning sour & loath
To labour like a turk
A tween the hour o' five & six
I took my corpse to work
Deuce take a labourers life thought I   5
They talk o slaves els where
I sees much choice in foreighn parts
As I do in Slavery here

[O THRICE LUCKY TOWN (THE MORE LUCKY POOR CREATU'RS)]

O thrice lucky town (the more lucky poor creatu'rs)
Who ere could have thought that such luck would be thine
Such a stranger as thou art to things o' like natur
But time bringeth all things to pass – so its sighn
& O' what a blessing o' poor peoples sides   5
Who just before this wer' near pineing to dead
That his L—d—ps great goodnes condecends to provide
An odd sort of something that they may be fed
What a good christian heart must his honour posess
To 'mean him so l—w when so high riches rank him   10
In giving this h—ge p—dge – they cant do no less
Then down on their knappers & twenty times thank him

And benevolent charity sure such as this is
'll set others a going for the good o poor ce'turs
And warm squeezing Mizers to open their fis'es   15
And soften the wit-leather hearts of our betters

17

[O FREEDOM FREEDOM SACRED NAME]

O freedom freedom sacred name
Thy lands a land of slaves
Tho many a town thy right proclames
But trust me they are knaves
Theres many a slave shows in his notes   5
In freedoms intrest bawling
Woud sell his consciense for a groat
O freedom thou art fallen

THE LAMENTATIONS OF ROUND-OAK WATERS

Oppress'd wi' grief a double share
Where Round oak waters flow
I one day took a sitting there
Recounting many a woe
My naked seat without a shade   5
Did cold and blealy shine
Which fate was more agreable made
As sympathising mine

The wind between the north and East
Blow'd very chill and cold   10
Or coldly blow'd to me at least
My cloa'hs were thin and old
The grass all dropping wet wi' dew
Low bent their tiney spears
The lowly daise' bended too   15
More lowly wi my tears

(For when my wretched state appears
Hurt friendless poor and starv'd
I never can withold my tears
To think how I am sarv'd   20
To think how money'd men delight
More cutting then the storm
To make a sport and prove their might
O' me a fellow worm)

With arms reclin'd upon my knee   25
In mellancholly form
I bow'd my head to misery
And yielded to the storm
And there I fancied uncontrould
My sorrows as they flew   30
Unnotic'd as the waters rowl'd
Where all unnoticd too

But soon I found I was deciev'd
For waken'd by my Woes
The naked stream of shade bereav'd   35
In grievous murmurs rose

'Ah luckless youth to sorrow born
'Shun'd Son of Poverty
'The worlds make gamely sport and scorn
'And grinning infamy   40
'Unequall'd tho thy sorrows seem
'And great indeed they are
'O hear my sorrows for my stream
'You'll find an equal there'

'I am the genius of the brook   45
'And like to thee I moan
'By Naiads and by all forsook
'Unheeded and alone
'Distress and sorrow quickly proves
'The friend sincere & true   50
'Soon as our happines removes
'Pretenders bids adieu'

'Here I have been for many a year
'And how My brook has been
'How pleasures lately flourish'd here   55
'Thy self has often seen
'The willows waving wi' the wind
'And here & there a thorn
'Did please thy Mellancholly mind
'And did My banks adorn'   60

'And here the shepherd with his sheep
'And with his lovley maid
'Together where these waters creep
'In loitering dalliance play'd
'And here the Cowboy lov'd to sit   65
'And plate his rushy thongs
'And dabble in the fancied pit
'And chase the Minnow throngs'

'And when thou didst thy horses tend
'Or drive the ploughmans team   70
'Thy mind did natturally bend
'Towards my pleasing stream
'And different pleasures fill'd thy breast
'And different thy employ
'And different feelings thou possest   75
'From any other Boy'

'The sports which they so dearley lov'd
'Thou could's't not bear to see
'And joys which they as joys approv'd
'Ne'er seem'd as joys to thee   80
'The Joy was thine couldst thou but steal
'From all their Gambols rude
'In some lone thicket to consceal
'Thyself in Sollitude'

'There didst thou Joy & love to sit   85
'The briars and brakes among
'To exercise thy infant wit
'In fancied tale or song
'And there the inscect & the flower
'Would court thy curious eye   90
'To muse in wonder on that power
'Which dwells above the sky'

'But now alas my charms are done
'For shepherds & for thee
'The Cow boy with his Green is gone   95
'And every Bush & tree
'Dire nakedness oer all prevails
'Yon fallows bare and brown
'Is all beset wi' posts & rails
'And turned upside down'   100

'The gentley curving darksom bawks
'That stript the Cornfields o'er
'And prov'd the Shepherds daily walks
'Now prove his walks no more
'The plough has had them under hand   105
'And over turnd 'em all
'And now along the elting Land
'Poor swains are forc'd to maul'

'And where yon furlong meets the lawn
'To Ploughmen Oh ! how sweet 110
'When they had their long furrow drawn
'Its Eddings to their feet
'To rest 'em while they clan'd their plough
'And light their Loaded Shoe
'But ah – there's ne'ery Edding now 115
'For neither them nor you'

'The bawks and Eddings are no more
'The pastures too are gone
'The greens the Meadows & the moors
'Are all cut up & done 120
'There's scarce a greensward spot remains
'And scarce a single tree
'All naked are thy native plains
'And yet they're dear to thee'

'But O ! my brook my injur'd brook 125
''T'is that I most deplore
'To think how once it us'd to look
'How it must look no more
'And hap'ly fate thy wanderings bent
'To sorrow here wi' me 130
'For to none else could I lament
'And mourn to none but thee'

'Thou art the whole of musing swains
'That's now resideing here
'Tho one ere while did grace my plains 135
'And he to thee was dear
'Ah – dear he was – for now I see
'His Name grieves thee at heart
'Thy silence speaks that Misery
'Which Language cant impart' 140

'O T[urnil]l T[urnil]l dear should thou
'To this fond Mourner be
'By being so much troubl'd now
'From just a Nameing thee
'Nay I as well as he am griev'd   145
'For oh I hop'd of thee
'That hadst thou stay'd as I believd
'Thou wouldst have griev'd for me'

'But ah he's gone the first o' swains
'And left us both to moan   150
'And thou art all that now remains
'With feelings like his own
'So while the thoughtles passes by
'Of sence & feelings void
'Thine be the Fancy painting Eye   155
'On by'gone scenes employ'd'

'Look backward on the days of yore
'Upon my injur'd brook
'In fancy con its Beauties o'er
'How it had us'd to look   160
'O then what trees my banks did crown
'What Willows flourishd here
'Hard as the ax that Cut them down
'The senceless wretches were'

'But sweating slaves I do not blame   165
'Those slaves by wealth decreed
'No I should hurt their harmless name
'To brand 'em wi' the deed
'Altho their aching hands did wield
'The axe that gave the blow   170
'Yet 't'was not them that own'd the field
'Nor plan'd its overthrow'

'No no the foes that hurt my field
'Hurts these poor moilers too
'And thy own bosom knows & feels   175
'Enough to prove it true
'And o poor souls they may complain
'But their complainings all
'The injur'd worms that turn again
'But turn again to fall'   180

'Their foes and mine are lawless foes
'And L—ws thems—s they hold
'Which clipt-wing'd Justice cant oppose
'But forced yields to G—d
'These are the f—s of mine & me   185
'These all our Ru—n plan'd
'Alltho they never felld a tree
'Or took a tool in hand'

'Ah cruel foes with plenty blest
'So ankering after more   190
'To lay the greens & pastures waste
'Which proffited before
'Poor greedy souls – what would they have
'Beyond their plenty given ?
'Will riches keep 'em from the grave ?   195
'Or buy them rest in heaven ?'

A FAMILLIAR EPISTLE TO A FRIEND

'Friendship peculiar boon of heaven
'The noblest minds delight & pride
'To men & angels only given
'To all the lower world deny'd
'Thy gentle flows of guiltless joys
'On fools & villians ne'er descend
'In vain for thee the tyrant sighs
'& hugs a flatterer for a friend'.
                    Sam. Johnson

This morning just as I awoken
A black cloud hung the south – unbroken
Thinks I just now we have it soaking
– I rightly guest
Feth glad wer' I to see the tokens   5
I wanted rest

& fex a pepsing day theres been on't
But caution'd right wi' what I'd seen on't
Keeping at home has kept me clean on't
Ye know my creed   10
Fool hardy work – I neer wer' keen on't
But lets proceed

I write to keep from mischief meerly
Fire side & comforts 'joying cheerly
& brother chip I love ye dearly   15
Poor as ye be
Wi' honest heart & soul sincerely
There all to me

This scrawl – mark thou the applicaton
(Tho hardly worth thy observation)   20
Meaneth a humble Invitation
On some days end
O' all 'rag'd muffins' i' the nation
Thou art the friend –

Ive long been agravated shocking   25
To see our gentry folks so cocking
But sorrows often catch'd by mocking
The truth I've seen
Their pride may want a shoe & stocking
For like has been   30

Prides power's not worth a roasted Onion
I'ds leave be prison mouse wi' Bunyan
As I'd be king o' our dominion
Or any other
When shoffl'd through – its my opinion   35
One's good as tother

Nor wou'd I gi' from off my cuff
A single pin for no such stuff
Riches besh—t a pinch o' Snuff
Woud dearly buy ye   40
Whos got ye keeps ye – thats enough
I dont envy ye

If fates so kind to lets be doing
Thats, just keep cart o' wheels fo' going
Oer my half pint I can be crowing   45
As wells another
But when theres this & that stan's owing
O curse the bother

For had I money like a many
I'd balance even to a penny –   50
Want, thy confinement make[sl me scrany
That spirits mine
I'd sooner gi' then take from any
But worth cant shine

O independence oft I bait thee   55
How blest I'd been to call ye Matey
– Ye fawning flattering slaves I hate ye
– Mad harum-scarum
If rags & tatters underrate me
Free still I'll wear 'em   60

What sc—d—ls honours light infesteth
Which her few votaries detesteth
Which honesty as vain arresteth
She cant be heard
In reasons proof she vain protesteth   65
Worth's no reward

By why these politicks & pluther
The muse ill knows such usless bluther
She turns old friend to greet a brother
& brags to name it   70
Just as one beggar owns another
Like wants they claim it

& soon as ere a change o' weather
Frees us from labours cramping tether
(Sorrow thrown by heart lights a feather)   75
Mind what I tell ye
A jovial crush we'll have to gether
– Ye plainly spell me

P—x take all Sorrows now I'll bilk em
Whats past may go so – time that shall come   80
Or's bad or worse or how it will come
I'll neer despair
Poor as I am friends shall be welcome
As rich on's are

So from my heart old friend I'll greet ye   85
No out side brags shall never cheat ye
Wi' what I have wi' such I treat ye
Ye may believe me
I'll shake ye're Rags when ere I meet ye
If ye decieve me   90

So mind ye friend 'whats what' I send it
My letters plain & plain I'll end it
Bads bad enough but worse wornt mend it
So I be happy
& while I've sixpence left I'll spend it   95
In cheering nappy

A hearty health shall crown my story
– Dear native England I adore thee
– Britons – may ye wi friends before ye
Neer want a quart   100
To drink your king & countrys glory
Wi upright heart

Postscript
Ive oft meant tramping oer to see ye
But d—d old fortune g—d forgi' me
She's so cross grain'd & forked wi' me   105
Be ere so willing
Spite o' my jingling powers – 'ti'n't i' me
To scheme a shilling

& poverty her cursed rigour
Spite o' Industry's utmost vigour 110
Dizens me out i' such a figure
I'm sham'd being seen
'Sides my old shoon – poor muse ye twig her
Waits roads being clean

Then here wind bound till fates confer'd on't 115
I wait ye friend – & take my word on't
I'll (spite o' fate) scheme such a hurd on't
As we wi'n't lack
So no excuses shall be heard on't
– Yours random Jack. 120

HELPSTON GREEN

Ye injur'd fields ye once where gay
When natures hand displayd
Long waving rows of willows grey
And clumps of awthorn shade
But now alas your awthorn bowers 5
All desolate we see
The woodmans axe their shade devours
And cuts down every tree

Not trees alone have ownd their force
Whole woods beneath them bowd 10
They turnd the winding riv'lets course
And all thy pastures plough'd
To shrub nor tree throughout thy fields
They no compassion show
The uplifted axe no mercy yields 15
But strikes a fatal blow

29

When ere I muse along the plain
And mark where once they grew
Rememb'rance wakes her busy train
And brings past scenes to view   20
The well known brook the favorite tree
In fancys eye appear
And next that pleasant green I see
That green for ever dear

Oer its green hills I've often stray'd   25
In childhoods happy hour
Oft sought the nest along the shade
And gatherd many a flower
And there with playmates often join'd
In fresher sports to plan   30
But now increasing years have coin'd
These childern into man

The greens gone too—ah lovely scene
No more the kingcup gay
Shall shine in yellow oer the green   35
And shed its golden ray
No more the herdsmans early call
Shall bring the cows to feed
Nor more the milkmaids evening brawl
In 'come-mull' tones succeed   40

Both milkmaids shouts and herdsmans call
Have vanish'd with the green
The kingcups yellow shades and all
Shall never more be seen
But the thick culterd tribes that grow   45
Will so efface the scene
That after times will hardly know
It ever was a green

Farwell thou favorite spot farwell
Since every efforts vain   50
All I can do is still to tell
Of thy delightful plain
But that pro[v]es short—increasing years
That did my youth presage
Will now as each new day appears   55
Bring on declining age

Reflection pierces deadly keen
While I the moral scan
As are the changes of the green
So is the life of man   60
Youth brings age with faultering tongue
That does the exit crave
There's one short scene presents the throng
Another shows the grave

THE VILLAGE MINSTREL (lines 924–1281)

99

& oft wi shepherds leaning oer their hooks
Hed stand conjecturing on the ruins round   925
Tho little skilld in antiquated books
Their knowledge in such matters seemd profound
& they woud preach of what did once abound
Castles deep moated round old haunted hall
& somthing like to moats still swamps the ground   930
As neath old cromwells rage the towers did fall
& bush & ivy creeps the hill & ruin hides it all

100

& ancient songs hes hung enrapturd on
Which herds men on a hill has sat to sing
Bout feats of robin hood & little john 935
Whose might was feard by country & by king
Such strength had they to twich the thrumming string
Their darts oft suckt the life blood of the deer
& sherwood forest wi their horns did ring
Ah these where such that he did joy to hear 940
& these where such that warmd when antique scenes did 'pear

101

Thy moat o woodcroft & thy time bleachd towers
Whose hughe head over looks the level green
He oft has viewd em as he pluckt his flowers
King cup & daisey ah & joyd has been 945
To list the passing netherds tale between
An ancient story scores of years by gone
Perils thou met wi in thy early days
In cromwells time or doubtless rebel john
The times he were not leard to know but let the tale go on 950

Woodcroft Castle
The Netherds tale
Tho night in yon castle now lulls the clowns sleep
& returns him in peace to his plough
Tho the shepherd unskard sits in rest wi his sheep
& the maid sings her song neath her cow
There once was an hour a most terrible hour 955
When the shepherd & ploughmen has fled
When the centinel stood wi his gun at the door
& the maiden was scard from her bed

2

Tho now ducks & geese they do swim i' the moat
& the beast at their cribs left to feed 960
Tho the tower nows of no other use then a coat

For the pigeons to roost in & breed
There once was a day a most terrible day
When that moat it flowd bloody wi all
When the top of yon tower saw the midst of the fray   965
& the cannons made totter the wall

3

It might be when charles our unfortunate king
Was disdaind by each rebel out law
That one michael Hudson his soldiers did bring
To keep our low country in awe   970
Tho few trusty fellows there was in the land
To royalty he was a friend
& valiant as ever was sword put in hand
Or master on man might depend

4

This very old castle he came to comand   975
A staunch set of servants brought he
Ere theyd loose it by rebels theyd loose their right hand
Or their legs lopped off to their knee
They 'fended it stoutJy & watchd at the gate
Where draw bridge there might be as then   980
& hudson I ween were up early & late
A watching the foe wi his men

5

Twas when dewy morn on the pasture did weep
From stamford the rebels did roam
Their tumults no doubt scamperd shepherds & sheep   985
& great rout they made as they come
They rallied thro helpstone ah helpstone I ween
Thou neer knew a rebel before
& great consternation no doubt thou wast in
As the marston chaps were on the moor   990

33

6

Ive heard gossips say when such news spread about
The maidens near fell into fits
& old women hearing the rebels were out
Was a'most scard out of their wits
The mizer tore slabs up & buried his coin   995
& granny she instantly fell
To hide what she thought the bold rogues woud purloin
Such as kettles & pots in the well

7

But surely if I had been then on the green
Employd (markd the herds man) as now   1000
Id took to my heels soon as rebels Id seen
& left em free choice of a cow
& doubtless the netherds might run – & the rout
Full easy came in for their prey
& as they flockt up to the castle no doubt   1005
Thought its tenants as easy as they

8

But hudson soon let em to know they was wrong
As his brandishd sword threats did despise
He told em that conquest wa'n't made by a tongue
But swords cut the way to the prize   1010
& instant the hot bloody battle begun
& hudson so heartnd his men
That the rebels repulsd stood on tiptoe to run
Tho numberd as thirty to ten

9

But vain are the swords & the deeds of the brave   1015
When cowards wi numbers oerpower
As vain hopes the flye to scape fish on the wave
Or thistle down float in a shower
They forded the moat & thought conquest was bought
Ah then came the terrible hour   1020

When the bold royal captives subdued as they thought
Pusht again from the top of the tower

10
Repulse so undaunted – the rebels dismayd
Offerd quarter for battle to end
& then was thy guardians o woodcroft betrayd   1025
Ah who woud on cowards depend
The valiant comander was cowardly flung
From off the tower top by the foe
His hand they slashd off on the tower as he hung
& his body fell bleeding below   1030

11
& one who had quakd coud he usd his right hand
As many at nelson has done
When he begd like a soldier to dye on dry land
Dashd him dead i the flood wi his gun
& this is the tale woud make any one weep   1035
Bout the towers thou so often has seen
That neerll be forgot while a shepherd tends sheep
Or netherd keeps cows on the green

102
Thus did the swain the dismal tale relate
While lubins breast wi tenderest woes did bleed   1040
Much did he sigh to hear the valiants fate
& marveld much that cruel wars shoud breed
So nigh his natal home the horrid deed
& soon the tale his wild research supplyd
Like artless maidens who romances read   1045
Each ruind heap was castles now discryd
Were other hudsons bore comand & fought as brave & dyd

103
But who can tell the anguish of his mind
When reformations formidable foes

Wi civil wars on natures peace combind   1050
& desolation struck her deadly blows
As curst improvment gan his fields inclose
O greens & fields & trees farwell farwell
His heart wrung pains his unavailing woes
No words can utter & no tongue can tell   1055
When ploughs destroyd the green when groves of willows fell

104

There once was springs when daises silver studs
Like sheets of snow on every pasture spread
There once was summers when the crow flower buds
Like golden sunbeams brightest lustre shed   1060
& trees grew once that shelterd lubins head
There once was brooks sweet wimpering down the vale
The brooks no more – king cup & daiseys fled
Their last falln tree the naked moors bewail
& scarce a bush is left around to tell the mournful tale 1065

105

Yon flaggy tufts & many a rushy nott
Existing still in spite of spade & plough
As seemly fond & loath to leave the spot
Tells where was once the green – brown fallows now
Where lubin often turns a saddnd brow   1070
Marks the stopt brook & mourns oppresions power
& thinks how once he waded in each slough
To crop the yellow 'horse blobs' early flower
Or catch the 'millar thumb' in summers sultry hour

106

There once was days the wood man knows it well   1075
When shades een echod wi the singing thrush
There once was hours the ploughmens tale can tell
When mornings beauty wore its earliest blush
How woodlarks carrold from each stumpy bush
Lubin himself has markd em soar & sing   1080

The thorns are gone the woodlarks song is hush
Spring more resembles winter now then spring
The shades are banishd all – the birds betook to wing

107
There once was lanes in natures freedom dropt
There once was paths that every valley wound   1085
Inclosure came & every path was stopt
Each tyrant fixt his sign were pads was found
To hint a trespass now who crossd the ground
Justice is made to speak as they command
The high road now must be each stinted bound   1090
– Inclosure thourt a curse upon the land
& tastless was the wretch who thy existance pland

108
O england boasted land of liberty
Wi strangers still thou mayst thy title own
But thy poor slaves the alteration see   1095
Wi many a loss to them the truth is known
Like emigrating bird thy freedoms flown
While mongrel clowns low as their rooting plough
Disdain thy laws to put in force their own
& every village owns its tyrants now   1100
& parish slaves must live as parish kings alow

109
Ye fields ye scenes so dear to lubins eye
Ye meadow blooms ye pasture flowers farwell
Ye banishd trees ye make me deeply sigh
Inclosure came & all your glories fell   1105
Een the old oak that crownd yon rifld dell
Whose age had made it sacred to the view
Not long was left his childerns fate to tell
Where ignorance & wealth their course pursue
Each tree must tumble down – old 'lea close oak' adieu   1110

110

Lubin beheld it all & deeply paind
Along the railed road woud muse & sigh
The only path that freedoms rights maintaind
The naked scenes drew pity from his eye
Tears dropt to mem'ry of delights gone bye   1115
The haunts of freedom cowherds wattld bowers
& shepherds huts & trees that tow[e]red high
& spreading thorns that turnd a summer shower
All captives lost & past to sad oppresions power

111

& oft wi shepherds he woud sit to sigh   1120
On past delights of many a by gone day
& look on scenes now naked to the eye
& talk as how they once were clothed gay
& how the runnel wound its weedy way
& how the willows on its margin grew   1125
Talk oer wi them the rural feats of may
Who got the blossoms neath the morning dew
That the last garland made & where such blossoms grew

112

As how he coud remember well when he
Laden wi blooming treasures from the plain   1130
Has mixt wi them beneath a dotterel tree
Drove from his cowslips by a hasty rain
& heard em there sing each delightful strain
& how wi tales what joys they usd to wake
Wishing wi them such days woud come again   1135
They lovd the artless boy for talking sake
& gave it out some future day a wondrous man hed make

113

& you ye poor ragd out casts of the land
That hug your shifting camps from green to green
He lovd to see your humble dwelling stand   1140

& thought your groups did beautify the scene
Tho blamd for many a petty theft yeve been
Poor wandering souls to fates hard want decreed
Doubtless too oft such acts your ways bemean
& oft in wrong your foes 'gen you proceed   1145
& brand a gipseys camp when others do the deed

114

Lubin woud love to list their gibberish talk
& view the oddity such ways display
& oft wi boys pursud his sunday walk
Where warpt the camp beneath the willows grey   1150
& its black tennants on the green sward lay
While on two forked sticks wi cordage tyd
Their pot oer pilferd fuel boils away
Wi food of sheep that of red water dyd
Or any nauceous thing their frowning fates provide   1155

115

Tho oft they gather money by their trade
& on their fortune telling art subsist
Where her long hurded groat oft brings the maid
& secret slives it in the sybils fist
To buy good luck & happiness – to list   1160
What occupys a wenches every thought
Who is to be the man – while as she wist
The gipsies tale wi swains & wealth is fraught
The lass returns well pleasd & thinks all cheaply bought

116

Full oft in summer lubins markt & seen   1165
How eagerly the village maids pursue
Their sunday rambles where the camps have been
& how they gi' their money to the crew
For idle stories they believe as true
Crossing their hands wi coin or magic stick   1170

How quakt the young to hear what things they knew
While old experiencd dames knew all the trick
Who said that all their skill was borrowd from old nick

117

& thus the superstitious dread their harm
& neer dare fail relieving their distress   1175
Lest they wi in their cot shoud leave a charm
To let nought prosper & bring on distress
Great depth of cunning gipseys do posses
& when such weakness in a dame they find
Forsooth they prove most terryfying guess   1180
& tho not one to charity inclind
They mutter black revenge & force her to be kind

118

His native scenes o sweet endearing sound
Sure neer a heart does beat howere forlorn
But the warmd breast has soft emotions found   1185
To cherish the dear spot where it was born
Een the poor hedger in the early morn
Chopping the pattering bushes hung wi dew
Scarce lays his mitten on a branching thorn
But painfull mem'ry banishd thoughts renew   1190
Reminding when't was young what happy days he knew

119

When the old shepherd wi his wooly locks
Crosses the green past joys his eyes will fill
Where when a boy he usd to tend his flocks
Each fringed rushy bed & swelling hill   1195
Where he has playd or stretchd him at his will
Freshning anew on lifes declining years
& jogs his memory wi their pleasures still
O how such things his native scenes endears
No spot throughout the world to him so pleasingly appears 1200

120

The toil worn thresher in his little cot
Whose roof did shield his birth & still remains
His dwelling place how rough so ere his lot
His toil tho hard & small the wage he gains
That many a child most piningly mentains   1205
Send him to distant scenes & better fare
How woud his bosom yearn wi parting pains
How woud he turn & look & linger there
& wish een now his cot & poverty to share

121

How dear to soldiers does the relic prove   1210
Took from his cot or gave by loves sweet hand
A box that bears a motto of true love
How will he take his quid & musing stand
Think on his native lass & native land
& bring to mind all those past joys again   1215
From which wild youth so foolish was trepand
Kissing the pledge that all these ways retain
While fancy points the spot far oer the barring main

122

O dear delightfull spots his native place
How lubin lookd upon the days gone bye   1220
How he tho young woud past delights retrace
Bend oer gulld holes where stood his trees & sigh
Wi tears the while bemoistning in his eye
How hed look for the green a green no more
Mourning to scenes that made him no reply   1225
Save the strong accents they in memory bore
'Our scenes that charmd thy youth are dead to bloom no more'

123

O samely naked leas so bleak so strange
How woud he wander oer ye to complain
& sigh & wish he neer had known the change   1230

To see the ploughshare bury all the plain
& not a cows lip on its lap remain
The rush tuft gone that hid the sky larks nest
Ah when will may morn hear such strains again
The storms beats chilly on his naked breast   1235
No shelter grows to shield him now no home invites to rest

124

'Ah' woud he sigh 'ye neath the churchyard grass
'Ye sleeping shepherds coud ye rise again
'& see what since your time has come to pass
'See neer a bush nor willow now remain   1240
'Looking & listning for the brook in vain
'Yed little think as such your natal scene
'Yed little now distinguish field from plain
'Or where to look for each departed green
'All ploughd & buried now as tho there nought had been   1245

125

But still they beamd wi beautys on his eye
& other scenes wa'n't half so sweet to view
& other flowers but strove in vain to vie
Wi his few tufts that scap'd the wreck & grew
& sky larks too their singing might pursue   1250
To claim his praise – he coud but only say
Their songs were sweet but not like those he knew
That charmd his native plains at early day
Whose equals neer was found where ere his steps might stray

126

When distant village feast or noisey fair   1255
Short abscence from his fields did him detain
How woud he feel when home he did repair
& mixt among his joys – the white spire fane
Meeting his eye above the elms again
Leaving his friends in the sweet summer night   1260
No longer lost on unknown field or plain

Far from the pad wi well known haunts in sight
Hed stray for scatterd flowers wi added new delight

127

As travellers returnd from foreign ground
Feels more endearments for his native earth   1265
So lubin cherishd from each weary round
Still warmer fondness for those scenes of mirth
Those plains & that dear cot which gave him birth
& oft this warmness for his fields hed own
Mixd wi his friends around the cottage hearth   1270
Relating all the travels he had known
& that hed seen no spot so lovly as his own

128

Nor has his taste wi manhood ere declind
Yell now oft see him on his lonly way
Oer stile or gate in thoughtfull mood reclind   1275
Or long the road wi folded arms to stray
Mixing wi autumns sighs or summer gay
& curious natures secrets to explore
Brushing the twigs of wood or copse away
To roam the lonely shade so silently   1280
Sweet muttering oer his joys from clowns intrusions free

ENGLAND

'England with all thy faults I love the[e] still
'My country & while yet a nook is left
'Where english minds & manners may be found
'Shall be constrained to love thee'
                              Cowper

England my country mong evils enthralling
Where is the name that is dearer then thine

43

Where is the heart so detests in thy falling
Or woud beat wi more sorrows to see it then mine
England my country theres villians woud crush thee 5
Thats shouting out freedom dissention to sow
In this hour of danger I heartily wish thee
That source of protection I cannot bestow

England thou word so enchantingly sounding
Thy name in my heart thrilling raptures renew 10
& may thy base natures their mother land wounding
Meet the resentment of those that are true
Sharp tho the rod of restriction may bind thee
& freedom may groan wi much load over powerd
Better keep laws that have ages confind thee 15
Then loose them to wolves & be instant devourd

England pretenders arise for thy freedom
Alas but false prophets the best of em be
Christians was warnd of such spys not to heed em
Most surely their secrets the ruin of thee 20
Cut throat assasins of vandal & tarter
Once over[r]an nations that hopd to be free
Be weak land & trust em & thou art the martyr
I tell thee their triumphs the ruin of thee

England return to past days for a caution 25
Where foul excesses have blotted thy page
Where rebel hypocrites maskd wi devotion
Showerd down upon thee the blackest of rage
Look at thy state in their power–was it freedom
Laws broke & kings murderd was that to be free 30
While basest of savages lurkd to succeed 'em
Ah look back & think what the present may be

England thoust reason such times to remember
Thy wounds then recieved never healed will be
& mark as in ashes there still lurks the ember 35

To stir up thy weakness & then ruin thee
Never again do thou forfeit thy glory
Wading thro bloodshed in hopes to be free
Never let hist'ry repeat such a story
Look at whats past as a caution for thee   40

England be patient your chains may be tiring
Still better slaves in a land of your own
Then yield up to traitors to vainess aspiring
& banishd as slaves into deserts unknown
England be patient & bear your chains lightly   45
Tho in gauld fetters bound down as ye be
Freedoms hid sunbeams may yet glitter brightly
Still may the day come as ye may be free

England my country I woud not decieve thee
Warm are my wishes that thou shoudst be free   50
England my voice in thy causes believe me
Are the souls echos entreating for thee
England as yet bear the yoke that is on thee
Still be thou peacfull as hard as it be
Wait & there doubtless may heroes be born thee   55
Yet may the day come when thou shalt be free

England my country mong evils enthralling
Where is the name that is dearer then thine
Where is the heart so detests in thy falling
Or woud beat wi more sorrows to see it then mine   60
England my country theres villians woud crush thee
Thats shouting out freedom dissention to sow
In this hour of danger I heartily wish thee
That source of protection I cannot bestow

LANGLEY BUSH

O Langley bush the shepherds sacred shade
Thy hollow trunk oft gaind a look from me
Full many a journey oer the heath Ive made
For such like curious things I love to see
What truth the story of the swain alows   5
That tells of honours which thy young days knew
Of 'langley court' being kept beneath thy boughs
I cannot tell–thus much I know is true
That thou art reverencd even the rude clan
Of lawless gipseys drove from stage to stage   10
Pilfering the hedges of the husband man
Leave thee as sacred in thy withering age
Both swains & gipseys seem to love thy name
Thy spots a favourite wi the smutty crew
& soon thou must depend on gipsey fame   15
Thy mulldering trunk is nearly rotten thro
My last doubts murmuring on the zephers swell
My last looks linger on thy boughs wi pain
To thy declining age I bid farwell
Like old companions neer to meet again   20

THE MORES

Far spread the moorey ground a level scene
Bespread with rush & one eternal green
That never felt the rage of blundering plough
Though centurys wreathed springs blossoms on its brow
Still meeting plains that stretched them far away   5
In uncheckt shadows of green brown & grey
Unbounded freedom ruled the wandering scene
Nor fence of ownership crept in between
To hide the prospect of the following eye

Its only bondage was the circling sky   10
One mighty flat undwarfed by bush & tree
Spread its faint shadow of immensity
& lost itself which seemed to eke its bounds
In the blue mist the orisons edge surrounds

 Now this sweet vision of my boyish hours   15
Free as spring clouds & wild as summer flowers
Is faded all – a hope that blossomed free
& hath been once no more shall ever be
Inclosure came & trampled on the grave
Of labours rights & left the poor a slave   20
& memorys pride ere want to wealth did bow
Is both the shadow & the substance now
The sheep & cows were free to range as then
Where change might prompt nor felt the bonds of men
Cows went & came with every morn & night   25
To the wild pasture as their common right
& sheep unfolded with the rising sun
Heard the swains shout & felt their freedom won
Tracked the red fallow field & heath & plain
Then met the brook & drank & roamed again   30
The brook that dribbled on as clear as glass
Beneath the roots then hid among the grass
While the glad shepherd traced their tracks along
Free as the lark & happy as her song
But now alls fled & flats of many a dye   35
That seemed to lengthen with the following eye
Moors loosing from the sight far smooth & blea
Where swopt the plover in its pleasure free
Are vanished now with commons wild & gay
As poets visions of lifes early day   40
Mulberry bushes where the boy would run
To fill his hands with fruit – are grubbed & done
& hedgrow briars – flower lovers overjoyed
Came & got flower pots – these are all destroyed
& sky bound mores in mangled garbs are left   45

47

Like mighty jiants of their limbs bereft
Fence now meets fence in owners little bounds
Of field & meadow large as garden grounds
In little parcels little minds to please
With men & flocks imprisoned ill at ease   50
Each little path that led its pleasant way
As sweet as morning leading night astray
Where little flowers bloomed round a varied host
That travel felt delighted to be lost
Nor grudged the steps that he had taen as vain   55
When right roads traced his journeys end again
Nay on a broken tree hed sit awhile
To see the mores & fields & meadows smile
Sometimes with cowslaps smothered – then all white
With daiseys – then the summers splendid sight   60
Of corn fields crimson oer with the 'head ach' bloomd
Like splendid armys for the battle plumed
He gazed upon them with wild fancys eye
As fallen landscapes from an evening sky
These paths are stopt – the rude philistines thrall   65
Is laid upon them & destroyed them all
Each little tyrant with his little sign
Shows where man claims earth glows no more divine
On paths to freedom & to childhood dear
A board sticks up to notice 'no road here'   70
& on the tree with ivy over hung
The hated sign by vulgar taste is hung
As tho the very birds should learn to know
When they go there they must no further go
Thus with the poor scared freedom bade good bye   75
& much the[y] feel it in the smothered sigh
& birds & trees & flowers without a name
All sighed when lawless laws enclosure came
& dreams of plunder in such rebel schemes
Have found too truly that they were but dreams   80

THE PARISH
A SATIRE

'No injury can possibly be done, as a nameless character can ever
be found out but by its truth & likeness'   Pope

The Parish hind oppressions humble slave
Whose only hopes of freedom is the grave
The cant miscalled religion in the saint
& Justice mockd while listning wants complaint
The parish laws & parish queens & kings   5
Prides lowest classes of pretending things
The meanest dregs of tyrany & crime
I fearless sing let truth attend the ryhme
Tho now adays truth grows a vile offence
& courage tells it at his own expence   10
If he but utter what himself has seen
He deals in satire & he wounds too keen
Intends sly ruin by encroached degrees
Is rogue or radical or what you please
But shoud vile flatterers with the basest lies   15
Attempt self interest with a wished disguise
Say groves of myrtle here in winter grow
& blasts blow blessings every time they blow
That golden showers in mercey all to bless
The half thatchd mouldering hovels of distress   20
That edens self in freedoms infant sphere
Was but a desert to our Eden here
That laws so wise to choke the seeds of strife
Here bless a beggar with an Adams Life
Ah what an host of Patronizers then   25
Woud gather round the motley flatterers den
A spotted monster in a lambkins hide
Whose smooth tongue uttered what his heart denied
Theyd call his genius wonderous in extream
& lisp the novel beautys of his theme   30
& say twas luck on natures kinder part

To bless such genius with a gentle heart
Curst affectation worse then hell I hate
Thy sheepish features & thy crouching gait
Like sneeking cur that licks his masters shoe   35
Bowing & cringing to the Lord knows who
Licking the dust for each approving nod
Were pride is worshiped like an earthly god
The rogue thats carted to the gallows tree
Is far more honest in his trade then thee   40
Thy puling whine that suits thy means so well
Piteous as chickens breaking thro its shell
That rarely fails to ope the closest purse
Is far more rougish then the others force
I dread no cavils for the clearest sink   45
When ere the bottoms stirred is sure to stink
So let them rail I envye not their praise
Nor fear the slander stung deciet may raise
Let those who merit what the verse declares
Choose to be vexd & think the picture theirs   50
On Lifes rude sea my bark is launched afar
& they may wish the wreck who dread the war
Then waves in storms their spite is nothing more
That lash rage weary on a heedless shore
A public names the shuttle cock of fame   55
Now up then down as fashion wills the game
At whom each fool may cast his private lie
Nor fears the scourge of satires just reply
While those that rail may do what deeds they list
They hide in ignorance & are never missed   60
Their scorn is envys imp conscieved by hate
That tortures worth in every grade & state
As mists to day as shadows to the sun
These stains in merits welfare ever run
Diseases that infect not but at last   65
Die of their own distempers & are past
Such friends I count not & such foes disdain
Their best or worst is neither loss nor gain

Friendship like theirs is but the names disgrace
A mask that counterfiets its open face   70
Cant & hypocricy disguise their ways
Their praise turns satire & their satire praise
Good men are ever from such charges free
To prove them friends is praise enough for me

Satire should not wax civil oer its toil   75
Tho sweet self interest blossoms on the soil
Nor like a barking dog betray its trust
By silence when the robber throws his crust
Till fear & mercey all its wrath divides
To feeble portraits buttered on both sides   80
Ill strive to do what flattery bids me shun
Tell truth nor shrink for benefits to none
Follys a fool that cannot keep its ground
Still fearing foes & shewing were to wound
A jealous look will almost turn her sick   85
& hints not meant oft gauls her to the quick
& hide or shuffle or do what she will
Each mask like glass reflects the picture still
As powder kindles from the smallest spark
Confusion buzzes & betrays the mark   90
From such frail scources every fact is drawn
Not sought thro malice or exposed in scorn
But told as truths that common sense may see
How cants pretentions & her works agree
I coud not pass her low deceptions bye   95
Nor can I flatter & I will not lye
So satires Muse shall like a blood hound trace
Each smoothfacd tyrant to his hiding place
Whose hidden actions like the foxes skin
Scents the sly track to were they harbour in   100
& each profession of this Parish troop
Shall have a rally ere the hunt be up
To none that rules I owe nor spite nor grudge
How just the satire be who reads may judge

That good old fame the farmers earnd of yore 105
That made as equals not as slaves the poor
That good old fame did in two sparks expire
A shooting coxcomb & a hunting Squire
& their old mansions that was dignified
With things far better then the pomp of pride 110
At whose oak table that was plainly spread
Each guest was welcomd & the poor was fed
Were master son & serving man & clown
Without distinction daily sat them down
Were the bright rows of pewter by the wall 115
Se[r]ved all the pomp of kitchen or of hall
These all have vanished like a dream of good
& the slim things that rises were they stood
Are built by those whose clownish taste aspires
To hate their farms & ape the country squires 120
The old oak table soon betook to flight
A thing disgusting to my ladys sight
Yet affectations of a tender claim
To the past memory of its owners name
Whose wealth prides only beauty stood her friend 125
& bought a husband that same wealth to spend
Laid it aside in lumber rooms to rot
Till all past claims of tenderness forgot
Bade it its honourable name resign
Transformed to stable doors or troughs for swine 130
Each aged labourer knows its history well
& sighs in sorrow the sad change to tell
The pewter rows are all exchanged for plate
& that choice patch of pride to mark them great
Of red or blue gay as an harlequin 135
The livried footman serves the dinner in
As like the squire as pride can imitate
Save that no porter watches at the gate
& even his Lordship thought so grand before
Is but distinguished in his coach & four 140
Such are the upstarts that usurp the name

Of the old farmers dignity & fame
& weres that lovley maid in days gone bye
The farmers daughter unreserved tho shye
That milked her cows & old songs used to sing 145
As red & rosey as the lovely spring
Ah these have dwindled to a formal shade
As pale & bed rid as my ladys maid
Who cannot dare to venture in the street
Some times thro cold at other times for heat 150
& vulgar eyes to shun & vulgar winds
Shrouded in veils green as their window blinds
These taught at school their stations to despise
& view old customs with disdainful eyes
Deem all as rude their kindred did of yore 155
& scorn to toil or foul their fingers more
Prim as the pasteboard figures which they cut
At school & tastful on the chimney put
They sit before their glasses hour by hour
Or paint unnatural daubs of fruit or flower 160
Or boasting learning novels beautys quotes
Or aping fashions scream a tune by notes
Een poetry in these high polished days
Is oft profained by their dislike or praise
Theyve read the Speaker till without a look 165
Theyll sing whole pages & lay bye the book
Then sure their judgment must be good indeed
When ere they chuse to speak of what they read
To simper tastful some devoted line
As somthing bad or somthing very fine 170
Thus mincing fine airs misconcieved at school
That pride outherods & compleats the fool
Thus housed mid cocks & hens in idle state
Aping at fashions which their betters hate
Affecting high lifes airs to scorn the past 175
Trying to be somthing makes them nought at last
These are the shadows that supply the place
Of farmers daughters of the vanished race

& what are these rude names will do them harm
O rather call them 'Ladys of the Farm'   180

Miss Peevish Scornful once the Village toast
Deemd fair by some & prettyish by most
Brought up a lady tho her fathers gain
Depended still on cattle & on grain
She followd shifting fashions & aspired   185
To the high notions baffled pride desired
& all the profits pigs & poultry made
Were gave to Miss for dressing & parade
To visit balls & plays fresh hopes to trace
& try her fortune with a simpering face   190
& now & then in Londons crowds was shown
To know the world & to the world be known
All leisure hours while miss at home sojournd
Past in preparing till new routs returnd
Or tittle tattling oer her shrewd remarks   195
Of ladys dresses or attentive sparks
How Mr So & so at such a rout
Fixd his eyes on her all the night about
While the good lady seated by his side
Behind her hand her blushes forced to hide   200
Till consious Miss in pity she woud say
For the poor lady turnd her face away
& young squire Dandy just returnd from france
How he first chose her from the rest to dance
& at the play how such a gent resignd   205
His seat to her & placed himself behind
How this squire bowd polite at her approach
& Lords een nodded as she passd their coach
Thus miss in raptures woud such things recall
& Pa & Ma in raptures heard it all   210
But when an equal woud his praise declare
& told young madam that her face was fair
She might believe the fellows truth the while
& just in sport might condescend to smile

But frownd his further teazing suit to shun   215
& deemd it rudeness in a farmers son
Thus she went on & visited & drest
& deemd things earnest that was spoke in jest
& dreamd at night oer prides uncheckd desires
Of nodding gentlemen & smiling squires   220
To Gretna green her visions often fled
& rattling coaches lumberd in her head
Till hopes grown weary with too long delay
Caught the green sickness & declined away
& beauty like a garment worse for wear   225
Fled her pale cheek & left it much too fair
Then she gave up sick visits balls & plays
Were whispers turnd to any thing but praise
All were thrown bye like an old fashiond song
Were she had playd show woman much too long   230
& condecended to be kind & plain
& 'mong her equals hoped to find a swain
Past follys now were hatful to review
& they were hated by her equals too
Notice from equals vain she tryd to court   235
Or if they noticed twas but just in sport
At last grown husband mad away she ran
Not with squire Dandy but the servant man

Young farmer Bigg of this same flimsey class
Wise among fools & with the wise an ass   240
A farming sprout with more then farmers pride
Struts like the squire & dresses dignified
They call him rich at which his weakness aimd
But others view him as a fool misnamed
Yet dress & tattle ladys hearts can charm   245
& hes the choice with madams of the farm
Now with that lady strutting now with this
Braced up in stays as slim as sickly miss
Shining at christmass rout & vulgar ball
The favourite spark & rival of them all   250

55

& oft hell venture to bemean his pride
Tho bribes & mysterys do their best to hide
Teazing weak maidens with his pert deciet
Whose lives are humble but whose looks are sweet
Whose beauty happen to outrival those   255
With whom the dandy as an equal goes
Thus maids are ruind oft & mothers made
As if bewitchd without a fathers aid
Tho nodds & winks & whispers urge a guess
Weakness is bribed & hides its hearts distress   260
To live dishonourd & to dye unwed
For clowns grow jealous when theyre once misled
Thus pointed fingers brand the passing spark
& whispers often guess his deeds are dark
But friends deny & urge that doubts mislead   265
& prove the youth above so mean a deed
The town agrees & leaves his ways at will
A proud consieted meddling fellow still

Nature in various moods pursues her plan
& moulds by turns the monkey or the man   270
With one she deals out wisdom as a curse
To follow fortune with an empty purse
The next in opposite extreams is bred
Oerflowing pockets & an empty head
Beggars in merit share a squires estate   275
& squires untitled meet a beggars fate
Fortunes great lottery owns nor rules nor laws
Fate holds her wealth & reason rarely draws
Blanks are her lot & merit vainly tryes
While heedless folly blunders on the prize   280

Young Headlong Racket to the last akin
Who only deals more openly in sin
& apes forged love with less mysterious guile
A high flown dandy in its lowest stile
By fashion hated with the vulgar gay   285

56

& deems it wit to tempt their steps astray
No maid can pass him but his learing eye
Attempts to prove her forward or too shy
He brags oer wine of loves his wits has won
& loves betrayed – & deems it precious fun   290
Horses & dogs & women oer his wine
Is all his talk & he believes it fine
For virtue now is such a trifling name
That vice can prey ont unexposed to blame
& fools may join him but to common sense   295
His head pleads empty & has no pretence
He courts his maids & shuns the better sort
& hunts & courses as a change of sport
& hates all poachers game destroying brutes
Altho with both the name as aptly suits   300
With this one difference darkness brings their prey
& he more brazen murders his by day
& thus he lives a hated sort of life
Loves wedded wantons while he scorns a wife
Prepares by turns to hunt & wh——e & shoot   305
Less then a man & little more then brute

Next on the parish list in paltry fame
Shines Dandy Flint Esqr whose dirty name
Has grown into a proverb for bad deeds
& he who reads it all thats filthy reads   310
Near did a single sentence more express
Of down right evil or of goodness less
Than Dandy Flint grown old in youthful shame
By loathed diseases which no words may name
& worn so spare that wit as passing bye   315
Swears Nick will thread him thro a bodkins eye
A sot who spouts short morals oer his gin
& when most drunk rails most against the sin
A dirty hog that on the puddles brink
Stirs up the mud & quarrels with the stink   320
Abusing others in his cants deciet

57

To come off victor when the rest are beat
His mask is but of lawn & every space
Lets in new light to show cants crimping face
He apes the lamb & is a wolf in grain   325
& guilty darkness dares the light in vain
Thus fools by making others failings known
Become the self accusers of their own
So Dandy Flint may rail it nothing weighs
Sense takes the slander of a fool for praise   330

These are the things that oer inferiors flirt
That spring from pride like summer flyes from dirt
& teaze & buzz their summer season bye
Bantering the poor & struggling to be high
& shall such knaves 'neath flatterys garment hide   335
Or fear damp truth to turn its glass aside
The plea is urgd not but to common sense
Reason & truth will stand its own defence
Whilst dark hypocrisy affects the cheat
The real bitter mocks a seeming sweet   340
But who so dealeth openly in shame
Must bear being noticed by his proper name
As he who thrusts his phiz in every glass
Meets a reflection be it man or ass
& can they thus who love themselves to view   345
Chuse to be vexd to find the picture true
Be as it will none but the base are bit
& satire shows them as they chuse to sit
Which if disliked they may improve with ease
& make the likeness [better] if they please   350
& satire stingless – follys & defects
While yet defective still its glass reflects
But when they cease to be as heretofore
It suits with others & is theirs no more

Some of the old school yet my verse coud tell   355
& one from boyhood I remember well

Who near aspired on follys wings to soar
A plain mean man scarce noticed from the poor
Who near expected as he walkd the street
Bows from inferiors whom he chancd to meet 360
Inferiors bred from fashions idle whim
Equals & neighbours all appeard to him
& tho wealth scornd in such low walks to go
& pride disdaind & called his manners low
He sought nor paid prides homage unto man 365
But lived unshining in his humble plan
& when his rights tyrannic power assaild
His courage triumphd tho his pocket failed
For he was doomd to feel that worldly curse
An upright spirit & an empty purse 370
Nor did he try the shamless fault to cure
Still keeping honest & remaining poor
But he has left & one of different race
Spoilt his old mansion & supplied his place
Nor left he there in seeking were to dwell 375
One heart save prides but inly wishd him well
Thus fortune oft dishousd by blinded guess
Bids honour starve & knavery meet success
Smiles on the wickeds ways their hopes to glad
& sinks the good man to maintain the bad 380

Proud Farmer Cheetum turnd a rogue by stealth
Whom prosperous times had ripend into wealth
Hunting & shooting had its ceasless charm
When his full purse cared little for a farm
A trusty hand was left to plough & plan 385
The double trade of master & of man
He kept his stud for hunts & races then
& dogs fed even better then his men
Bought loves & changed them when the freak was old
& drank his wine without a wife to scold 390
& gaind a dashing name & livd in style
& wore a mask to profit byt the while

For he who dares to do a deed of shame
Feels none & only knows it by the name
& made large credit while his name was good   395
For all woud trust him draw on whom he woud
A man so stylish none coud dream to doubt
Till changing times the secret brought about
The grains sunk price oer knaverys tricks was thrown
& others failings well excused his own   400
The times he said & frownd disturbd & sad
Needed no comment to explain them bad
So ere he broke he honestly confest
His wealth all gone & credit had the rest
& proved to all a smuggling rogue too late   405
Cheat creditors – turnd bankrupt – & still great
Hunts shoots & rackets as he did before
& still finds wealth for horses dogs & whore
& dogs & wh—— & horses in his train
Are all that have no reason to complain   410
These show his kindness in their varied ways
& gild his rotting name with dirty praise
Like as when brooks are dry the village sinks
Boast their full dingy tide that flows & stinks
That seems to boast when other streams are dry   415
'Neath summer suns how brave a dyke am I'

Old Saveall next whose dirty deeds & fame
Might put a young bards silken lines to shame
But my plain homespun verse lets none escape
Nor passes folly in its rudest shape   420
When satires muse puts on a russet gown
Tho vermin start as game she runs them down
So Saveall shall have place whom fortunes smiles
Unmixed with frowns hath made him known for miles
Famous for riches & by knavery prized   425
& famed for meaness & by worth despised
Who trys to buy a good name & decieve
With fair pretentions that but few believe

Who seldom swears & that but now & then
A smuggled oath when vexd by better men   430
That beard hypocrisy with honest grace
& tears the mask from cants decieving face
Yet in religion he is made elect
& buys with wine the favours of the sect
Making each spouter welcome when he comes   435
& turning beggars from their fallen crumbs
Pleading up charity in whining tones
& driving dogs at dinner from the bones
The scraps which beggars plead for serve his swine
So their lorn hopes seek other doors to dine   440
The broken bones enrich his land for grain
So dogs beneath his table wait in vain
On neighbourly good will he often dwells
& in dry times locks up his very wells
& if twas but of worth we might suppose   445
Hed even save the droppings of his nose
Such is this Saveall first of fortunes fellows
Famous for wealth great farms & small beer cellars
With the elect most saintish or most civil
& with the rest a cunning knave or devil   450

Poor honour now yields to the stronger side
A wrinkld maid turnd stale & past her pride
Knavery & cant in triumph take her place
Unblushing strumpets with a tempting face
Religion now is little more then cant   455
A cloak to hide what godliness may want
As painters deaths to make the terror less
Wrap their dry bones within a cheating dress
The world is of a piece words mostly make
The little difference for distinctions sake   460
Vice must own bad so virtue takes the best
Coarse is the one mere cobweb is the rest
& when encroaching vice with cunning deeds
To make a hole in virtues garb succeeds

Tis but indeed a customary case   465
She darns it up as none may spy the place
& if once caught by slanders jealous eye
Tho breaches double & holes multiply
Virtue awhile turns penitent & then
Like rifled maid her title claims agen   470
Their prayers are read as old accustomd things
& offerd up for all souls save the kings
They love mild sermons with few threats perplexd
& deem it sinful to forget the text
Then turn to business ere they leave the church   475
& linger oft to comment in the porch
Of fresh rates wanted from the needy poor
& list of taxes naild upon the door
Little religion in each bosom dwells
& that sleeps sound till sundays chiming bells   480
When from each shelf is regularly took
The weekly wanted pious dusty book
Seeking the church an hours good prayers they read
& hear a sermon as the all they need
Then read when home the reccolected text   485
& lay religion by till sunday next
Some with reform religions shade pursue
& vote the old church wrong to join the new
Casting away their former cold neglects
Paying religions once a week respects   490
They turn from regular old forms as bad
To pious maniacs regular[l]y mad
A chosen race so their consciet woud teach
Whom cant inspired to rave & not to preach
A set of upstarts late from darkness sprung   495
With this new light like mushrooms out of dung
Tho blind as owls i' th' sun they livd before
Consiet inspired & they are blind no more
The dru[n]ken cobler leaves his wicked life
Hastes to save others & neglects his wife   500
To mend mens souls he thinks himself designd

& leaves his shoes to the uncalld & blind
He then like old songs runs the scriptures oer
& makes discoverys never known before
Makes darkest points as plain as A B C   505
& wonders why his hearers will not see
Spouts facts on facts to prove that dark is light
& all are blind till he restore their sight
& swears the old church which he cast away
As full of errors & as blind as they   510
& offers prayers no doubt as prayers are cheap
For chosen shepherds to his worships sheep
Thinking the while if such the will of fate
Self might become a hopeful candidate
& doubtless longs shoud reformation call   515
To leave his own & take his neighbours stall
Part urgd as scripture more as self consiet
To suit his ends each passage he repeats
& in as various ways each fact he weaves
As gossips riddles upon winter eves   520
Now storming threats now pleading comforts mild
In puleing whine soft as a sucking child
The[y] cant & rave damnations threats by fits
Till some old farmer looses half his wits
Looks back on former sins tho loath to doubt   525
Groans oer a prayer & thinks himself devout
Then learnings lookd on as an idle jest
& the old cobler preaches far the best
Who smooths with honied hopes the deep dyd sinner
& earns reward – a lodging & a dinner   530
Their former teachers as blind guides they mock
Nor think them chosen for the crazy flock
The crazy flock believe & are depraved
& just in time turn ideots to be saved

The Ranter priests that take the street to teach   535
Swears god builds churches where so ere they preach
While on the other hand protestant people

Will have no church but such as wears a steeple
Thus creeds all differ yet each different sect
From the free agents to the grand elect   540
Who cull a remnant for the promised land
That wear heavens mark as sheep their owners brand
Each thinks his own as right & others wrong
& thus keeps up confusions babel song
While half the tribes at bottom are no more   545
Then saints skin deep & devils at the core
Who act by customs & as custom shows
Lay bye religion with their sunday cloaths
Religions aim is truth & different creeds
By different channels for that aim proceeds   550
But many wander muddy by the way
& dark with errors struggle far astray
Till weary with the toil they fainter creep
& then like stagnant waters stink & sleep
Religions truth a plain straight journey makes   555
Which falshoods wandering never overtakes
As gold when purified flows free from dross
& leaves the worthless mixture without loss
So from black errors truths eternal morn
Mounts into light & smiles the night to scorn   560

Tis not religion but its want when sects
Rail at each other to hide their own defects
For calmness quiet cheerfulness & love
Its essence is to aid our hopes above
Tis vain philosophy that would decieve   565
The[y] heer too much to doubt or to believe
What is & was we feel – what is to be
Truth nothing knows tis guess pretends to see
Een earths least mysterys are above our skill
& would-be-gods are but her childern still   570
Wisdom still searching with her flickering flame
Lost in her mysterys dwindles to a name
Whence goeth light when evening hides the sun

& whence the darkness when the night be done
Hither it cometh – aye – & there it goes   575
Is the whole sum which mighty wisdom knows
So resignation should the worst befall
& faith to hope the best is best of all

Old Ralph the veriest rake the town possesd
Felt sins prick deep & all his crimes confest   580
Groand oer confessions to his ranting priest
& prayd & sang & felt his soul released
The new births struggles made him wonderous wan
& feebly prayd at first the baby man
Twixt doubts & fears yet viewd the cured complaint   585
& scarce percieved the devil from the saint
But soon the 'outward man' grown godly mad
Felt the good spirit triumph oer the bad
& cants dull prayers too lame to visit heaven
Lookd oer past sins & fancied all forgiven   590
He then whind lectures in a happier strain
& coaxd poor sinners to be born again
Shund old companions once beloved so well
As condemnd transports on the way to hell
& prayd & sang from sin & pain releasd   595
& smoothd his hair & fashiond for a priest
Old women heard him with oerjoyd delight
Some cryd & sind & others turnd out right
Theyd read the gospel studied good St Paul
But ralp[h]s good doctrine was the best of all   600
From him they found their old religions stuff
Was nought but like a play at 'blind mans buff'
A pathless journey in a starless night
Till good St Ralp[h] restored the way to light
& thus as priest he exercised his wits   605
Forcd men to prayers & women into fits
& heard & cured each difficult complaint
& midst his flock seemed little less then saint
But hell untired with everlasting watch

(The fox grows cunning when preys hard to catch)   610
Crept into Ralphs new planted paradise
& met success in tempting him to vice
A simpering eve did in his garden dwell
& she was fair & he grew fond – & fell
Twas love at first but een when that began   615
The sinking saint grew more & more the man
& with his eve so treache[r]ously fair
Coud feel more joy then kneeling down to prayer
Yet still he prayd nor deemd his case so bad
As stone blind sinners tho his heart was sad   620
The bible still he read with saintly looks
& deemd all others as ungodly books
Unless a patch of scripture here & there
Redeemd each page & made them godly ware
Tho sinfull love had overpowerd his skill   625
With other sins he kept unspotted still
He drank nor swore & when a lye was told
Twas just gains trifle when he bought & sold
When bretheren met he woud his joys express
Groand while they prayd & said amen by guess   630
Then 'da—— & blame ye' hed no further dare
Hell coud not urge the fallen man to sware
Till the compleation of his serpent sin
Urgd by the devil sunk him to the chin
Eve tho beguild forbidden fruit to taste   635
Had lovd an adam ere she loved the priest
& ere disgrace had ripend into light
Ralph had no power to wed her & be right
His fate was evident it came at last
His sheep was judge & shepherd ralph was cast   640
Then drink & rackett joind their former friends
& new born saint in the old sinner ends

Next comes a name who spite of all controuls
Reigns oer the bodys ills as Ralph the souls
A mighty doctor – what so thickly sown   645

That een the Parish can a doctor own
Yes own one too whose power so splendid shines
As een to name illuminates my lines
For every mouth is puckered with his skill
So sing his patients & so say his bill   650
The worst disease he does so quick subdue
That makes some think the devil helps him through
But what care they who helps – if pain endured
So long before he rose can now be cured
By reading in their water all their ails   655
& conjuring medicines up that never fails
Thus all the country join his fame to raise
& few but Dr Urine gets the praise
So now for skill the parish rules the roast
Renowned for Quacks that Citys cannot boast   660
– Ah where in City or in Town can dwell
Famed Dr Urine thy rare parrarell
No where indeed to match at once with thee
Thy mighty fame & humble pedigree
But can that taint the Laurel on thy brows   665
'Cause thou wert wont to docter Swine & cows
& rose to fame as fame was took by force
From giving judgment on a cholicked horse
To read the water of poor sickly clowns
& ease them not of illness but their crowns   670
Tho every ill swims on thy majic glass
& at thy conjuring bidding rise & pass
Like Mackbeths murdered spirits grimly on
& thou thy powers scheme cures for every one
Een from the boasting of thy self – & thine   675
Thy duped deciples – such thy fame doth shine
As if the dead were not beyond thy skill
But might be quickened from thy power & pill –
The poor old woman now half blind & lame
With age – has room to curse thy greedy fame   680
For she herself had fame ere thou hadst thine
& did as doctress of the Village shine

Tho one rare salve was cure for every sore
That Salve & that famed Doctress' race is oer
Say Dr Urine why – (& dont deride   685
My gossiping enquirey) shouldst thou hide
In such poor paltry Parish this renown
As seems well worthy of the finest town
Nay rather City for Im sure thy name
& Waterbottles might extend thy fame   690
To every patient that had death to fear
Then say good Docter why so linger here
Thourt no great 'schollard' that the learned tell
& all that buy thy drugs might know as well
But it so turns & lucky for thy pelf   695
Thy patients are less 'schollards' then thyself
– But what of learning words mispelt is small
Drawbacks on knowledge that gives cures for all
Distempers & diseases as he wills
& almost cures a broken limb with pills   700
The learned faculty are tools to thee
& from thy powers like thy complaints will flee
Then why thus linger in the worst of towns
To cure & hear the praise of foolish Clowns
But fools perhaps may be thy only game   705
To feed thy pockets & encrease thy fame
If so think not in greater towns to shine
Where skill would bid thy juggling tricks decline
& bright eyed reason send thee hasty back
Proving thee what thou really art a quack   710
So Dr Urine in thy nest remain
& till the dull dark age of fools be past
As conjuror & Water Doctor reign
Then drop into thy grave – a Quack at last

In politics & politicians lies   715
The modern farmer waxes wonderous wise
Opinionates with wisdom all compact
& een coud tell a nation how to act

Throws light on darkness with excessive skill
Knows who acts well & whos designs are ill 720
Proves half the members nought but briberys tools
& calls the past a dull dark age of fools
As wise as solomons they read the news
Not with their blind forefathers simple views
Who read of wars & wishd that wars woud cease 725
& blessd the king & wishd his country peace
Who markd the weight of each fat sheep & ox
The price of grain & rise & fall of stocks
Who thought it learning how to buy & sell
& he a wise man who coud manage well 730
No not with such old fashiond idle views
Do these news mongers trafic with the news
They read of politics & not of grain
& speechify & comment & explain
& know so much of parliment & state 735
Youd think them members when you heard them prate
& know so little of their farms the while
That can but urge a wiser man to smile

Young Brag a 'jack of all trades' save his own
From home is little as the farmer known 740
He talks with all the equal & the high
Equally ready to tell truth or lie
His betters view him in his just deserts
But equals deem him one of mighty parts
Opinions gratis gives in mens affairs 745
Fool in his own but wonderous wise in theirs
Upon his talents friends were strongly bent
Mistook his parts & off to school he went
A young aspiring hopeful youth at least
Whose parents deemd him fashiond for a priest 750
Twas somthing urgd the dissapointed view
With which religion had the least to do
Tho they baskd blessd in fortunes wealthy sun
They yearnd for more to bless their hopeful son

Whom school & colledge both had vainly taught   755
& learnd young hopeful to be fit for naught
His friends decievd beheld the faded charm
Resignd weak hopes & placed him in a farm
& there he lives & to great skill pretends
& reigns a god among his farming friends   760
Scrats paragraphs & sends them to the News
Signd 'constant reader' lest they shoud refuse
The illspelt trash on patriotic cavils
Leaving correction to the printers devils
Skits upon those by whom theyre never read   765
Who might as well write Letters to the dead
Or puffs upon himself in various ways
Whom none but self will either read or praise
& Poems too the polishd patriot chimes
Stanzas to Cobbets truth & Comic Ryhmes   770
To which he fits a hacknied tune that draws
From patriot dinners echoes of applause
& in the next weeks news out comes the treat
From 'constant reader' of the drunken feat
Were so much wine is lavishd in the strain   775
As even to make the reader drunk again
Were every dish on which the knaves regale
Find places there but common sense & ale
For common sense is grown too tame to teach
& ales too low to aid a patriots speech   780
& morts of speeches made to back reform
That raised applauses like a thunder storm
& almost loosd the rafters from their pegs
While chairs & tables scarce coud keep their legs
Reeling amid the hiccups & hurra's   785
& glass[es] rung & almost dancd applause
Nor will he pass his comic singing oer
For they too set the table in a roar
& then concludes it with the pompous clause
– Success to patriots & the good old cause   790
A hacknied tune which patriots daily sing

An Election Squib.

Like variations of 'God save the King'
But when election mobs for battle meet
& dirty flags & ribbons throng the street
Hunting for votes some little borough town   795
Tis there his genius meets the most renown
When on the hustings bawling spouters throng
Who fight & war like women with the tongue
All speakers & no hearers were the crys
Piles up confusions babel to the skys   800
& croaking at the top in proud renown
Each party sits till tother pulls him down
Here shines our orator in all his plumes
Nor prouder bantum to a dung hill comes
Then he to crow & peck & peck & crow   805
& hurl bad english at retorting foe
No hungry magpie round a rotten sheep
A longer song of nonsence up can keep
Were small words all their utmost powers engage
& monnysyllables swell mad with rage   810
Who martyrs like to freedoms noble cause
Are choaked by scores in hiccups & hurras
The rest awhile in thick disorder flye
& from his mouth like crackers bounce & dye
'I said' – 'says I' & – 'then' – 'he said' – 'says he'   815
Are the chain balls of his attillery
That storm & threaten at the deadly breach
& link the weapons of his broken speech
The head & tail piece setting off & close
That throws each sentence at his sneering foes   820
& when his monny syllables have spent
Their rage & given his utmost fury vent
& wore the cant thread bare that serves the throng
Like summers cuckoo tune for every song
Of 'Rotten boroughs' – 'bribery' – 'tyrants' – 'slaves'   825
Were selfs a patriot & opposers knaves
To fill the void his lack of words will cause
He bawls out freedom & expects applause

Then bows his head in oratorial grace
& exit makes to give new speakers place 830
So have I seen the schoolboy in his sport
(When playing soldiers) honours praise to court
Spout to his fancied army on parade
Bawling of valour ere the assault was made
Then drew his 'wooden sword' & led the way 835
To storm their castles & commence the fray
Pointing their pellets at unconsious foes
At bantum cocks that on the dung hill crows
When pop each gun went to commence the quarrel
Nor scared the flye that settled on the barrel 840
He ryhmes election squibs & meet[s] applause
From party critics that support his cause
His fustian wit trots wild on broken feet
Jostling the readers patience from his seat
Half prose half verse they stagger as they go 845
& after fashions follys dribbling flow
One line starts smooth & then for room perplext
Elbow along & knock against the next
& half its neighbour then a stop marks time
To close the sense – what follows is for ryhme 850
Pert forwardness & insolent consiet
In bard & patrons close as circles meet
All that is bad from one to tother jumps
Both play at cards & turn up knaves as trumps
& his bad wares in credits way to push 855
He boasts theres nought to make the modest blush
Tho common sense he neither fears or heeds
Who finds a cause to blush at all she reads
To see its name with fools as partners shown
& cursed with trash which dullness shrinks to own 860
Yet in the columns of the weekly News
They shine as laureat odes to 'Pinks' or 'Blues'
Where humbug patron of cants tinsel gauds
Reads & with Fudge so sanctions & applauds
One blows the bubble up with puffing sides 865

& tother marks till stiff necked how it rides
Bawling aloud till hoarse 'look here now there'
Till mobs throng round to wonder & to stare
Then flattery puffs a critique in their cause
& gain throngs in with interest & applause 870
So boys with their tobacco pipes & suds
Play while one bubble after tother scuds
Look there a fine one goes & there another
How bubble two beats bubble one his brother
Then blows again with cheeks distended wide 875
Till like the frog he almost bursts with pride
Then out goes bubble three & instant out
From gaping mouths come the applauding shout
That makes his pride & happiness redouble
& soap baloons flye up in many a bubble 880
Humbug still hailing with excess of joy
Who condescends to feed both men & boy
With this small difference the boys sports are stinted
Tho humbug praises theres no puff to print it
He games & drinks & rackets up & down 885
A low livd mocker of high life in town
& sips his wine in fashionable pride
& thrusts in scorn the homely ale aside
His fathers riches bought such foolish airs
But wasting fortunes een must need repairs 890
As parching summer checks the runnels haste
The greatest wealth will lessen spent in waste
Tho credit proves him poor his stubborn pride
Oer acts his purse & struggles dignified
Yet stung with tidings that his consience vents 895
He rails at tythes & hopes for falling rents
Curses all taxes as tyrannic things
& hates the pride of government & kings
Forgetting self tho on the brink to fall
A shade of mightier consequence then all 900
Turnd radical in spirit & in purse
He prays reform & deems the laws a curse

Speaks treasonous things before his friends & cousins
& toasts reforming patriots by dozens
& aping wit with ignorant delight   905
A village politician turns out right
Burdett & Brougham his Bibles place supplys
& these he reads & studys & applys
But choaks their wit to pass his narrow brains
& steals the stingless carcass for his pains   910
Like to the Daw dressed in the Peacocks coat
He gives proud utterance to each stolen note
While laughter roars he seems on clouds to walk
For laughter is the chorus of small talk
Election hums & Placards on the throne   915
He mars the joke & makes the rest his own
Runs reason mad in his unreasoning matters
& twists & tears poor common sense to tatters
Yet while he mimics second hand & storms
& mocks each echo hooting for reforms   920
& rants with oratorial pause & start
Each stale grown speech of patriots oer by heart
He meets applause in every spouting fit
By those who take impertine[n]ce for wit
Friends gape & wonder while they hear him preach   925
& swear it Ciceronian every speech
But others view him in wits sneard remark
A toothless puppy that can only bark
He hails his countrys foes his only friends
D—mns peace & prays for war that never ends   930
Its ruins lookd on as the way to wealth
& grace for all meals is reforms good health
& why is all this hubbub for reforms
This anxious looking for expected storms
That turns each fireside into parliments   935
In strong debates of taxes tithes & rents
Is aught of general good or general views
Sketchd in the pathway which reform pursues
Or is the rich mans lands or misers pelf

But grudgd in others to be claimd by self   940
Doubtless the reasons far more plain then good
Is far more true as such then understood
Our village politicians clings no doubt
To one sole cause that moves the rest about
His general good perhaps is small akin   945
To self a core that smuggles in that skin
Taxes no doubt might be at peace & stand
If theyd sink claims on his conserns & land
& such forcd things as Landlords yearly claims
He hates no doubt – tho fear but inly blames   950
& views reform in but a selfish light
To make a level far as self is right
Turn Lords to farms or farmers change to Lords
Is the dear wish that with his heart accords
Or when all laws are ruind with the throne   955
Just but to make the farm he rents his own
Thus far no farther tho with reasons leave
Want pleads for times of adam & of eve
This must not be they toild for bread before
& some must still be rich & some be poor   960
To sink the many & exalt the few
Is still his creed in an extended view
Reform thus leveld to brags selfish will
Want still might toil & be contented still
With other nations mid tyranic strife   965
This miscalld mania struggles oft to life
Fair is the mask that hides its visage first
But soon the infant to a fiend is nursd
That like a wolf howls hungerly & high
A cry for blood – & freedom apes that cry   970
For Freedom unrestraind forsakes her cause
& lawless pleasures are her only laws
Like as high tempests reckless whom they harm
Come headlong on their pleasures to perform
Too late the trees beneath their burthen groan   975
The lawless storm feels treason in that tone

& down its whole artillery lightning hail
& thunder comes the rebels to assail
Prostrate at once the groves in ruins lye
Their torn roots pleading pity from the sky   980
So with the tyrant whom he wills he blames
Mere treason is whatere his vengance names
& where that falls – defence – complaints – aye sighs
Are discontents & treasons in disguise
Thus laws grow lawless & the patriot dies   985
Dies & above his poor insulted dust
Fears made to sanction that the deed was just
Such is the case when freedom like a flood
Bursts out in mischief what was meant as good
So thy proud lilys haughty france was torn   990
Whose whitness dared the insulted light to scorn
& scorn did come & thou wert weak indeed
Torn down & trampled like the meanest weed
Thy laws a tyrants scoffing stock became
& thy white Flag blushed red for very shame   995
When by a tyrants pompous threats unfurled
To show its former weakness to the world
Who mocking liberty where none remained
With stronger fetters former rights enchained
Heaven shield thee England in thy ancient cause   1000
From tyrant governments & broken laws
Since freedom came & crowned thee free none dare
As yet to rouse thy Lion from its lare
Threats have assailed thee but as like the wind
They roared & into nothing rage resigned   1005
& they may roar & bluster but in vain
So barks the Masstiff at his clanking chain
Nations in bonds can never cope with thee
For they alone are mighty who are free
& mayst thou ever be the same as now   1010
With victorys laurels blooming on thy brow
That scource from which thy every glory springs
A land of liberty as well as kings

Thus village politics – & hopes for pelf
Live in one word & centre all in 'self'   1015
Thus village politicians urge repairs
& deem all governments as wrong but theirs
Cants juggling wisdom spurning reasons rules
The reasoning jargon of unreasoning fools
Versd in low cunning which to handle brief   1020
Is but a genteel title for a thief
Nay start not reader such harsh words to hear
Nor deem the pen of Satire too severe
What is that shuffling shadow of a man
Were selfs deceptions shine in every plan   1025
Who spouts of freedom as the thing he craves
& treats the poor oer whom he rules as slaves
Who votes equallity that all may share
& stints the pauper of his parish fare
Who damns all taxes both of church & state   1030
& on the parish lays a double rate
Such is our heroe in his tyrant pride
Then is his honours title misapplied
Such with one breath scoff at the poors distress
& bawl out freedom for their own redress   1035
True Patriotism is a thing divine
& far above a theme so mean as mine
To higher powers due praises may belong
But patriotism is above my song
Not that which tells its emptiness aloud   1040
Like quacks & pedlars to a gaping crowd
That pleads foul robbery in an honest stile
& feeds poor hope on honied words the while
That deems it honour urgd in knaverys cause
& highest merit to evade the laws   1045
With words of peace & plenty thickly sown
Deceptions aimd at ignorance alone
Empty as frothing bubbles on the stream
Or shadowy banquets in a beggars dream
Ruins the mark the motly monster bears   1050

& vile hypocrisy the mask it wears
Cant as high priest around its alter prays
& preaches loud its mockery of praise
Oer blinded minds its poison quickly runs
But shrinks in mist from reasons searching suns   1055
To those gilt Dagons knaves & fools may raise
Deceptions alters of decieving praise
& paint their claims as interest wills to paint
Call each a god a devil or a saint
Truth will his godships mighty claims betray   1060
& prove like Daniel that hes made of clay
These soft politic saints may freedom preach
& vacant minds believe the lies they teach
Who think them walking canaans flowing oer
With milk & honey for the starving poor   1065
& sure enough their wants may richly fare
If like camelions they can feed on air
Their promises sown thick degenerate run
& mildew into broken ones when done
& tho a plentious seed time dreams of gains   1070
A blighted harvest falsifys the pains
Such promises to day to morrow straight
Like an old almanack is out of date
& they who break them no more credit breaks
Then Moors new year does for the olds mistakes   1075
Thus freedom preaching is but knaverys game
& old self interest by a different name

But they alone are worthy of its claims
Who midst the storm that sanctions or defames
Firm like the Oak on their first ground sojourn   1080
Neath suns & winds that shines & shocks in turn
Who fear no scoffs nor hunt the cloak of bribes
Those smiling tempters of declaiming scribes
Meteors that dazzle with a vapours flame
That rise in gilded praise & set in shame   1085
Tho barren vineyards patriots labour in

Their countrys good is all they strive to win
Tho rough the road they struggle to the last
& look with joy upon the journey past
Their very faults are blessings misapplied   1090
'& een their failings lean to virtues side'
Tho crowds be found to scorn & few to raise
The 'still small' anthem of deserving praise
Yet consience triumphs like a setting sun
& self illumined feels its best was done   1095
For men like these the heathens praise did claim
Seats with the Gods & gave their deeds the name
& still for such fame pulls from freedoms tree
A bough that blossoms with posterity
& twines like Ivy gathering strength with time   1100
Green round the ruins of their native clime

& such art thou – but why shoud I proclaim
Thy worth that hideth from the gaze of fame
& in the conscience of a noble cause
Shrinks like a hermit from the worlds applause   1105
Yet worth like thine a share of fame shall meet
That falls like sunshine on thy calm retreat
That fame that found the Roman at his plough
Follows thy footsteps & applauds thee now
& little need hath verse of mine to tell   1110
Of one respected & beloved so well
& lest my humble muse unused to shine
Shoud with presumptive theme dishonour thee
I'll leave thy name to worthier songs then mine
& pledge this offering to thy memory   1115
Titles & power & riches & estate
All at thy birth conspired to make thee great
But these are baubles which distinction breeds
& are as shadows to thy noble deeds
Pomp is an insect that but makes display   1120
For one poor season & so fades away
Tho flattery fawns by wealth & titles moved

True worth alone can make the man beloved
& worth is thine that through thy life hath won
The praise of many & the scorn of none   1125
For foes grow silent when they hear thy name
& sanction praises were they cannot blame
For thy whole life hath sought one common end
The slave to free the feeble to befriend
No pompous speechs which ambition vents   1130
Made thy name popular in parliments
No court intrigues a fawning hope to raise
Gilt thy first entrance with newspaper praise –
Mans general welfare & thy countrys good
Deeds on which honours noblest base hath stood   1135
Were the first struggles of thy patriot skill
& wears through life thy whole ambition still
Labouring along in each unshining part
With simple truth & such an upright heart
That when the poor hear thee their rights defend   1140
They feel thee more their brother then their friend
& in such hearts thy name so good & just
Shall live behind & 'blossom in the dust'
& may thy names successors ever be
Branches proved worthy of their parent tree   1145
To bloom unblighted on a glorious race
Shineing unsullied on the page of fame
& like the sunrise on an ancient place
Gild the past memory of thy worthy name
Names without worth may be by beggars bought   1150
Shadows of nothings that are less then naught
These will grow old like garments time will tear
Poor honours tinsel & make worse for wear
The proudest trials to prolong their date
When scut[c]heond pride turns rags & mocks in state   1155
Aye marble bye & bye with sculpture deckt
Shall mingle with the ashes they protect
Brass eat its self away in fretting rust
& names on adamant shall fret to dust

Worth & worth only has the longest run   1160
& virtue graves it on the golden sun
Eternitys escutcheon there it shines
With every day renewed which nothing lines
Piering its influence on the happy day
While bad ones moulder in the night away   1165
What is mere honour that so charms the sight
A bauble gilt a shadow cloathed in light
A pompous nothing pride extolleth high
A boast of blood that runs its channels dry
To stagnate upon common shores at last   1170
Honour in state what is the Farce when past
A veil death rends exposing tyrant knaves
To eke the refuse of ignoble graves
Honour in war the cannon vaunts so loud
What but poor insect weaving its own shroud   1175
A danger where the bravest dare & die
For the cold praise that marble tombs supply
& such is honours all in every game
Like faithless friend she soon forgets their fame
& as a laccquey unto shame will turn   1180
With littleness & meaness to sojourn
So what was Pompeys Cesars in the past
Race horses dogs & coaches heir at last

Mere titles without worth are withered bays
& paper crowns that mock at honours rays   1185
The meanest tradesman in his flash attire
Struts from behind his counter an Esqr
Een knighthood from its throne is hurled afar
& fortune caught for clowns the fallen star
What honour wore times past Sir Ralph wears now   1190
Whose feats of prowess sprung from flail & plough
Whose grandame spun & darned the cloaths she wore
& rob[b]ed the dung hill to increase her store
Thus sprang the means that feed his present fame
& silver stars gild oer his little name   1195

& just as much of honours light they leave
As pewter crests upon a paupers sleeve
The little odds thats hardly worth the name
Lie in the metal for the mans the same
While a good name however poor or small   1200
Grows great in value & outshines them all

A shadow man between the two extreams
Of fat & lean like pharoahs hungry dreams
With visage such as frighted childern dread
When gossip stories haunt their dreams abed   1205
In heart & head vain ignorant & dull
& fierce in visage as a baited bull
Appears the village constable who bears
The affairs of state & keeps them in repairs
Foremost in meetings he resumes his place   1210
& gives opinions upon every case
Reigning & ruling in the mighty state
A jackall makeshift for a majistrate
Keeping the tools of terror for each cause
When the starved poor oerstep his pigmy laws   1215
To mark the paupers goods the parish brand
Is in his mansion ready at command
Titles around his name their honours bring
Like rags & tatters round the 'beggars king'
Knight of the black staff master of the stocks   1220
& hand cuff-keeper – tools that sadly mock
His dignity – for common sense will sneer
& half acknowledge in his passing ear   [1245]
That such like tools & titles near was known
To grace a name so aptly as his own   1225
For though with natural cunning fortified
His deeds will often grow too large to hide
Tho' like a smugglers dealings shunning light   [1250]
They peep thro' rents & often sprout in sight
Thus summons oft are served in hopes of pelf   1230
To overcharge & get a fee for self

& village dances watched at midnight hours
In the mock errand of his ruleing powers [1255]
With feigned pretence good order to preserve
Only to break it if a chance shoud serve 1235
For married clowns his actions closely mark
& jealous grow at whispers in the dark
Whence broils ensue – then from the noisey fray [1260]
Himself hath made sneaks unpercieved away
Like to the fox whom yard dogs barks affright 1240
When on the point of robbing roosts at night
Such is this Sancho of the magistrates
& such are most knaves of those petty states [1265]
Where cunning fools are only reckoned wise
Who best can hide their faults from others eyes 1245
& bold assurance forging merits place
Takes credit to be bad were all are base
Whose Staff becomes his law & succour too [1270]
The stoutest village rabble to subdue
Soon as he holds it in his mighty hand 1250
It grows as potent as a magic wand
Clowns look & grow submissive at the view
As if the mighty weapon froze them thro [1275]

Churchwardens Constables & Overseers [1220]
Makes up the round of Commons & of Peers 1255
With learning just enough to sign a name
& skill sufficient parish rates to frame
& cunning deep enough the poor to cheat
This learned body for debatings meet [1225]
Tho many heads the parliment prepare 1260
& each one claims some wisdom for its share
Like midnight with her vapours tis so small
They make but darkness visible withall
Their secretary is the Parish Clerk [1230]
Whom like a shepherds dog they keep to bark 1265
& gather rates & when the next are due
To cry them oer at church time from his pew

He as their 'Jack of all trades' steady shines
Thro thick & thin to sanction their designs [1235]
Who apes the part of King & Magistrate 1270
& acts grand segnior of this turkish state
Who votes new laws to those already made
& acts by force when one is disobeyd
Having no credit which he fears to loose [1240]
He does what ever dirty jobs they chuse 1275
For when a Hudibrass oersteps the laws
A Ralph is ready to defend his cause
Tasking the pauper [his] labours to stand
Or clapping on his goods the Parish Brand
Lest he shoud sell them for the want of bread 1280
On parish bounty rather pind then fed
Or carrying the parish book from door to door
Claiming fresh taxes from the needy poor
& if ones hunger overcomes his hate
& buys a loaf with what shoud pay the rate 1285
He instant sets his tyrant laws to work
In heart & deed the essence of a turk
Brings summons for an eighteen penny rate
& gains the praises of the parish state
Or seizes goods & from the burthend clown 1290
Extorts for extra trouble half a Crown
Himself a beggar that may shortly take
A weekly pittance from the rates they make
But the old proverb suits the subject well
Mount such on horseback & theyll ride to hell 1295
Such is this fussy cur that well deserves
The business of the master whom he serves
The vilest thing neer crawled without its brother
& theyre as like as one Ass gets another
One sets no job but tother barks to do't 1300
Both for self interest lick the foulest foot
& spite of all the meaness & the stink
Picks up gains crumbles from the dirtiest sink
One name serves both & that I need not name

85

For all may by the color know the game   1305
As hungry dogs know carrion by the smell
So all may know them by their ways as well
Coarse as such images but nought would do
But coarsest stuff to make the picture true
As when some muse weeps over Tyburn tree   1310
Hard words & hanging make the melody
So as they reign here let them hang together
Stinking when met like sinks in stormy weather
Tho natures marks are deep that all may scan
A knaves delusions from an honest man   1315
Oppression often mourns the vile abuse
& flyes to justice – deemd of little use
Truth that coud once its own redresses seek
Is now deemd nothing & forbid to speak
Driven like an exild king from past renown   1320
Power took its place & keeps it with a frown
But tis well known that justice winks at crimes
A saying thats in season at all times
Or why should the poor sinning starving clown
Meet jail & hanging for a stolen crown   1325
While wealthy thieves with knaverys bribes endued
Plunder their millions & are not pursued
Nay at the foot of Tyburns noted tree
They do deserving deeds & still go free
Where others suffer for some pigmy cause   1330
They all but murder & escape the laws
Skulking awhile in briberys dirty den
Then start new gilt & pass as honest men
Gold is a mighty substitute it buys
The fool sufficient credit to seem wise   1335 [ ]
The coward laurels Harlots a good name
A mask for villany for titles fame
Buys knaves an office Traitors trust & powers
Buys lies & oaths & breaks them every hour
Buys cant its flattery Hypocrites their paint   1340 [ ]
Making a very devil seem a saint

Buys asses panegarics & what not
Buys pride its worship & leaves God forgot
In fact buys all & every thing forsooth
But two poor outcasts honesty & truth   1345 [ ]
& why shoud power or pride betray its trust
Is it too old a fashion to be just   [1335]
Or does self interest inclinations bend
Aye Aye the Farmer is his worships friend
As parish priest from him he meets his tythes   1350
Punctual as harvest wakes the tinkling sythes
Tho often grudgd yet he their hopes to glad   [1340]
Prays better harvests when the last was bad
& as he deals so honestly with him
It must be malice in the poor or whim   1355
Who seek relief & lay on them the blame
& hopless seek it & return the same   [1345]
Within the church where they on sabbath days
Mock god with all the outward show of praise
Making his house a pharisees at best   1360
Gods for one day & Satans all the rest
The parson oft scarce puts his sermon bye   [1350]
Ere neath his pulpit & with mighty cry
The clerk anounces – what ? – commandments meet
No – when these parish vestrys next shall meet   1365
To fleece the poor & rob with vile command
Want of its bread too feeble to withstand   [1355]
Altho its aching heart too often knows
Knaves call it debtor where it nothing owes
For in these Vestrys cunning deep as night   1370
Plans deeds that would be treason to the light
& tho so honest in its own disguise   [1360]
Twould be plain theft exposed to reasons eyes
For the whole set just as they please can plan
& what one says all sanction to a man   1375
Self interest rules each vestry they may call
& what one sticks for is the gain of all   [1365]
The set – thus knavery like contagion runs

& thus the fathers card becomes the sons
Both play one game to cheat us in the lump   1380
& the sons turn up shows the fathers trump
Here shines the man of morals Farmer Finch   [1370]
Smooth tongued & fine an angel every inch
In outward guise & never known as yet
To run in Taverns Brothels or in debt   1385
In public life all punctual honest true
& flattery gives his graces double due   [1375]
For pitys gifts are never public made
But there his name & guinea is displayed
In double views to answer prides desire   1390
To purchase praise & to be dubbed Esquire
A sunday never comes or foul or fair   [1380]
That misses him at church throughout the year
The priest himself boasts as the mans reward
That he near preached a sermon but he heard   1395
Such is the man in public all agree
That saints themselves no better men could be   [1385]
But now of private life lets take the view
– In that same church & in that very pew
Where he each sabbath sings & reads & prays   1400
He joins the vestry upon common days
Cheating the poor with leveys doubly laid   [1390]
On their small means that wealth may be defrayed
To save his own & others his compeers
He wrongs the poor whom he has wrongd for years   1405
Making the house of prayer the house of sin
& placing Satan as high priest within   [1395]
Such is this good church going morral man
This man of morrals on deseptions plan
So knaves by cant steer free from sins complaints   1410
& flatterys cunning coins them into saints
Tho justice Terror who the peace preserves   [1400]
Meets more of slander then his deeds deserves
A blunt opinionated odd rude man
Severe & selfish in his every plan   1415

THE CLERICAL MAGISTRATE.

" *The Bishop.* Will you be diligent in Prayers—laying aside the study of the world and the flesh ?——*The Priest.* I will.
The Bishop. Will you maintain and set forwards, as much as lieth in you, quietness, peace, and love, among all Christian People ?——*Priest.* I will.
¶ The Bishop laying his hand upon the head of him that receiveth the order of Priesthood, shall say, RECEIVE THE HOLY GHOST."
The Form of Ordination for a Priest.

———— " The pulpit (in the sober use
Of its legitimate peculiar pow'rs)
Must stand acknowledg'd, while the world shall stand,
The most important and effectual guard,
Support, and ornament of virtue's cause.
  *   *   *   *   *
Behold the picture ! Is it like?

THIS IS A PRIEST,

made ' according to Law',

Or right or wrong his overreasoning heart
Believes & often overacts his part [1405]
Tho pleading want oft meets with harsh replies
& truths too often listend too as lies
Altho he reigns with much caprice & whim 1420
The poor can name worse governers then him
His gifts at Christmass time are yearly given [1410]
No doubt as toll fees on the road to heaven
Tho charity or looses byt or wins
Tis said to hide a multitude of sins 1425
& wether wealth-bought-hopes shall fail or speed
The poor are blest & goodness marks the deed [1415]
Tho rather leaning to the stronger side
He preaches often on the sins of pride
& oft while urging on the crimes of dress 1430
His looks will tell the jealous were to guess
Vain offering mercys plea in hopes to cure [1420]
How wasted pride might feed the wanting poor
& wether just or not his own whole plan
Sets the example as a plain drest man 1435
His three cockt hat & suit in colour met
Were youths first fashion & he sticks it yet [1425]
The same spruce figure traced in memorys back
Een strangers know him as 'the man in black'
While playing boys on sundays without guess 1440
Will scent their foe a furlong by his dress
Tho to complaints his aid is oft denyd [1430]
Tho said too oft to shun the weaker side
Yet when foul wrongs are utterd in his ear
Farmers themselves meet reprimands severe 1445
Poor trembling maids too learn his looks to dread
By sad forcd errands to his mansion led [1435]
His worships lectures are so long & keen
Theyre dreaded now as pennance once has been
Tho it is said what will not rumour say 1450
There een was seasons when the priest was gay
That now & then in manhoods lusty morn [1440]

90

His maids turnd mothers & were never sworn
Yet still he reigns what ever faults they find
A blunt odd rude good picture of his kind   1455
Who preaches partial for both church & king
& runs reform down as a dangerous thing   [1445]
& oft like hells its mystic deeds unravels
& dreads its name as childern dread the d——ls
Yet mixes often in election dinners   1460
& takes his seat 'with publicans & sinners'
Drinks healths & argues wether wrong or right   [1450]
Nor ever flinches to be deemd polite
But healths gave out by young reforming sparks
He drinks in silence & disdans remarks   1465
Or puts the profferd wine untasted bye
& waits some wiser speech to make reply   [1455]
Anothers faults with him are quickly known
Yet needs a micriscope to find his own
He deems all wrong but him unless they be   1470
Of the same cloth & think the same as he
Thus self triumphant both in light & dark   [1460]
He oft leaves reason & oer shoots the mark
& while he deems reform a knave & cheet
Extreams in both as equals nearly meet   1475
For he who gains on reasons race the start
& good or bad thus overacts his part   [1465]
Is quite as radical in reasons cause
As he who trys to trample oer the laws
What ever cause he banters or defends   1480
Enthuseism baffles not befriends
The wild mad clamours that its votarys raise   [1470]
Urge those to ridicule who meant to praise
& hurts religion tho it wears a gown
As bad as deists who woud pull it down   1485
& thus his reverence often sinks in faults
& dashes on & never own[s] nor halts   [1475]
Ranters & Methodists his open foes
In person & in sermons hell oppose

With superstition hell brook no pretense   1490
& deems them catholics in all but sense
They in their turn oppose the urgd remark   [1480]
& deem his worship grovling in the dark
Sifts the opinions which he puts in force
& strives to wreck him with his own discourse 1495
Deeming the plan to which his pride doth cling
'That little learning is a dangerous thing'   [1485]
From whence reformd opinionists proceed
That near had been had they not learnd to read
They prove such plans in arguments at length 1500
A very pope in every thing but strength
& tho the cobler priest lacks no consiet   [1490]
His worship tires him & will not be beat
When the old snob despairing not resignd
Sighs while he sneers & pitys one so blind   1505
Still with each rude assault he preseveres
Nor heeds the Coblers cant nor cares nor fears [1495]
& now & then his sermons length prolongs
To guard his flock against decietful tongues
& takes much trouble on a sabbath day   1510
To lecture drunkards & drive boys from play
& tho from year to year unknown to use   [1500]
To keep his peace & sunday from abuse
Beside the circling cross upon the hill
The dareing Stocks maintain their station still 1515
& as derision & decaying time
Weaken their triumph oer abuse & crime   [1505]
The priest still mindfull of his ruling cares
Renews their reign in threatning repairs
Laws or religion or be what they will   1520
Self will not yield but stickles to it still
& still he rules in every baffling plan   [1510]
The same head strong opinionated man

But now grown old in reading sundays prayers
& keeping village morals in repairs   1525

Till een his very spectacles refuse
To see the largest print that age can chuse   [1515]
He seeks a curate to supply his place
A kinsman of his worships sacred race
Who ages back sought priesthoods place to teach   1530
The only spot were bankrupts cannot reach
& meeting riches in prosperity   [1520]
Still chuse a scion from the family
To graft upon religions fruitful stock
Were blights near come ambitions hopes to mock   1535
That bends with fruit when ere they like to pull
& bears all seasons & is ever full   [1525]
So this young kinman of his worships troop
That like to Levi keeps the charter up
Now fills with mighty lungs the plenteous place   1540
Whose love of gain makes up for want of grace
Who wears his priesthood with a traders skill   [1530]
& makes religion learn to make her bill
Who ere he cures his sheep of their disease
Like lawyers studys oer the churches fees   1545
Who ekes new claims on customs ancient price
When reason ruled & priests were not so nice   [1535]
& sets on registers his raising mark
That used to fetch their sixpence to the clerk
& from the age enquiring staring clown   1550
Extorts the monstrous charge of half a crown
& if a wanderer leaves his wants to roam   [1540]
& dies on other ills he meets from home
His church yard common for a bed is lost
& forfeits must be paid by double cost   1555
& his jack all the clerk in double sense
Who sings his sunday task & counts his pence   [1545]
Hies to his post instructed in his trade
To claim the fees before the grave is made
& marriage pays its earnest for a bride   1560
Offering her fees before the knott is tyd
& new made mothers that with thanks repairs   [1550]

93

Seek gods kind love but pays the priest for prayers
With him self interest has a face of brass
A shameless tyrant that no claims surpass 1565
Who shrinks at nothing & woud not disdain
To take a farthing in the ways of gain [1555]
Or less what ere his claims [&] fees enjoin
If such a fraction was a current coin
Such is the substitute put on to keep 1570
The close shorn remnant of his worships sheep
& bye & bye hopes at his friends decay [1560]
To be sole shepherd & recieve full pay
& is religion grown so commonplace
To place self interest foremost in the race 1575
& leave poor souls in Satans claws confind
Crawling like crabs a careless pace behind [1565]
Excuse the priest he's prest with weighty cares
& tho the pauper dyes without his prayers
What if such worthless sheep slip into hell 1580
For want of prayers before the passing bell
The priest was absent twas a daily song [1570]
Yet none except the vulgar thought it wrong
Perhaps when death beds might his aid desire
His horse was sick & might a drink require 1585
Or friends for just nessesitys might claim
His shooting skill to track the fields for game [1575]
& when they needed patridges or hares
The parish pauper coud not look for prayers
Or if he did indulge the foolish whim 1590
What cared the priest – dye & be d——d for him
& he had land to shepherd where the wheat [1580]
In a sly way the churches profit beat
Tho he kept one to manage of his kin
Yet self was foreman when the gain dropt in 1595

& dwells no memorys in the days gone bye
No names whose loss is worth a present sigh [1585]
Yes – there was one who priesthoods trade profest

94

"I venerate the man, whose heart is warm,
Whose hands are pure, whose doctrine, and whose life
Coincident, exhibit lucid proof
That he is honest in the SACRED CAUSE."

THIS IS

A PRIEST

made according to Truth,
The guide of Old Age—
the Instructor of Youth;

'One whom the wretched & the poor knew best'
& in yon house that neighbours near the show   1600
Of parish huts a mellancholy row
That like to them a stubble covering wears   [1590]
Decayd the same & needing like repairs
Superior only was the mansion known
Instead of mud by having walls of stone   1605
There lived the Vicar once in days gone bye
When pride & fashion did not rank so high   [1595]
Ere poor religion threw her weeds away
To mix in circles of the worldly gay
Ere hunting Parsons in the chace begun   1610
& added salarys kept their dog & gun
To claim & tresspass upon ground not theirs   [1600]
The game for shooting well as tythe for prayers
Ere sheep was driven from the shepherds door
& pleasure swallowed what might feed the poor   1615
In that same time whose loss was keenly felt
The good old Vicar in this mansion dwelt   [1605]
Plain as the flock dependant on his cares
Their week day comforts & their sunday prayers
Hed no spare wealth to follow fashions whim   1620
& if he had she'd little joys for him
He kept no horse the hunting sports to share   [1610]
He fed no dogs to run the harmless hare
Hed nought to waste while hunger sought his shed
& while he had it they near wanted bread   1625
His chiefest pleasure charity possest
In having means to make another blest   [1615]
Little was his & little was required
Coud he do that twas all the wealth desired
Tho small the gift twas gave with greatest will   1630
& blessings oer it made it greater still
On wants sad tale he never closed his door   [1620]
He gave them somthing & he wishd it more
To all alike compassions hand was dealt
& every gift tho small was deeply felt   1635

The beggars heart dismantled of its fears
Leapd up & thankd him for his crust with tears [1625]
& ownd was worth rewarded as it ought
Hed claims to thousands were hed but a groat
Muttering their blessing as they turnd to part 1640
Wishing his purse an equal to his heart
Ah weres the heart so hardend at its core [1630]
Or eye so dead on what it pauses oer
That times sad changes fail to be severe
That sees his havoc & near drops a tear 1645
The Vicars greensward pathways once his pride
His woodbine bowers that used his doors to hide [1635]
& he himself full often in his chair
Smoaking his pipe & conning sermons there
The yard & garden roods his only farms 1650
& all his stock the hive bees yearly swarms
Are swept away – their produce & their pride [1640]
Were doomed to perish when the owner dyd
Fresh faces came with little taste or care
& joyd to ruin what was his to rear 1655
His garden plants & blossoms all are fled
& docks & nettles blossom in their stead [1645]
Before the door were pinks & roseys stood
The hissing goose protects her summer brood
& noisey hogs are free to wallow oer 1660
What once was gravelld & kept clean before
The corner seat were weary hinds had rest [1650]
The snug fire side that welcomd many a guest
Not fashions votarys these disdaind his door
But plain old farmers & the neighbouring poor 1665
The one in harmless leisure to regale
To crack his wallnutts & to taste his ale [1655]
With miserys humble plea the other led
To tell his sorrows & to share his bread
These are decayed as comforts will decay 1670
As winters sunshine or as flowers in may
These all are past as joys are born to pass [1660]

Were lifes a shadow & were flesh is grass
Een memorys lingering features time shall rot
& this good man is nearly now forgot 1675
Save on his tomb & some few hearts beside
Greyheaded now left childern when he dyd [1665]
Who from their parents all his goodness knew
& learnd to feel it as they older grew
When he was vanishd & the world was known 1680
& troubles evil days became their own
Then woud they talk in sorrows gushing joys [1670]
Of the good priest that preached when they were boys
& shake their heads & wish such godly men
& good old times woud come about agen 1685
Full well may they regret the seasons gone
Such happy times that pride hath trampld on [1675]
Well may the past warm in the peasants praise
& dwell with memory as the golden days
When the old vicar with his village dwelt 1690
Ere prides curst whimseys was so deeply felt
When farmers used their servants toils to share [1680]
& went on foot to market & to fair
Not like the present petty ruling things
Disdaining ploughs from whence their living springs 1695
& looking high among their betters now
Claim with the parson labours passing bow [1685]
Ere titled homage wore no vulgar names
Nor made a mockery to pretending claims
Yon cot when in its glory & its pride 1700
Maintaind its priest & half the poor beside
These were the times that plainess must regret [1690]
These were the times that labour feels as yet
Ere mockd improvments plans enclosed the moor
& farmers built a workhouse for the poor 1705
& vainly feels them & as vainly mourns
As no hopes live betokening like returns [1695]
The cottage now with neither lawn or park
Instead of Vicar keeps the vicars clerk

Wolves may devour oppressions fiends may reign 1710
Nones nigh to listen when the poor complain
Too high religion looks her flocks to watch [1700]
Or stoop from pride to dwell in cots of thatch
Scenes too important constant business brings
That lends no time to look on humbler things 1715
Too much of pleasure in her mansion dwells
To hear the troubles which the pauper tells [1705]
To turn a look on sorrows thorny ways
Like good samaritans of former days
To heal in mercy when foul wrongs pursue 1720
& weep oer anguish as she once woud do
Distress may languish & distress may dye [1710]
Theres none that hears can help them when they cry
Compassion cannot stoop nor pride alow
'To pass that way' with oil or honey now 1725
Still there are some whose actions merit praise
The lingering breathings of departed days [1715]
Tho in this world of vainess thinly sown
Yet there are some whom fashion leaves alone
Who like their master plain & humble go 1730
& strive to follow in his steps below
Who in the Wilderness as beacons stand [1720]
To pilgrims journeying to the promised land
To give instructions to enquiring souls
& cheer the weak above the worlds controuls 1735
To tend their charge & wanderers back restore
To rest the weary & relieve the poor [1725]

The past & present always disagree
The claims of ruin is what used to be
Old customs usuage daily disappears 1740
& wash to nothing in the stream of years
The very church yard & its ramping grass [1730]
& hollow trees remain not as it was
Far different scenes its nakedness displays
To those familiar with its guardians days 1745

Tho holy ground & trees that round it grew
Ownd claims sufficient to be holy too   [1735]
Religions humble plea was felt in vain
When ruin enterd with the hopes of gain
Its weak defence was trampled under foot   1750
& all its pride laid level to its root
Its awthorn hedges surely sacred things   [1740]
That blushd in blossom to a many springs
Its hollow trees that time decayd in tears
& left to linger in the blight of years   1755
Whose mossy finger scarrd on every grain
The trace of days that never come again   [1745]
These old inhabitants are now no more
Oppression enterd & their reign was oer
Sure shades like these a natural end bespoke   1760
Who'd thought their peace was ripening to be broke
Till other hearts the vicars place supplyd   [1750]
That preachd a life that practice oft belied
Then ancient tenants of a sacred spot
They fell like common trees & were forgot   1765

Ah sure it was a mellancholly day
That calld the good man from his charge away   [1755]
Those poor lorn outcasts born to many cares
That shared his table welcome as his prayers
To them the bells worse tidings never gave   1770
Then that which calld their guardian to the grave
To them no prayers so near their bosoms reachd   [1760]
As the sad lecture oer his coffin preachd
Theyd no more harvests now of hopes to reap
Een children wept to see their mothers weep   1775
& pulld their gowns to ask & question when
Hed wake & come to give them pence agen   [1765]
'Hell not sleep there for ever sure he wont
'Wholl feed & cloath us if the Vicar dont'
Thus lispd the babes & while their parents sighd   1780
Muttering their blessings by the pasture side

Warm repetitions of their griefs was given [1770]
& they hoped too to meet their friend in heaven

Beside the charnell wall in humble guise
A small stone noteth were the vicar lyes 1785
Were age slow journying on the sabbath day
Oft potters up to wipe the weeds away [1775]
& show enquiring youth with mournfull pride
That good mans name that once its wants supply'd
To hear it read & bring back days to view 1790
& feel his goodness & his loss anew
Blessing his name & praying as they weep [1780]
To be full soon companions of his sleep
To share with him the churchyards lonely peace
Were pride forgets its scorn & troubles cease 1795
Were povertys sad reign of cares is oer
Nor tells its wants to be denyd no more [1785]
The last lorn hope & refuge that appears
Thro the dull gloom of lifes declining years

Shoved as a nusiance from prides scornfull sight 1800
In a cold corner stands in wofull plight
The shatterd workhouse of the parish poor [1790]
& towards the north wind opes the creaking door
A makeshift shed for misery – no thought
Urgd plans for comfort when the work was wrought 1805
No garden spot was left dull want to cheer
& make the calls for hunger less severe [1795]
With wholsome herbs that summers might supply
Twas not contrived for want to live but dye
A forced consern to satisfy the law 1810
Built want this covering oer his bed of straw
Een that cheap blessing thats so freely given [1800]
To all that liveth neath the face of heaven
The light of day is not alowd to win
A smiling passage to the glooms within 1815
No window opens on the southern sky

A luxury deemd to prides disdainful eye [1805]
The scant dull light that forcefull need supplyd
Scorn frownd & placed them on the sunless side
Here dwell the wretched lost to hopless strife 1820
Reduced by want to skelletons in life
Despised by all een age grown bald & grey [1810]
Meets scoffs from wanton childern in their play
Who laugh at miserey by misfortune bred
& points scorns finger at the mouldering shed 1825
The tottering tennant urges no replye
Turns his white head & chokes the passing sigh [1815]
& seeks his shed & hides his hearts despair
For pity lives not as a listner there
When no one hears or heeds he wakes to weep 1830
On his straw bed as hunger breaks his sleep
& thinks oer all his troubles & distress [1820]
With not one hope that life shall make them less
Save silent prayers that every woe may have
A speedy ransom in the peaceful grave 1835
Close fisted justice tho his only friend
Doth but cold comforts to his miserys lend [1825]
For six days only it alows its fee
Pay scarce sufficient for the wants of three
& for the seventh which god sent to rest 1840
The weary limbs of labouring man & beast
He too may pay for what blind justice cares [1830]
Theyve nought for sunday but the parsons prayers

He lived not from his cradle thus forlorn
Both friends & kindred blest his early morn 1845
But kindred now are vanished all & gone
His friends turned foes & thus he lives alone [1835]
A Farm he rented in his prosperous days
& prides mouth never opened but to praise
Misfortune crossed his path he tried in vain 1850
& sunk like Job but never rose again
His kindred pitied but no help supplied [1840]

His friends were sought but friends their aid denied
Kin turned away & left his wants forlorn
& prides eye never heeded but to scorn 1855
To him the whole wide world contained no friend
His griefs to sooth his weakness to defend [1845]
Look where he may all he possessed is fled
& he himself tho living seems as dead

Old Farmer Thrifty reigns from year to year 1860
Their tyrant king yclypd an overseer
A sad proud knave who bye a cunning plan [1850]
Blindfolds his faults & seems an honest man
He rarely barters when he buys or sells
But sets a price & there his honour dwells 1865
He rails at cheating knaves for knaverys sake
& near asks double what he means to take [1855]
Shuns open ways which lesser rogues pursue
An outside christian but at heart a Jew
Each smooth deciet his blackend heart belies 1870
& consience blushes thro the thin disguise
He seems so honest so says Farmer Slye [1860]
That even childern may his bargains buy
& pays all debts too with a feignd good will
& rarely frowns to read a trades mans bill 1875
While those deemd moderate charges rarely fail
To buy a welcome & to taste his ale [1865]
Upright & punctual every bargains made
A very quaker in affairs of trade
He preaches down the faults in neighbours known 1880
Scorns others roguery just to hide his own
Thus he mocks honour on deceptions creed [1870]
But let us read the riddle in the deed
Tho wealth nor makes nor want bemeans the man
With nought but luck the world & he began 1885
Old men will tell you when the boy was small
How he blackd shoes & waited at the Hall [1875]
But natural cunning shone in early youth

& flatterys tongue which pride mistook for truth
Raisd by degrees the youngster into fame   1890
& blotchd fates stigma from his little name
Gilding like blemished fruit his failings oer   [1880]
Thats fair without & rotten at the core
Thro all the names that wait on wealth & pride
From shoe black vile to valet dignified   1895
He rose successively without a fall
& ownd the cunning power to please in all   [1885]
& as the serpent yearly changed his skin
Some old face fled to take the youngster in
At length power blessd him with its highest stretch   1900
Which good mens merits might despair to reach
No longer doomd in servitude to wait   [1890]
Next to the squire he managed his estate
Yclypd a Steward – strangers made their bow
& the squire took him as an equal now   1905
While to neglect his former steward fell
For no one crime unless twas acting well   [1895]
& soon the tyrant threw the mask aside
When wealth throngd in & power was gratified
Soon cloakd deciet that placed its owner there   1910
To grasp at riches threw its visage bare
He raisd the rents of all the tennants round   [1900]
& then distrest them as in duty bound
& then askd leave of the contented squire
To rent the farm & had his hearts desire   1915
The storm at first must burst upon the poor
That urgd wants curses as they passd his door   [1905]
The humble hind that kept his cow before
& just kept want from creeping to his door
He viewd their comforts with a jealous heart   1920
& raised their rents & bade their hopes depart
Yet loath to leave – their cows was sold for rent   [1910]
& the next year left nothing but complaint
Twas just as wished his plans was quickly known
Each spot was seized & added to his own   1925

Others resignd & the half starving poor
Laid down their sufferings at their masters door   [1915]
Unused to such complaints the easy squire
Was rousd to listen pity & enquire
The knave still ready up his sleeve to creep   1930
Proved all as right & land as still too cheap
But friends familiar swore the squire was mad   [1920]
To think of reasoning with a man so bad
To see & suffer such uncloakd abuse
From one whose plans was shuffle & excuse   1935
Such whispers urgd the easy Squire to shift
& Steward Thrifty then was turnd adrift   [1925]
But not before his purse was filld with pelf
For knaves work quick & near loose sight of self
His nest was featherd ere his fame was old   1940
& land was bought when farms was cheaply sold
He now retires at ease & sells his grain   [1930]
& strives to be an honest rogue in vain
With big round belly & sleek double chin
He reads the news & smokes & drinks his gin   1945
& studys all the week oer gains affairs
& once a week at Chappel reads his prayers   [1935]
& seems as striving former deeds to mend
Mild to a foe & coaxing to a friend
But to the poor his ways are still severe   1950
Dwindled in Office to an overseer
Still deaf to want that seeks him to be fed   [1940]
He gives them curses in the lieu of bread
Or scoffing at their hopes tells them theyre free
To seek a law as tyranizd as he   1955
Thus want still proves the stewards cankerd heart
& wealth beholds him ape 'the goodly part'   [1945]
The one in nursing vengance while he starves
Is urged to curse him as he still deserves
The other blinded by his alterd plan   1960
Forgives & takes him as a d——d good man
Why art thou, beggars king wants overseer   [1950]

105

To helpless poverty alone severe
On their dependance thou hast fatly fed
& can thy niggard hand deny them bread   1965
He pleads bad times when justice chides his ways
Tho justice self is ill deserving praise   [1955]
& is bad times the cause of such despair
Go ask the wretches who inhabit there
If past good times their hopes had ever blest   1970
& left them thus so wretched & distrest
Ask if their griefs can better times recall   [1960]
Their startled tears tell plenty as they fall
& pitys heart can easy comprehend
That Farmer Thrifty never was their friend   1975

Art thou a man thou tyrant oer distress
Doubtless thy pride woud scorn to think thee less   [1965]
Then scorn a deed unworthy of that name
& live deserving of a better fame
Hurt not the poor whom fate forbad to shine   1980
Whose lots were cast in meaner ways then thine
Infringe not on the comforts they posses   [1970]
Nor bid scant hope turn hopless in distress
Drive not poor freedom from its niggard soil
Its independance is their staff for toil   1985
Take that away which as their right they call
& thourt a rogue that beggars them of all   [1975]
They sink in sorrow as a race of slaves
& their last hope lives green upon their graves
Remember proud aspiring man of earth   1990
Prides short distinction is of mortal birth
However high thy hated name may be   [1980]
Death in the dust shall humble pride & thee
That hand that formd thee & lent pride its day
Took equal means to fashion humbler clay   1995
One power alike reigns as thy god & theirs
Who deaf to pride will listen humbler prayers   [1985]
He as our father with the world began

& fashiond man in brotherhood with man
& learn thou this proud man tis natures creed   2000
Or be thou humbled if thou wilt not heed
The kindred bond which our first father gave   [1990]
Proves man thy brother still & not thy slave
& pride may bluster in its little life
To tyranize with overpowering strife   2005
Its turn shall come when proud insulting death
Shall bid it humble & demand its breath   [1995]
& cannot these fierce tyrants of vain deeds
Dare in their pomp to intercept his speed
As well may rushes stiffen in the storm   2010
& try to wear the oaks unyielding form
As well may feathers float against the stream   [2000]
& shadows grow to substance in a dream
Or clouds in tempests struggle to be still
As pride to tamper & so baulk his will   2015
He meets them in their strength & torn from ease
They groan & strive like tempests thro the trees   [2005]
While want from lifes dull shadows glad to run
As pride went foremost & claimed all the sun
Slips from the bitterness of mortal clay   2020
As calm as storms drop on an autumn day
Death is the full stop that awaits to tell   [2010]
The period of our earthly chronicle
The closing Finis that doth end the rude
Essay of life & bids its tales conclude   2025
With all its failings in the lowly grave
Existance ceases with the all it gave   [2015]
Wealth want joy anguish all do cease & lye
More blank then shadows neath the smiling sky
Leaving eternity to keep the key   2030
Till judgment sets all hopes & terrors free
Pride & oppression here all meet their end   [2020]
& find their weakness when too late to mend
With noiseless speed as swift as summer light
Death slays & keeps his weapons out of sight   2035

Here thousands stript of earthly pomp & powers
Met death & perished in unlooked for hours [2025]
Their wealth availed not one in all the tribe
Death hath no ears to listen to a bribe
The rich fall poor into the grave & there 2040
The poor grow rich an equal claim to heir
Deaths gloomy mansions owns no hall or throne [2030]
But all lye equal – Death is lord alone
Pomps trickerys in the grave are all forgot
& worms & eyless skulls distinguish not 2045
The pomp that rotting in prides tomb doth lye
From rubbish that fills up the slaves just bye [2035]
Here tyrants that outbraved their God tho clay
& for earths glory threw the heavens away
Whose voice of power did like the thunder sere 2050
As anger hurried on the heels of fear
Ordaining hosts of murders at a breath [2040]
How silent here doth sleep their rage in death
Their feet that trampled freedom to its grave
& felt the very earth they trod a slave 2055
How quiet here they lye in deaths cold arms
Without the power to crush the feeble worms [2045]
Who spite of all the dreadful strife they made
Crept there to conquer & was not afraid
The warrior from wars havoc here detered 2060
Bows before death lame as a broken sword
His power wastes all to nothingness away [2050]
As showers at night wash out the steps of day

Still lives unsung a race of petty knaves
Numerous as wasps to sting & torture slaves 2065
The meanest of the mean a servile race
Who like their betters study to be base [2055]
Whose dung hill pride grows stiff in dirty state
& tho so little apes the little great
The Workhouse Keeper as old Thriftys man 2070
Transacts the business on the tyrants plan

Supplys its tennants with their scanty food [2060]
& tortures misery for a livlihood
Despised & hated by the slaves he wrongs
& een too low for satires scourging songs 2075
So may they yet sink down more viler things
& starve as subjects were they reign as kings [2065]
Or when on earth their dirty triumph ends
May hells obscurity reward its freinds

A thing all consequence here takes the lead 2080
Reigning knight errant oer this dirty breed
A Bailiff he & who so great to brag [2070]
Of law & all its terrors as Bumtagg
Fawning a puppy at his masters side
& frowning like a wolf on all beside 2085
Who fattens best where sorrow worst appears
& feeds on sad misfortunes bitterest tears [2075]
Such is Bumtagg the bailiff to a hair
The worshipper & Demon of despair
Who waits & hopes & wishes for success 2090
At every nod & signal of distress
Happy at heart when storms begin to boil [2080]
To seek the shipwreck & to share the spoil
Brave is this Bumtagg match him if you can
For theres none like him living save his man 2095
As every animal assists his kind
Just so are these in blood & business joined [2085]
Yet both in different colors hide their art
& each as suits his ends transacts his part
One keeps the heart bred villian full in sight 2100
The other cants & acts the hypocrite
Smoothing the deed where law sherks set the gin [2090]
Like a coy dog to draw misfortune in
But both will chuckl[el oer their prisoner's sighs
& are as blest as spiders over flyes 2105
Such is Bumtagg whose history I resign
As other knaves wait room to stink & shine [2095]

109

& as the meanest knave a dog can brag
Such is this lurcher that assists Bumtagg

Born with the changes time & chance doth bring 2110
A shadow reigns yclypd a woodland king
Enthrond mid thorns & briars a clownish wight [2100]
My Lords chief woodman in his titles hight
& base & low as is the vulgar knave
He in his turn for tyrant finds his slave 2115
The bug-bear devil of the boys is he
Who once for swine pickt acorns neath the tree [2105]
& starving terror of the village brood
Who gleand their scraps of fuel from the wood
When parish charity was vainly tryed 2120
Twas their last refuge – which is now denyd
Small hurt was done by such intrusions there [2110]
Claiming the rotten as their harmless share
Which might be thought in reasons candid eye
As sent by providence for such supplye 2125
But turks imperial of the woodland bough
Forbid their trespass in such trifles now [2115]
Threatning the dithering wretch that hence proceeds
With jail & whipping for his shameless deeds
Well pleased to bid their feeblest hopes decay 2130
Driving them empty from the woods away
Cheating scant comfort of its pilferd blaze [2120]
That doubtless warmd him in his beggars days
Thus knaves in office love to show their power
& unoffending helplessness devour 2135
Sure on the weak to give their fury vent
Were theres no strength injustice to resent [2125]
As dogs let loose on harmless flocks at night
Such feel no mercy were they fear no bite

Here comes one different to mere parish stuff 2140
A host of talents met in Mr Puff
Knowing in all things ignorant of none [2130]

To him mere genius is but farce & fun
While talent drops as from his finger ends
He knows all names – the greatest are his friends   2145
& tho he never saw your face before
Hell jest at wit & run his nonsense oer   [2135]
Familiar stuff so thick your shame assails
That even dogs to hear it wag their tails
He is so full of wisdom you would swear   2150
Hed robbed the tree of knowledge till twas bare
& not contented with its store of fruits   [2140]
Had seized the trunk & grubbed it by the roots
& as for quoting Puffs the man to quote
As if hed read all that was ever wrote   2155
Yet like his coat his taste must ape the fashion
So Shakspears pages are his greatest passion   [2145]
Nor can a beggar even scrat his head
But theres what Shakspears on the matter said
To show by trifles how the fool has read   2160
Are you a Bard – write prose too – very well
Puff deals in all & does in all excell   [2150]
& what he will not boast of having done
He casts that crumb of credit at his son
Mechanical pursuits to spout & write   2165
'My son sir' rivals copper plate out right
Themes when a boy at school was never won   [2155]
But foremost tho an infant stood 'My son'
& so between them knowledge is possest
Like Pharoahs kine they swallow all the rest   2170
Sir Walter, Byron, as his friends he styles
& at your ignorance thumbs his chain & smiles   [2160]
Tho at the top of Fame[s] high towering tree
These share the worlds applause – poh so does he
If not in print he tells you bye & bye   2175
He has a M.S. shall climb as high
Do you know half the Poets – thats as none   [2165]
He strokes his chin & knows them every one
Poet Philosopher Mus[i]cian

111

In fact all fames are bound in his Edition   2180
What ere is great Puff is – but nothing small
All greatness dwells in Puff & Puff in all   [2170]
If chance ere throws a Poet in his way
He worms him in their notice untill they
Half think theyve seen the smirking fiend before   2185
With so much confidence he tongues them oer
But the mere Barber who is daily led   [2175]
To clean his chin & drab his fustian head
If he but comes when he with friends hath got
He scorns the fellows speech & knows him not   2190
Thus all small matters meet a rude rebuff
From this self oracle renowned Hal Puff   [2180]
& all thats great he treats as his compeers
A downright Ass in every thing but ears

Others of this small fry as mean as base   2195
May live unknown a pigmy reigning race
& sink to hell from whence their knavery came   [2185]
As namless tribes unworthy of a name
Left on the dung hill were they reignd to rot
Hated while living & when dead forgot   2200
Here ends the Song – let jealousy condemn
& deem reproofs they merit aimd at them   [2190]
When pride is touchd & evil consience bit
Each random throw will seem a lucky hit
– If common sense its ears & eyes may trust   2205
Each pictures faithful & each censure just
So let them rail – the proverbs truth is known   [2195]
'Were the cap fits theyll wear it as their own'
Full many knaves sharp satires wounds have met
Who live in aqufortis dying yet   2210
In burning Ink their scarecrow memorys dwell
Left to the torture of lifes earthly hell   [2200]
As markd & lasting as the thieves burnt brand
Who lives & dies with villian on his hand

DEATH

Why should mans high aspiring mind
Burn in him with so proud a breath
When all his haughty views can find
In this world yields to death
The fair the brave the vain the wise   5
The rich the poor & great & small
Are each but worms anatomys
To strew his quiet hall

Power may make many earthly gods
Where gold & briberys guilt prevails   10
But deaths unwelcome honest odds
Kicks oer the unequal scales
The flattered great may clamours raise
Of power & their own weakness hide
But death shall find unlooked for ways   15
To end the farce of pride

An arrow hurtled eer so high
From een a jiants sinewy strength
In times untraced eternity
Goes but a pigmy length   20
Nay whirring from the tortured string
With all its pomp of hurried flight
Tis by the sky larks little wing
Out measured in its height

Just so mans boasted strength & power   25
Shall fade before deaths lightest stroke
Laid lower than the meanest flower
Whose pride oer topt the oak
& he who like a blighting blast
Dispeopled worlds with wars alarms   30
Shall be himself destroyed at last
By poor despised worms

Tyrants in vain their powers secure
& awe slaves murmurs with a frown
But unawed death at last is sure   35
To sap the babels down
A stone thrown upward to the sky
Will quickly meet the ground agen
So men gods of earths vanity
Shall drop at last to men   40

& power & pomp their all resign
Blood purchased thrones & banquet halls
Fate waits to sack ambitions shrine
As bare as prison walls
Where the poor suffering wretch bows down   45
To laws a lawless power hath past
& pride & power & king & clown
Shall be deaths slaves at last

Time the prime minister of death
Theres nought can bribe his honest will   50
He stops the richest tyrants breath
& lays his mischief still
Each wicked scheme for power all stops
With grandeurs false & mock display
As eves shades from high mountain tops   55
Fade with the rest away

Death levels all things in his march
Nought can resist his mighty strength
The pallace proud triumphal arch
Shall mete their shadows length   60
The rich the poor one common bed
Shall find in the unhonoured grave
Where weeds shall crown alike the head
Of tyrant & of slave

GREECE

A voice from the ocean
  Is pealing around
& Europe in motion
  Stirs glad at the sound
Keen swords are unsheathing   5
  Warm hopes they increase
For free hearts are breathing
  Success unto Greece

Who feels but 'God speed 'em'
  That land of the brave   10
Tis the cradle of freedom
  Never meant for her grave
More than glorys aspirants
  Her childern proclaim
In the blood of their tyrants   15
  They are worthy her fame

Over ocean & dry land
  Over mountain & plain
Lost Scios green island
  Breathes vengance amain   20
& vengance is brewing
  For it threatend so loud
Freedom sleeping in ruin
  Burst the folds of her shroud

& heard in her wonder   25
  What she doubted to be
Her war cry in thunder
  Bidding slaves to be free
She knew not greece nourished
  That fame that still runs   30
From the heroes she cherished
  To the hearts of their sons

Till she saw the lorn laurel
  Which tyrannys breath
Had blighted – glow sterile   35
  & triumph oer death
So she wreathed her a garland
  Of leaves from the tree
Showing inland & farland
  Greece had dared to be free   40

& refreshed from long slumbers
  She sallies again
& proud are the numbers
  That join in her train
With weapons unbearing   45
  To challange their own
& hearts full of daring
  To tyrants unknown

Fame spreads out her pages
  Their herrald to be   50
To tell future ages
  Who fight to be free
Her trumpets are sounding
  For battle aray
& war steeds are bounding   55
  To burst in the fray

The mighty in spirit
  Collect like a flood
Resolved to inherit
  Their rights with their blood   60
What hearts are not wishing
  Their comrades to be
Nor feels their blood rushing
  To on with the free

All despots may tremble 65
  Tho they frown in their fear
Slaves only disemble
  While in peace they appear
Every pulse leaps for freedom
  Every gauling chain speaks 70
More than words tho few heed 'em
  All in feeling are Greeks

Freedoms Standard bids muster
  The injured & slave
Tho tyrants may bluster 75
  Who would not be brave
They fight for lifes glory
  Its birthright & name
& poor is the story
  That shrinks from their fame 80

" 'Tis Liberty alone, that gives the flow'r
Of fleeting life its lustre and perfume;
And we are weeds without it."

THE GIPSEYS SONG

The gipseys life is a merry life
& happy boys we be
We pay no rent nor tax to none
But live untythd & free
None cares for us for none care we   5
& were we list we roam
& merry boys we gipseys be
Tho the wild woods are our home

& come what will brings no dismay
Were with few cares perplext   10
For if todays a swaily day
We hope for luck the next
& thus we sing & kiss our mates
While our chorus still shall be
Bad luck to tyrant majistrates   15
& the gipseys dwelling free

To mend old pans & bottom chairs
Around the towns we tramp
When a day or two our purse repairs
& plenty fills our camp   20
& our songs we sing & our fiddles sound
Their cat gut harmony
While eccho fills the woods around
With gipsey liberty

The green grass is our softest bed   25
The sun our clock we call
The nightly sky hangs over head
Our curtains house & all
Tho housless while the wild winds blow
Our joys are uncontrould   30
We bare foot dance thro winters snow
When others dye with cold

Our maidens they are fond & free
& lasting are their charms
Brown as the berry on the tree   35
No suns their beauty harms
Their beautys are no garden blooms
That fade before they flower
Unshelterd were the tempest comes
They smile in sun & shower   40

& they are wild as the wood land hare
That feeds on the evening lea
& what care we for ladys fair
Since ours are fond & free
False hearts hide in a lily skin   45
But ours are coarse & fond
No parsons fetters link us in
Our hearts a stronger bond

Tho the wild woods are our house & home
Tis a home of liberty   50
Free as the summer clouds we roam
& merry boys we be
We dance & sing the year along
& loud our fiddles play
& no day goes without a song   55
With us all months are may

The crow that haunts the fallow grounds
& round the common feeds
The fox that tracks the wood land bounds
& in the thicket breeds   60
These are the neighbours were we dwell
& all the guests we see
That share & love the quiet well
Of gipsey liberty

The elements are grown our friends 65
& leaves our huts alone
The thunder bolt that rocks & rends
The cotters house of stone
Flyes harmless bye our blanket roofs
Were the winds may burst & blow 70
For our camps tho thin are tempest proof
& buffet rain & snow

May the lot weve met our lives befall
& nothing worse atend
So heres success to gipseys all 75
& every gipseys friend
Go were we will may kindred fate
Our friendly partners be
Protect us from the magistrate
& keep our dwellings free 80

& we will sing & dance around
With a heart that never fails
Tho magistrates like hungry hounds
Still threaten us with jails
& while the ass that bears our camp 85
Can find a common free
Around old Englands heaths we'll tramp
In gipsey liberty

THE POACHERS

Come prime your Guns your belts throw on
  Thro the forest softly tread
The sun is set & the day is gone
  & all our foes are fled
The Pheasant to his roost doth flee 5
  The Hare is on her seat
The Bucks at lare & we are free
  To take the first we meet

We hide by day & roam by night
  Yet know not how to fear   10
& a shining night is our delight
  At the season of the year
& we have freedom in our cause
  Tho we hide in gloomy caves
Twas tyrant knaves that made the laws   15
  To keep the cowards slaves

The moon may shine the clouds may lower
  Our chanses we can trust
While we have caves to shun a shower
  & keep our guns from rust   20
Our flints are good the fire is free
  & our eye will brook no blame
For the sound of the Gun as sure as fate
  Is the death knell of the game

Thus sung the chief of the Poacher band   25
  Carousing in the cave
As he held the Flaggon in his hand
  & their night health gaily gave
Success to Poachers one & all
  & he who dares the most   30
Be first upon the list to call
  For the tomorrows toast

The frowns of heaven fell b[l]ack in each face
  As clouds fled by the moon
Not one in the band ere slackened his pace   35
  The night had paused as soon
The storm approached the winds did blow
  Some comrades funeral knell
But no one paused or cared to know
  What day would have to tell   40

BALLAD

Boys bring the booty from the cave
Which night fall made our fee
& a brave carousing we will have
All under the green wood tree
The Priest for his life might beg & pray   5
He but wished to save his wine
Of which well have our fill today
& merrily we'll dine

So said our king bold Robin Hood
When we robbed the priest of Lorn   10
& sure in merry Sherwood
A richer neer was shorn
Gold Rings & Jewels many a one
Rich gifts at holy shrine
Which this vile knave miscalled his own   15
We took them with his wine

They call us out laws for our deeds
& viler names have we
But we are loyal to our king
& Robin Hood is he   20
So let us now our bonds renew
While our masters praise we sing
In Sherwood first his bugle blew
& here we crown him king

In famed old merry Sherwood   25
He owns both beast & bird
& whoso flaunts at Robin Hood
Shall rue his haughty word
The fat priest tho a crafty fox
Soon as he left his stall   30
& dared to stray thro Sherwood oaks
We made him pay for all

He counted beeds & said his prayers
For old priest hidden deeds
But had he hid his purse or wares   35
His life wa'nt worth his beeds
Spite of their bells & books to curse
Well fleeced such knaves shall be
But if we take a good mans purse
Well return him twice the fee   40

Our bows are of the toughest wood
& so tight we lace the string
That arrows drink the wild deers blood
Ere the Hawk can move his wing
& swifter then the glancing sun   45
Breaks thro the morning skyes
The shaft is sped & the work is done
& down the fat buck lies

Our only laws are our kings will
& Robin Hood is he   50
So Little John the flaggon fill
& drink to majesty
Let the old health go round the ring
To crown him king again
& while weve strength to twitch the string   55
Here Robin Hood shall reign

ROBIN HOOD & THE GAMEKEEPERS A BALLAD

As under Sherwoods snubbled oaks
In musing wise lay Robin Hood
A losel lout him thus bespoke
Fast pricking thro the pleasant wood

Up knave as idle as a bird   5
An out laws man I trow ye be
With Robin Hood I want a word
So up & tell me who ye be

Feth then say on quoth Robin Hood
None other Robin reigns but me   10
The stranger like a statue stood
& stonied turned aloof to flee

Nay say thou on & speed not hence
Abusions I nor heed nor fear
I will abet mine own defence   15
Aguise thou not what Im to hear

My masters Locksly Abbeys heir
I trow ye know his dignity
Quoth Robin I nor know nor care
Tell thou his message unto me   20

Out laws in sooth he reckons all
That stroye the game wherere they dwell
& those without his paddock wall
Among these woods he claims as well

In sooth gif ye your sports pursue   25
& dare another string to draw
In heeding not yell sorely rue
I heed quoth Robin not one straw

Albe his mind was ettled sore
& by his forrest liberty   30
& by his bowmen all he swore
The abbot should ameded be

The majistrate laws overseer
What is he but an out law grown
Who breaks good laws without a fear   35
To punish those who break his own

Id lever be a motley fool
Then lout me at his caytive throne
Kings made the laws & Kings shall rule
For I none other lord will own   40

I never did the needy wrong
Nor knelt to curse a soul in prayers
Beshrew this abbots heart & tongue
But he hath dont & well he fares

I never woke fair lemans sighs   45
Beshrew the knave as he hath done
Nor forced a tear from lemans eyes
For deeds that dare not see the sun

His monks & he are all akin
One swears all right the others do   50
& troth can I the abbey win
They for their evil deeds shall rue

So go thy ways thou seely man
The abbots fool I trow ye be
Tell him if he would rule my clan   55
To fet himself the taunt to me

& sure he shall aby the deed
In troth this tell him – here he swore
Thy self may take his place indeed
For he shall join his monks no more   60

Full swift the losel prickt the plain
Right glad the outlaws leave to hear
To wear a whole skin home again
Which he erewhile did sorely fear

Then up bold Robin rose that day   65
Resolved the Abbots game to trim
& swore the first that said him nay
Should rue the hour they met with him

Bad laws said he are lawless food
To feed a tyrants appetite   70
I will but reverence the good
& break thro wrong to get at right

The game they are a lawless breed
That keep no bounds to feed upon
They tresspass upon all to feed   75
& are for all as well as one

& to the Abbots park Ill go
To shoot whatever may betide
Then up he took his trusty bow
& slung his arrows by his side   80

The pheasant left his perch & crowed
But never found his perch again
& all that came in Robins road
Both hares & pheasants soon were slain

& when a good fat buck or doe   85
Did leave the lares they met no more
Bold Robin bent his sturdy bow
& down they fell upon the floor

Thus Robin did his sports pursue
Till near the Abbey he espied   90
Ten lusty keepers full in view
& vassals near a score beside

When him they saw they hastened on
Thinking to make him rue the deed
For when ten bows are bent to one   95
There bides no fear to check the speed

But Robin Hood his bugle blew
& ere one eccho had the sound
Still to the call & signal true
A hundred bowmen gathered round   100

Well sped said he my merry men
See where they come to spoil my play
But stand by me good bowmen ten
& we will make them rue the day

Ten strung their bows the rest obeyed   105
& vanished in the fern like deer
Or flock of birds in forrest shade
That meet the eye & dissapear

Bold Robin & his bowmen ten
Bent with their bows upon the stretch   110
The keepers shot like fearfull men
Before they came in arrows reach

Now let their skill again be tryed
We will not throw a shot away
They shot again an ell too wide   115
Said Robin they shall rue the day

Then shot bold Robin & his men
Who faced the keepers like their game
Their eyes no fear could baulk or bann
So death near sped a surer aim   120

& neer a man that stood his ground
But had a wound to tell the fray
& some were slain & many found
Too much mishap to run away

All fled that could none staid I wot   125
That had their leggs left free to run
Bold Robins men rued near a shot
To him the strife was cheaply won

Unkend away the wounded crept
The slain god rest their souls for aye   130
& Robin swore before he slept
The abbot for their deaths should pay

His heben bow he swore therebye
That neer did baulk its masters will
To locksley Abbey he would hie   135
His every promise to fullfill

His bowmen left their hidden lare
Like to a flock of bounding deer
& off to locksleys monks they fare
But di'el a monk was tennant there   140

Bad news & sorrow deffley speeds
The monks lean fay had ceased to pray
Unbidden hung their idle beads
They fled for saftey far away

The Abbot thought of Robins threat 145
& feeling he should rue therebye
Nor could he run he was so fat
So dyed with very fear to dye

What ere was worth they took at will
& morts of booty got therebye 150
Much wine they drank & more did spill
& thus they feasted merrily

Undrained full many a barrel stood
When every bowmans thirst was staid
By halidom said Robin Hood 155
This Abbots was a thriving trade

Then Robin & his bowmen all
Fared to the forrest with their cheer
& every town & every Hall
Was smote with bane & mickle fear 160

Fair lemans wept & sore did blame
The Abbot for this deadly strife
& wailing mothers cursed his game
That robbed their lusty bairns of life

But Robins rage is paid & so 165
God save & speed our goodly king
& grant sike sports may leave no mo
Sike deadly bouts to sing

[HONESTY THOUGH KINGS REVILE THEE]

Honesty though kings revile thee
Thou art still a heavenly gem
Tyrants by a name defile thee
Thoust no heritage with them
Bowed & bruised & often broken   5
By the proud & insincere
Still thou ownst the unbought token
That all upright hearts revere

Scoffed & scorned & rudely handled
By the tyrants rude decree   10
Yet howere thy bodys mangled
Still thy mind is with the free
Yet howere thy name is hated
By the sycophants of slaves
Yet howere thy power is rated   15
By the tyrant – hearken knaves

Ye may fume & ye may bluster
Boast of steal & try the deed
Ye may cant of God & muster
Powers – ye hypocrites – but heed   20
Poor honesty – though rags surround her
No bribes could work her overthrow
Nor slaverys chains hath ever bound her
Dare ye to talk of slavery – No

Ye talk of peace – & mean oppression   25
Ye talk of liberty for slaves
But whisper in your black transgression
That they shall have it in their graves
Ye talk of bible faith & duty
Aye duty is your bait ye knaves   30
But not to God – it would not suit ye
Unless God taught us to be slaves

Poor honesty makes blank your honour
Yeve threatened till ye dare no more
Ye now set cants smooth dogs upon her   35
But tyrant knaves your reign is oer
Your steel like to a reed is broken
Your forcefull scorn all weak as dreams
Poor honesty wears its own token
& justice only she esteems   40

Tyrants & hypocrites are for ye
They glorify your brutish deeds
But truth & humane hearts abhor ye
They shudder at your canting creeds
They pity – but they never fear ye   45
Your idle threats their hearts contemn
If good your cause they would revere ye
For honestys their diadem

Rouse but the lion from its slumber
Rouse but old charters from their graves   50
& freedom soon shall disencumber
All shackles from the hands of slaves
The mind is free & stirred to motion
Twill like a flood its channels find
Like waves upon a stormy ocean   55
Like sands upon a desert wind

Can natures warnings make you see
Can danger teach you right from wrong
Let nature then your teacher be
& only listen to her song   60
Free but the bird from out the cage
It instant seeks the highest tree
This proves beyond your tyrant rage
That nature at her heart is free

ON SEEING A SKULL ON COWPER GREEN

One morn I wandered forth neath spirits high
Those moods that mornings peering breath instills
& like my shade my mind in ecstasy
Stretched like a jiant oer the pasture hills
I mused on reasoning mans exalted sway   5
Oer the brute world – pride made my feelings brave
Creations lord to me he seemed that day
I felt as if all nature was his slave
But times glass soon did mock my visioned might
I saw & shrunk an insect at the sight   10

For as I wandered by a quarrys side
Where an old hoary weather beaten swain
Was delving sand – in lifes rude troubles tried
An humble pittance natures boon to gain
He stopt his toil & with a feeble hand   15
Pointed to where a human skull lay bare
& mingled with the refuse of the land
Fallen from life & pride to moulder there
I looked upon the relic with deep awe
While silence seemed to question what I saw   20

What wert thou upon earth perhaps a king
For such the relics of earths best renown
Thou pompous shadow thou proud trifling thing
Bare is the brow that triumphed neath a crown
By rank forsaken stript of prides attire   25
Deaths sad reality fate only claims
All else like shadows bidden to expire
Time keeps the wreck to mock at earthly fames
To show vain glory in its golden birth
Of what poor value it is held by death   30

Wert thou a tyrant that disdained though clay
The laws of God & man & with vain power
For earths vain glorys threw the heavens away
How art thou fallen at this lonely hour
Thy vengance that did like the thunder sear   35
Ordaining hosts of murders at a breath
Hath vanished & the slave forgot his fear
Beneath the banner of that tyrant death
Even the little ant now undismayed
Creeps oer thy skull & feeleth not afraid   40

A warrior thou who sped in victorys ways
As over bearing as a mighty wind
Ah little thought thy pride that victorys praise
So soon would leave her heroes fame behind
From war & all its havoc long deterred   45
Thy courage withering in its mad career
Bowed before death tame as a broken sword
& ah how silent doth it harbour here
Its fame all sunk to nothingness away
As showers by night was[h] out the steps of day   50

Wert thou a lover ah what else so warm
As lovers thoughts that lead the heart to bliss
How sad the change in deaths oertaken storm
Cold wrecked & stranded in a place like this
Love that will nestle neath the eagles wing   55
& find a dwelling in the lions den
Hath long forsaken thee thou lonely thing
Of mystery & knows thee not agen
Warm hopes gay thoughts rapt joys & fond desires
Have lost their home death put out all their fires   60

Wert thou a poet who in fancys dream
Saw immortality throw by her veil
& all thy labours in fames temple gleam
In the proud glory of an after tale
If so how cheated thy ambition died   65
How vain the hopes the muses visions gave
Death with eternity scarce took one stride
Ere thou wert left forgotten in the grave
Chilled all thy powers with thoughts oerflowing full
& nought left extant but this empty skull   70

Wert thou of poor descent & like to me
A toiling worm to earn lifes daily bread
If so death made thee rich as well as free
& left thee equal with the noblest dead
Emperors & kings no more by flattery fed   75
Poor as thou art their condescension spares
Even to thee a portion of their bed
& thines as soft a pillow now as theirs
& who could grudge the mightys guest to be
Where kings grow kind & share their pomp with thee   80

In vain I question nought will answer me
Of what thou wert yet know I that thou art
A faithful portrait of what life shall be
Thus much thy mystic vision doth impart
King Tyrant Warrior Lover Bard & all   85
Shall into nothing every name resign
& fames proud scroll at last shall be the pall
To hide them as oblivion hideth thine
While virtues deeds shall longest live & be
A wreath to girdle vast eternity   90

NELSON & THE NILE

Great Nelsons glory near the nile
Set fames bright scroll on fire
& raised a flame in englands isle
That never shall expire
His empire was the ocean-world   5
The heart of war his throne
Where ever Englands flag unfurled
He riegned & ruled alone
Wherever he wars vengance hurled
There victory was his own   10

With heart of fire that burnt the mind
& found its peace in strife
With thoughts that did outspeed the wind
& met from terror life
Upon the sea his element   15
In danger he grew strong
To battle as a feast he went
Its thunder loud & long
Was music & his hearts assent
Beat welcome to the song   20

The stubborn storms whose fury rends
Full many a gallant mast
His valour won them into friends
They worshiped as he passed
He led his fleet along the sea   25
The flying foe to hail
His daring filled with merry glee
The spirit of the gale
Who deemed him neptunes self to be
& spread his every sail   30

Yet long he sought till fortunes day
The first of august came
When Nelson bore into the bay
That deified his name
But day when dared & year when won   35
My pen need not defile
For victory wrote it while the sun
Did hold his light & smile
To see how Nelson fought & won
The battle of the Nile   40

The taunting foe of safety vain
Their anchors cast aground
Untill the mighty of the main
Like a tempest gathered round
& they that did the world deride   45
Now trembled at his name
While rocks & shores & seas defied
& danger dared his fame
To all in thunder he replied
& terror shrunk in shame   50

Full soon their colours & their fleet
Did ruins throne bedeck
Till weary ocean at his feet
Seemed sinking with the wreck
Their pompous ships were hurled on high   55
& on their wings of flame
Told to the wondering blushing sky
His glory & their shame
While mars in ecchoes made reply
& marvelled at his name   60

The elements supprised & won
To view so grand a fight
Drew nights black curtains from the sun
Who smiled upon the sight
The sea forgot its waves & lay 65
Quite still the sight to see
& neptune from his caves that day
Looked out amazedly
& threw his coral crown away
For Nelson ruled the sea 70

THE COTTAGER

True as the church clock hand the hour pursues
He plods about his toils & reads the news
& at the blacksmiths shop his hour will stand
To talk of 'Lunun' as a foreign land
For from his cottage door in peace or strife 5
He neer went fifty miles in all his life
His knowledge with old notions still combined
Is twenty years behind the march of mind
He views new knowledge with suspicious eyes
& thinks it blasphemy to be so wise 10
Oer steams almighty tales he wondering looks
As witchcraft gleaned from old black letter books
Life gave him comfort but denied him wealth
He toils in quiet & enjoys his health
He smokes a pipe at night & drinks his beer 15
& runs no scores on tavern screens to clear
He goes to market all the year about
& keeps one hour & never stays it out
Een at St Thomas tide old Rovers bark
Hails dapples trot an hour before its dark 20
He is a simple worded plain old man

Whose good intents take errors in their plan
Oft sentimental & with saddend vein
He looks on trifles & bemoans their pain
& thinks the Angler mad & loudly storms   25
With emphasis of speech oer murdered worms
& hunters cruel – pleading with sad care
Pitys petition for the fox & hare
Yet feels self satisfaction in his woes
For wars crushed myriads of his slaughterd foes   30
He is right scrupelous in one pretext
& wholesale errors swallows in the next
He deems it sin to sing yet not to say
A song a mighty difference in his way
& many a moving tale in antique ryhmes   35
He has for christmass & such merry times
When Chevychase his master piece of song
Is said so earnest none can think it long
Twas the old Vicars way who should be right
For the late Vicar was his hearts delight   40
& while at church he often shakes his head
To think what sermons the old vicar made
Down right [&] orthodox that all the land
Who had their ears to hear might understand
But now such mighty learning meets his ears   45
He thinks it greek or latin which he hears
Yet church recieves him every sabbath day
& rain or snow he never keeps away
All words of reverence still his heart reveres
Low bows his head when Jesus meets his ears   50
& still he thinks it blasphemy as well
Such names without a capital to spell
In an old corner cupboard by the wall
His books are laid – though good in number small
His bible first in place – from worth & age   55
Whose grandsires name adorns the title page
& blank leaves once now filled with kindred claims
Display a worlds epitome of names

Parents & childern & grand childern all
Memorys affections in the list recall 60
& Prayer book next much worn though strongly bound
Proves him a churchman orthodox & sound
The 'Pilgrims Progress' too & 'Death of Abel'
Are seldom missing from his reading table
& prime old Tusser in his homely trim 65
The first of bards in all the world with him
& only poet which his leisure knows
– Verse deals in fancy so he sticks to prose
These are the books he reads & reads again
& weekly hunts the almanacks for rain 70
Here & no further learnings channels ran
Still neighbours prize him as the learned man
His cottage is a humble place of rest
With one spare room to welcome every guest
& that tall poplar pointing to the sky 75
His own hand planted when an idle boy
It shades his chimney while the singing wind
Hums songs of shelter to his happy mind
Within his cot the 'largest ears of corn'
He ever found his picture frames adorn 80
Brave Granbys head De Grasses grand defeat
He rubs his hands & tells how Rodney beat
& from the rafters upon strings depend
Bean stalks beset with pods from end to end
Whose numbers without counting may be seen 85
Wrote on the Almanack behind the screen
Around the corner upon worsted strung
Pootys in wreaths above the cupboards hung
Memory at trifling incidents awakes
& there he keeps them for his childerns sakes 90
Who when as boys searched every sedgey lane
Traced every wood & shattered cloaths again
Roaming about on raptures easy wing
To hunt those very pooty shells in spring
& thus he lives too happy to be poor 95

While strife neer pauses at so mean a door
Low in the sheltered valley stands his cot
He hears the mountain storm – & feels it not
Winter & spring toil ceasing ere tis dark
Rests with the lamb & rises with the lark   100
Content is helpmate to the days employ
& care neer comes to steal a single joy
Time scarcely noticed turns his hair to grey
Yet leaves him happy as a child at play

MONARCHY OF NATURE

Ive often thought me that a king should be
The head of every empire when Ive seen
The little toilings of the honey bee
Who forms a colony & owns a queen
& hurds his stores for winter in his hive   5
While wild & straggling tribes in bank & wall
Bore little holes – nor further store contrive
Then what themselves may want – & may be all
May be consumed ere winters storms are past
& then with famines tribes they pine & die   10
While tempest proof against the rudest blast
The hive bees monarchy doth live & thrive
Like popolous citys & when winters bye
Crowds upon crowds again their busy labours ply

HONESTY

There is a valued though a stubborn weed
That blooms but seldom & thats found but rare
In sunless places where it cannot seed
Would earth for truths sake had more room to spare
Cant hates it – hypocrites condemn it – & the herd   5
Seeking self interest frown & pass it bye
Tis trampled on – tis bantered – & deterred
Tis scoffed – & mocked at – yet it doth not die
But like a diamond for a century lost
Buried in darkness & obscurity   10
When found again it looses not in cost
But keeps its value & its purity
By time unsullied – still the prince of gems
& first of jewels in all diadems

The rich man claims it – but he often buys   15
Its substitute that is not what it seems
While poverty enobled in disguise
Its simple bloom oft worships & esteems
Knaves boast possesion – but they forge its name
Mobs laud & praise it – but with them tis noise   20
Or the mere passport for some hidden game
Beneath whose garb self interest lurks & lies
Tis by the good man only deemed a prize
Too valued to be scoffed at or opprest
Tis ever more respected by the wise   25
Though thousands treat it as a common jest
& that thou mayest not slight so grand a dower
Tis honesty go thou & wear the flower

THE SUMMONS

Twas once upon a certain time
No matter where & when
For sure as ere that time hath been
That time shall be agen
A strange old man he went about   5
& acquaintance claimed with all
& wheresoere his errand led
On poor & rich would call

He went into a village where
The people was but few   10
Who went to church the year about
Yet none his presence knew
Both young & old he met but none
Would treat him with respect
So he waxed wrath against the priest   15
Their morals to neglect

& this meddlesome old man
Went the Parsonage to find
When he heard a drunken noise
In a rude house close behind   20
One to limber his old joints
Would have had him danced & one
Held a foaming flaggon up
As his strength seemed nearly gone

He shook his head & passed   25
But revenge was in his eye
To think such strife should be alowed
& the Parson living bye
So he looked his summons out
& he never rang the bell   30
When he rudely entered in
Where this man of God did dwell

The Priest had dined & drank
& to prove his village power
No soul was eer admitted   35
Till hed slept his usual hour
But in the old man went
& full loudly did he spake
While the Priest waxed wonder wrath
When he found himself awake   40

& to mark the rude old man
Neer so much as touch his hat
When the priest he talked of manners
& the stocks to teach him that
& his wrath the more increased   45
When the old man rude of speech
Confessed he knew the village
Yet had never heard him preach

& he called the old man rogue
Tho hed never proved him one   50
For the Parson owned three livings
& the old man hadn't one
Tho his hair was thin & grey
Age met with no respect
So the old man he waxed wrath in turn   55
To witness the neglect

'Presumptuous Priest' said he
'You preach & practice not
'Read this it is for thee'
& scarce through one line he got   60
Ere he tryed to ring the bell
& then for help to call
But neither strength or voice remained
To ring or speak at all

& the old man laughed aloud   65
When he saw him try to pray
For he knew it was the first attempt
Without book many a day
& he laughed more loudly still
To see that altered plan   70
For the priest to whom the village bowed
Bowed low to that old man

Then he sought wants huts & found
A sick widow on her seat
With a cruise of water by her side   75
& a crust too hard to eat
& he marveled much to find
That charitys warm lore
Long as it had been preached at church
Had never reached her door   80
Tho the Parsons was the next but one
& he wondered much the more

& he tryed her heart to cheer
Ere her eye the summons saw
& told her she should change away   85
Her crust & bed of straw
To be equal with the best
Where the wealthiest men were sent
Shareing beds with queens to sleep
So she smiled her hearts consent   90
Then the old man left his summons
& upon his errand went

His heart was softened now
& to show the poors distress
He look[ed] out for the magistrate   95
A summons of redress
He soon was in the justice hall
Tho no quorams seat had he

With not so much as by your leave
What a bold man it should be   100

The majistrate he frowned
When he saw the old man stand
With his hat upon his head
& a summons in his hand
& he answered him in wrath   105
& 'you vagrant vile' said he
& coughed for rage 'dares any one
'Send summonses to me'

'Yes' said the bold old man
'Tho Ive neither place nor pelf   110
'I know you make men keep the law
'& brake every one yourself'
Twas truth indeed – the man of law
Into lawless passions ran
& to send the rude old man to jail   115
He his mittimus began

'Stay read your summons first'
Was the old mans bold command
The majistrate he turned to frown
But the pen dropt from his hand   120
& the old man laughed aloud
To see his passions fail
& thought how weak a knave to send
An honest man to jail

'Turn the wind another way   125
'Stop the tide the tempest still
'But never' said the bold old man
'Think to dispute my will'
Then he strided from the hall
& smiling shook his head   130
To see the man of power & law
Led like a child to bed

Then the old man sought the city
For his work was never oer
& Summonses were left almost 135
At every other door
The rich man with his titles
The labourer with none
Was served for bribes from that old man
Were never bought or won 140

At a most unwelcome season
On a lady he did call
As she sat before her mirror
Making ready for a ball
She would have scorned his errand 145
But in spite of her array
Beauty fled its painted shadow
& her cheeks chilled into clay

Then the old man passed a prison
& in passing made a call 150
He thought the folks in such a place
Were knaves & robbers all
Yet he found to his supprise
What he knew not all his time
That those sent there for speaking truth 155
Exceeded those for crime

For politics were running high
& noisey was the storm
Of those who managed state affairs
& those who wished reform 160
The ship of state was deemed a wreck
& savage were the broils
For some said those who manned her deck
Were those who shared her spoils

'The body of the people, I do think,
         are loyal still,'
But pray My L—ds and G—tl—n,
         don't shrink
From exercising all your care
         and skill,
Here, and at home,
   TO CHECK THE CIRCULATION

OF LITTLE BOOKS,

Whose very looks—
Vile *'two-p'nny trash,'*
         bespeak abomination.
Oh! they are full of blasphemies
         and libels,
And people read them
         oftener than their bibles

& those who nothing said at all 165
Were still suspected sore
& they who nothing said but truth
Were suspected much the more
& the old man sighed for pity
That worth should want esteem 170
But vowed that every knave ere long
Should serve on board with him

Then he sought a splendid mansion
& efeth was rated well
Cause he rung & waited not 175
For the answer of the bell
But he kept his summons up
& in further quest he went
For the Lord was making speeches
In an ancient parliment 180

The lacquey cloathed in lace
Sneered with disdainful eye
When the old man said hed seek him
For he thought hed told a lye
An insolent old man 185
Who could think he had the face
To go without a title on
Commission to his grace

Yet to parliment he went
Nor admission sought to win 190
He cared not for the houses rules
Nor fashions not a pin
Tho they frowned from either side
& the great Lord stopt his speech
To say the rude old man 195
In their rules had made a breach

The old man showed his summons
& that Lord fell at his feet
& parliment that instant saw
The stranger take his seat   200
He took the seat & said
That they lyed like evil elves
& by wishing well their country
They only meant themselves

& they no denials muttered   205
Or without a sound they fell
While the old man boldly utterd
What I dare not even tell
Tho he told when truth should triumph
Over falshood that decieves   210
& some who thought her freedom nigh
Did quake like aspin leaves

Some talkd of cold in their dismay
Tho the dog days they were neer
& the old man laughd as he went away   215
Such excuses vile to hear
& soon again there terror fled
& falshood closed the door
To plead as loud & far from truth
As ere hed done before   220

Now the old man sought a pallace
All untitled & alone
& ettiquette with all its pomp
Fell like a rotten stone
In vain they taught him homage   225
In vain they deemed him bold
Just like a flood he rushed along
Tho a feeble man & old

'God save the king' said every voice
As first in their esteem   230
But the old man laughd at such a choice
& called himself supreme
Tho the king was on his throne
Decked in his robes of state
He seemed no more to that old man   235
Then the porter at the gate

For he up & showed his summons
& alack & well aday
The throne was all a nothing then
The mighty nought but clay   240
Treason they would have said but all
That moment gasped for breath
For the strangers mask fell from his face
& that old mans name was death

TRIUMPHS OF TIME

Emblazoned vapour half eternal shade
That gatherest strength from ruin & decay
Emperor of empires for the world hath made
No substance that dare take thy shade away
Thy banners nought but victorys display   5
In undisturbed success thourt grown sublime
Kings are thy vassals & their scepters lay
Round thy proud footstool – Tyranny & crime
Thy subjects are then hail victorious Time

The elements that wreck the marble dome   10
Proud with the polish of the artizan
Thunders that torture the poor trifling home
Traced with the insignificance of man
Are architects of thine & proudly plan

Rich monuments to show thy growing prime 15
Earth quakes that rend the rocks with dreadful span
Lightnings that write in characters sublime
Inscribe their labours all unto the praise of time

Thy pallaces are kingdoms lost to power
The ruins of ten thousand thrones thy throne 20
Thy crown & scepter the dismantled tower
A place of kings yet left to be unknown
Now in triumphing ivy overgrown
Ivy oft pluckt on victorys brows to shine
That fades in crowns of kings prefering stone 25
It only prospers where they met decline
To flourish oer their fate & live alone in thine

Thy dwellings are in ruins made sublime
Impartial monitor no dreams of fear
No dread of treason for a royal crime 30
Deter thee from thy purpose – every where
Thy power is shown thou art arch emperor here
Thou soilst the very crown with stains & rust
On royal robes thy havoc doth appear
The little moth to thy proud summons just 35
Dares pomp to scorn & eats it into dust

Old shadows of magnificance where now
Where now & what their grandeur come & see
Busts broken & thrown down with wreathless brow
Walls stained with colours not of paint but thee 40
Moss lichens ferns & lonely eldern tree
That upon ruins gladly climb to bloom
& add a beauty where tis vain to be
Like the sweet shadow of a painful doom
A lovely maid in youth death smitten for the tomb 45

What now are grandeurs heirs things dull & drear
The vassals of thy mockery & will

Like banquos ghosts to pride their forms appear
& turns ambitions memory wintry chill
Where kings once ruled now spiders work their skill   50
In cobwebs nor yet feel their royal fate
There mopes the bat with triumph small & shrill
& wise satiric owl pops out elate
From trellised architrave to show who slept in state

Pomp may build pallaces & splendid halls   55
Power may display its victories & be brave
The eye finds weakest spots in strongest walls
& meets no strength that can out wear the grave
Nature thy hand maid & imperial slave
For pomp or splendours finery never heeds   60
Kings reign & die pride may distinctions crave
Yet she in barreness neer mourns thy deeds
Graves poor & rich alike she over runs with weeds

Honours mere bauble charmeth not thy sight
Poor pompous nothing pride extolleth high   65
A bauble gilt a shadow cloathed in light
A boast of blood that runs its channels dry
To stagnate upon common shores & die
Honours of state that honours right enslaves
Thou rendst the veil where vile exposures lye   70
Disclosing tyrant deeds & viler knaves
To eke the refuse still of more ignoble graves

Honours in war the cannon vaunts so loud
Dangers where at the bravest dare & die
With thees an insect weaving its own shroud   75
For the cold praise that marble tombs supply
& such are honours all low born or high
Thy powers their lesser glorys soon oercast
& as shrunk lacqueys unto farce they flye
So what was Pompeys Cesars in the past   80
Race horses even dogs & coaches heir at last

In thy proud eye imperial chronicle
An insect small to prize appeareth man
His pomp & honours share with thee no spell
To win thy purpose from the little span 85
Allotted unto life in natures plan
Trifles to him thy favours can engage
High he looks up & soon his race is ran
While the small daisy upon natures page
On which he sets his foot gains endless heritage 90

Look at the farces played in every age
By puny empires vaunting vain display
& blush to read the historians flattered page
Where kings was worshiped like to gods in clay
Whose pride the earth disdained & swept away 95
By thee a shadow worsted of their all
Leigons of soldiers battles dread array
Kings speeches golden bribes nought saved their fall
All neath thy feet are laid thy throne their funeral pall

How feeble & how vain compared to thine 100
The glittering insignificance of kings
Tho in their little light they would out shine
Thy splendid sun – yet soon thy vengance flings
Its gloom around them – then poor puney things
What then remains of all their great hath been 105
Tatters of state that as a mockery hings
Of greatness to conclude the idle scene
In life how mighty thought & found in death how mean

How hath the mighty has beens of the earth
Shrunk into insignificance & shame 110
Jiant powers that waked new empires into birth
Now scarcely own their skeletons & name
Time walks in scorn oer vain ambitions game
Oer ruins vast & vague an idle tome
That but record the fall & not the fame 115

Mothers of gods go witness greece & rome
By thee all exiled now & left without a home

The proudest empire boasting in its strength
No keener satire ever pens then praise
Eves shadows grow to jiants in their length   120
Greatness in both their hastening end betrays
Athens to highest power her head did raise
Then to the meanest fall she hastened on
Yet thou in sport a lower fall betrays
Covering with thy lean finger laid there on   125
A name the all thats left of what was Babylon

Thus Athens lingers on a nest of slaves
& babylon an almost doubted name
Thou with thy finger writes upon their graves
On one obscurity another shame   130
The richest greatness & the proudest fame
Thy sport concludeth as a farce at last
They were & would be but are not the same
Tyrants that made all subject where they past
Become a common jest for laughter at the last   135

Here where I stand thy voice breaths from the ground
A buried tale of sixteen hundred years
Fragments of roman pavements littered round
In each new rooted mol hill thick appears
Ah what is fame that honour so reveres   140
& what is victorys laurel crowned event
When thy grand powers intollerance interferes
Een Ceasars deeds are left in banishment
Indebted een to moles to show us where he went

Yet mighty poet thou & every line   145
Thy grand conseption traces is sublime
No language doth thy god like praise confine
Thy voice is earths grand polyg[l]ot o time

Known of all tongues & read in every clime
Changes of language make no change to thee   150
Thy works have worsted centurys of their prime
Yet new editions every day we see
Ruin thy theme its moral end eternity

Keen satirist too thy pen is deadly keen
Thou turnest things that once did wonder claim   155
To jests ridiculous & memorys mean
The egyptian pyramids without a name
Stand monuments to chaos not to fame
Stone jests of kings which thou in sport did save
As towering satires of prides living shame   160
Beacons to prove thy overbearing wave
Will make all fame at last become its owners grave

Even here I mark thy finger point in scorn
To yon stone column thou art fain to spare
Smiling upon the rosey face of morn   165
As if twas doomed for thy eternal heir
Tho not ordained mans mighty deeds to wear
Dolphin a dog deemed worthy to oerspan
Its little lot in life reposes there
Ah jesting time forgo thy scornfull plan   170
The dogs remembered still but all forgot the man

Thy tide rolls on mortality must share
A mortal fate & feeble each design
To prop distinctions fall none none can dare
To keep their offerings from thy mighty shrine   175
Where some few volunteer & thousands pine
With loathing to give up thy princley claim
Yet without stooping pride may well resign
Its all where Homer grows a doubtful name
Obscurity with thee is surely kin to fame   180

Mighty surviver thou shalt see the hour
When all the mightiness the earth contains
Its pomp its splendour & its hollow power
Shall waste like water from its weakened veins
Nor even leave a shadow for remains   185
When names & fames of which the earth is full
& books with all their knowledge urged in vain
When dead & living shall be void & null
& natures pillow be at last its human skull

Een temples raised to worship & to prayer   190
Sacred from ruin in all eyes but thine
Are laid as level & are left as bare
As spots with no pretentions to resign
Nor lives one relic that was deemed divine
By thee great sacriligious shade – all all   195
Are swept away & common weeds enshrine
That place of tombs & memorys prodigal
Itself a tomb at last the record of its fall

All then shall mingle fellowship with one
& earth be strewn with wrecks of human things   200
When tombs are broken up & memorys gone
Of proud aspiring mortals crowned as kings
Mere insects sporting upon waxen wings
That melt at thy oerpowering energy
& when theres nought to govern thy fame springs   205
To new existance conquered yet to be
An uncrowned partner still of dread eternity

Tis done oerpowering vision & no more
My simple numbers struggle in thy fame
Tis gone the spirit of thy voice is oer   210
Adventuring praises to thy mighty name
To thee an atom am I & in shame
I shrink from these aspirings to my doom
For all the world contains to praise or blame

Are but a garden hastening out of bloom   215
To fill up natures wreck mere rubbish for the tomb

Imperial moralist thy every page
Like grand prophetic visions doth install
Truth to all creeds the savage saint & sage
In unison may listen to thy call   220
Thy voice as universal speaks to all
It tells us what all were & are to be
That evil deeds will evil hearts inthrall
& virtue only change the dread decree
That whoso righteous lives shall win eternity   225

[JUST LIKE THE LION IN ALARMS]

Just like the lion in alarms
Roused from beneath the english arms
This trumpet sounding prince o' Thumbs
Roars 'Ceberus' & out he comes
With all the fuss & all the roar   5
That twaddles breed hath done before
While all his friends poor gaping flats
In sable coats & shovel hats
Began to clap & share the fun
As butchers oer their dogs have done   10
But ah alack & well a day
That such a thing for such a fray
Should eer be brought to make a match
& led in triumph to the scratch
To face game Sleafords honest John   15
That laid so hard & heavy on
Poor 'Ceberus' back that he
Who roared at first so lustily
A challange now from one blow cries
'Enough' & from the battle flies   20

Nor turns again – alas for H[an]t[hor]p
Friends shout in vain 'Do all you can T[hor]p
New nib your pen for one turn more
You'll fright him if you can but roar'
Yet like a mouse from pussey freed   25
Such noises but increased his speed
His friends at home rubbed down their shins
& stroaked cares wrinkles from their chins
While shovel hats were pulled adown
Oer many a nose to hide the frown   30
Dear heart said one of these anointed
I own Im somthing dissapointed
Our lion roared at first od' rot him
As well as eer did weaver Bottom
& sure enough I thought he'd play   35
The devil with them in the fray
Nay never so said neighbour Sly
& Reverend Sir Ill tell you why
Your Ceberus roaring dog was beat
As soon as eer he had a meet   40
For plain J[oh]n B[ed]f[or]d like a shark
Thrust home beyond his power to bark
& then twas seen through all his spite
The puppy had no teeth to bite
So H[an]t[hor]p 'woe is in thy rooms'   45
Thy guests look blue & bite their thumbs
& By——l—ms pr[ies]t in silence deep
Twixt news & sermon falls asleep
All find alas with heavy heart
That he who roared a lions part   50
Had not the wit tho cloathed in sattin
'To play the part to tear a cat in'

Caw thorp   B.

[OCH BY JASUS HES A IRISH LAD]

Och by jasus hes a irish lad
& he owns an irish heart
Hell be to none a sneaking cad
But act a princely part
By jasus judy fill the bowl   5
While whiskeys to be had
For I told you hed an irish soul
& Ill drink the soldier lad
 Whoop boy whoo
 Spite of every botheration   10
 The prince of waterloo
 Has gave emancipation
 & has kilt some taxe[s] too
 So drink round to the soldier lad
 & make no more to do   15

Come smoke about your whiskey stills
Round bogs & mountains all
Come judys scour your whisky gills
For taxes they shall fall
So drink in the reeking stuff   20
& in the largest bowl
For sure I tould ye right enough
 He had an irish soul
 Whoop boys boys whoo
 Spite of every botheration   25
 The prince of waterloo
 Has gave emancipation
 & has kilt some taxes too

The english swill their ale about
& sing like ony mad   30
The scotch too join the drunken rout
& hail the solder lad
& shall old irelands heart be still

Who bred the bonny boy
No well die oer the whiskey gill   35
But what well drink him joy

Old england makes a ranting row
Joy drunk wi the soldier boy
Who unmuzzled the ox to tread the mow
& she kicks up her heels for joy   40
Old mother excise may go – mad if she will
Hes already set fire to her tail
& hell raise the siege round the whisky still
As he's done by the copper of ale

So arrah my honey dont bother my joys   45
For Ill mortgage the hide of my cow
Ere Ill want a drop of the cratur boys
To drink to the soldier now
Och arrah my darling & shall it be said
That an irishmans backward in joy   50
When a double tooths drawn out of Taxes head
& all by the soldier boy

1830

These vague alusions to a countrys wrongs
Where one says 'aye' & others answer 'no'
In contradictions from a thouseand tongues
Till like to prison cells her freedoms grow
Becobwebed with these oft repeated songs   5
Of peace & plenty in the midst of woe
& is it thus they mock her year by year
Telling poor truth unto her face she lies
Declaiming of her wealth with gibe severe
So long as taxes drain their wished supplies   10

& will these gaoler[s] rivet every chain
Anew – yet loudest in their mockery be
To damn her into madness with disdain
Forging new bonds & bidding her be free

[GEORGE 4TH DEATH]

They gathered round thee every day
Their praise was loud & long
& blessings in thy powers display
Rushed forth from every tongue
They mourned as bees would mourn their queen   5
    When absent from the hive
Which if but half as true would show
    Thee the most beloved alive

But thou art gone & mourning too
Hath left the idle crowd   10
Self interests walk they still pursue
& shouts are long & loud
As when thou wert in pomp & power
    & <   > rejoicings gave
Still they rejoice tho thour[t]   15
    All lonely in the grave

Well thou wert such that even foes
When free to speak their mind
<   >
<   > kind   20

The knave may buy a gilded fame
Till follys scene shall close
The tyrant he may win a name
But thou wert none of those
& better far it is for thee   25

Now moved from fears distrust
So to have reigned that thousands try
   To honour thee in dust

Alive – the god of fashions sphere
The muse of all their songs 30
But dead thourt lost to every ear
& mute on every tongue

THE BLUES & THE SAILORS

Hoist up your blue my boys the brave & true
Are least in number yet but howsomiver
Heres two bold sailors – down right bits of blue
They'll join the free – so liberty for ever
By G[od] they never heed us boys or hail us 5
They dont know Tennison & theyre no sailors

Yet look theyre mighty stout & gallant men
& blues the turn pike road to liberty
& sure enough nine chances out of ten
Is that theyll join their courage with the free 10
For tho their trowsers are not over new
Tis blue & thats the colour for the true

Hail wandering britons wither do ye roam
Ye both seem hardy as the heart of oak
We too as britons bid ye welcome home 15
– & then one sailor to the tother spoke
Now d[am]me me Jim are these land lubbs to fright us
Theyve hoisted colours & are going to fight us

No no good strangers you for once mistake us
We will not war with britons such as you   20
No roast us boil us fry us burn us bake us
Well all die maryters for our bit of blue
The Bloody ches nuts & the 'lectoneering
Thats what we fight for – here they fell a cheering

The sailors stood agast – now Jim g[o]d[am]me   25
Weve both seen danger tho weve seldom cackled
But these same roasting lubbers want to cram ye
& make us robbers just to get us shackled
My grannys blue bag might make lecture hearers
But baked or boiled Jim bl[as]t em theyre no heroes   30

Nay nay good strangers we are heroes all
Tho not so great as sailors we are nixt you
So take the quart of beer tis ale not small
& drink to blue & soak it all betwixt you
The sailors took it – & no longer jealous   35
The mob roared out that they were glorious fellows

& France & Belgium & Tennison
Went forth in shouts from many a beardless lip –
But d[a]mme Jim that here rum Mr Anyson
Wor never mixed in grog on board our ship   40
So heres to england still – & france & belgam
Are no tars likings let em go to h—ll Jim

The blues right bluely took the empty quart
& vext as Turpins – masons cobblers tailors
All swore blue trowsers were not worth a f[ar]t   45
& small beer even were too good for sailors
But then the sailors had got out of hearing
& so the mob as victors fell a cheering

163

FAMILIAR EPISTLE TO A FRIEND

When evening takes the night for mate
   I met your friendly letter
& feth Ill scribble soon or late
   To own my self your debtor
Tho Id gan rest my weary pate   5
   & ceased from every labour
Burning ones shins beside the grate
   & chatting to a neighbour

Your kindness needs but little say
   Of how it was accepted   10
Ive been to see you many a day
   & made one vow & kept it
Good ale my fancy ever wins
   & had want stronger tethers
Id brake their links or brake my shins   15
   To crack our cups together

Neighbour & I were trying tricks
   About the royal riddle
The ravelled skein of politics
   A tune for every fiddle   20
That yearly wisdom doth explain
   Into a greater puzzle
Sweeping the circle round again
   What taxes yearly guzzle

Im neither wig nor tory clean   25
   To swear knaves act uprightly
But just a water mark between
   That skims opinions lightly
I guess nones got their game to seek
   With all their raving bother   30
& one thing both will often speak
   & as often mean another

Self interest is a rude maschine
    Of very old invention
& still the wheels run smooth & clean   35
    With many a fair pretention
& trust me boy the torys puff
    & patriots clitter clatter
Are samples of a kindred stuff
    As nigh as makes no matter   40

& let one plead & tother still
    Rave over freedoms charter
Theyre both at best a grinding mill
    That waits a windy quarter
Their countrys good is all my eye   45
    Theres Brougham almost crazy
With his reform – & bye & bye
    He'll list with 'Corporal Cazy'

Ive little faith in shifting creeds
    To sanction stranger faces   50
The old ones must be – knaves indeed
    If worse cant take their places
Tho patriots start a fussy tale
    Like Butlers Bear & Fiddle
Their good beginnings always fail   55
    & finish in the middle

& theres religion bless the saint
    I never wish to wound her
But shes so hipt with cants complaint
    A rotten pear is sounder   60
Theres different saints in different packs
    All urging different reasons
& if you cant swear white is black
    You hazard gospel treasons

Now ranting madmen take the street 65
   A sort of saintish smugglers
Who bawl their cant to all they meet
   Like Mountebanks & jugglers
Poor sinners like to you & I
   With terrors they regale us 70
Of brimstone drink when h—lls adry
   As if nick kept an alehouse

Yet let them bother how they may
   & preach up nice restrictions
Their practice often gets the sway 75
   & mars by contradictions
The lawyer guards the law yet lives
   Defending rougish actions
The patriot unions lesson gives
   & joins opposing factions 80

The priest that daily prays for good
   Owns h—ll gets daily fuller
& while he rails at satans brood
   Wears cloth the very colour
So let one plead & tother pray 85
   & greet the good that shall come
Lets you & I but have our way
   They may have theirs & welcome

& true as two & two make four
   Tho saints make few concessions 90
Like tavern chalks behind a door
   Theres knaves in most professions
That d——d sweet hussey madam sin
   At once so fair & civil
Theres scarce a heart she cannot win 95
   At times to join the d——l

& there are knaves – nay often worse
   Becolledged & begrammered
Just as a nail that never stirs
   No further then its hammered   100
Grow into saints in hopes of cash
   & cunning tythe besiegers
Fat livings with their notions clash
   & so theyre gospel teachers

Theres Dandy xxx of polished cits   105
   At once the pink & pattern
Who oft to show his colledge wits
   Swears both in greek & lattin
He games & runs a bankrupt bill
   & still to keep the farce on   110
Six days a week hes what you will
   & the seventh hes a – parson

Cant raves & pleads & every trade
   Hath some tirade of canting
Theyve all their lessons ready made   115
   & cash is all thats wanting
Tis that inspires some saints to stand
   For canaans milk & honey
& souls might lye like fallow land
   If t'were not for the money   120

Tis that which makes the mare to go
   & sports all sorts of cunning
Tis that gives weakness wit to know
   & read his interest running
It is the art of cant that gives   125
   Plain lessons without labour
& thus the greatest fool that lives
   Finds wit to cheat his neighbour

& common sense could chant a stave
    Nor need a second Daniel
To show broad cloath will hide a knave
    As oft as carsey flannel
& workhouse paupers tho disgraced
    By wants degraded station
Are good as paupers all belaced
    & pensioned on a nation

& honesty with pewter badge
    No deed of honour quarters
Is great as is the proud adage
    Beguilt on stars & garters
The brags of pride in pomp & pen
    Plain common sense will settle
Theres no degrees of honest men
    Tis only in the mettle

Im fain to praise the world but still
    Each hamlet town & city
Is so mad oer that golden pill
    That praise woud d——n the ditty
& sly time serving is a game
    I neer could venture in fort
Tho many see nor sin nor shame
    To wade rouges to the chin fort

So George the fourth was once the thing
    & up went many a beaver
From heads who if old nick was king
    Would wish him king for ever
But George the fourth is in his grave
    & fortune hunting strappers
Are dumb with praises pealing stave
    As bells withouten clappers

130

135

140

145

150

155

160

King William now is all the cry
  & up go hats & praises
God save the king – & so say I
  & so say all that pleases
But there is many a loyal knave   165
  That I could easy mention
Would never chaunt a single stave
  If the tune was not a pension

Self interest now lays plans so big
  In cunning apt & able   170
She with her friends plays thimble rig
  & the worlds a gaming table
Shell worship Dagons feet for place
  & flatter gall for honey
Shell swear lyes true before your face   175
  Or any thing for money

A psalm may be a psalm indeed
  As a ballad is a ballad
But self is still the rougish weed
  To garnish every sallad   180
& there'll be many a loyal guest
  At next years coronation
But countrys good & all the rest
  Is still a botheration

So heres to our King Will the fourth   185
  & every honest fellow
& may he never miss the worth
  Of ale to make him mellow
& heres farewell to politics
  & clamours cunning 'vermint'   190
– & d——n all knaves & roguish tricks
  So ends your humble servant

THE HUE & CRY
A TALE OF THE TIMES

Swords trumpets blunderbusses fires & thunder
Are up in arms & wonder wars with wonder

Bards doat upon Epics in numbers to suit
With a high sounding title & name
Of muses they borrow a harp & a lute
& kneel to apollo for fame
My fancys flye low & the tale to be told   5
I know not if epic or riddle
I ask not for harps from a muse young or old
Nor care if its sung to a fiddle

I sing of a man & a crooked old man
Thats seen in each village & town   10
Thats done more in mischief then any man can
& honestys running him down
If people are robbed hes the whole of the fame
& the old man he pockets the pelf
If fires they are raised hes the whole of the blame   15
As none comes to tell of himself

So they swore in the yeomanry troops horse & foot
& marched them for twenty miles round
& the yeomanry swore that the crooked old brute
Should very soon yield & be found   20
If he hadnt got into the sea in his fear
Or hid himself under the ground
& first he was yonder & then he was here
But they neer got the pig in the pound

Arms right was the signal – some used the wrong hand   25
Never mind they were gallant men all
& many who leapt on their war horses backs

From their war horses backs got a fall
But honour tho smotherd in dirt never felt
It a stain to his cloath any way   30
The crooked old man they considered their foe
& they fell into battle array
But the crooked old man was as far from a sword
As he was in the first of the fray

Old rumour was up – other stories were out   35
& all the world leaving his bed
Had witches by majic set fire to the sky
More wonders could not have been read
Some body at first had the end of the string
& it might be the man in the moon   40
Tho hed never been heard of to do such a thing
Yet northern lights tokened it soon

Thus rumours new stories kept stirring the row
& hue & cry spread far & wide
Till the farmer in fear loosed the team from his plough 45
& girded a sword by his side
To follow the rout of the crooked old man
Which none under heaven could find
Altho he was seen in ten places at once
They might as well follow the wind   50

For some said his clothing was light lackaday
& some said his cloathing was black
Some saw him as two in a Gig that was green
Some as one on a horse that was black
Today he sold matches & begged for a crust   55
To keep a poor beggar alive
To morrow he scares all the dogs in a town
Driving hard as a devil can drive
While a day or twos wonder goes buzzing about
Like a swarm of bees leaving a hive   60

The majistrates threatened – twas all of no use
No fear the old rebel could tame
The majistrates promised – he saw the excuse
Was to trap him so nobody came
Still deeds they were doing which nobody did   65
& none but the devil could plan
Who like a sly fox in his covert lay hid
& the blame fell upon the old man

Fair speakers got up of real goodness to teach
They had said – & done nothing before   70
& danger like steam might force good in the speech
Which might fall when the danger was oer
For the law it still looked upon wrong as its right
The placeman still hankered for spoil
& some were for taxes & some were for tythes   75
While labour was starving at toil

Some turned to past times when a 'general fast'
Was alowed to do good to the nation
& others bewailed that their fitness was past
As fasting had caused the vexsation   80
Persuation was lost though twas hinted in prayer
To persuade the poor flocks to get thinner
For all they desired was a subject for grace
To repeat oer a plentiful dinner

Thus 'fasts & thanksgivings' they got rather flat   85
& were dreaded as plagues by the nation
& the people when threatened by this sort & that
Grew in anger & silent vexation
For when a thanksgiving was published they knew
It a notice for troubles & crosses   90
& when a new fast was proclaimed twas a shew
To bear with new taxes & losses

& the crooked old man like a meddlesome thing
Had whispered some things to the people
Declaring such things did their wants as much good   95
As the bells noisey songs in the steeple
Nay worse – for he littered his libels about
To say that 'fast prayers' while a printing
Brought one man a harvest in roast & in boiled
That would serve ten a year without stinting   100

Some said the old man was a foreigner bred
Some had made him a duke if they could
Some said that hed nothing but deeds in his head
& some said his errand was good
No matter – the crooked old man was about   105
Some described him as bent as a bow
& some as a jiant whod put to the rout
Every idle pretention below

& people all stared as a wonder will stare
& looked on each other again   110
Every man of his neighbour seemed thinking beware
Still the crooked old man wasnt taen
One said it was Bouneparte risen again
One believed he had never been dead
& guess as they would still the crooked old man   115
Was the only thing noticed or read

Some said it was Cobbett some said it was Paine
Some went into france to Voltair
& when they got there why they got back again
To discover that nothing was there   120
Some rummaged old sermons some printed new Tracts
& handbills like messengers ran
Conjectures were many but few were the facts
As to who was the crooked old man

174

" This is some fellow,
Who, having been prais'd for his bluntness, doth affect
A saucy roughness — ——— ———
These kind of knaves I know, which in this plainness
Harbour more craft, and more corrupter ends,
Than twenty silly ducking observants,
That stretch their duties nicely."

" As one, who lay in thickets and in brakes
Entangl'd, winds now this way and now that
His devious course uncertain, seeking home."

THIS IS
WILL COBBETT,
with Thomas Paine's bones,

Still hard swearing fellows at Cobbett would stick 125
& the crooked old fellow was he
For Hunt & O Connel could neer be old nick
Since each had been made an M P
So it couldnt be them – well – & who could it be
Why none but the bones of Tom Paine 130
& some were for tarring a bundle of rags
To burn him for treason again

& some said the strange & the crooked old man
Cast a shadow that strutted like pride
& some swore it went as no shadow could do 135
Bolt upright by the old fellows side
& wherever that shadow it wended or past
Ruin seemed its infallable guide
& wherever that shadow it rested a time
There was trouble – & little beside 140

& there was an alderman making a rout
About mobs & their evil intentions
& there was the newspapers flying about
With rumours great lies & inventions
& the crooked old man he was first in the fray 145
Yet they neer could catch hold of his tail
For he always was first to get out of the way
When ever they talked of a jail

& the mob fell a laughing & hissing at last
& their jokes they grew bitter & many 150
For they knew that to make a poor alderman fast
Was the cruelest torture of any
& a warrior sore vext that his soldiers were beat
Not daring to make the mob sinners
Threatened Orator Hunt in his quiet retreat 155
In revenge for the loss of their dinners

The crooked old man grew a regular strife
& was all oer the world in an hour
& great speculators were left at an ebb
Who argued that money was power   160
For the old man proved not & their plans they all fell
Like the tinsel from tyrannys thrones
& many a one who had riches today
On the morrow was knocking of stones

Northern lights they were flashing their spears in the sky 165
Till midnight as morning grew wan
& people all said with a dread in their eye
Twas the work of the crooked old man
& many were sought to be swore on the watch
& rumour was up in the cry   170
But from that night to this why the crooked old man
Could never be seen in the sky

But his work it went on like a jiant refreshed
& they hunted him just like a fox
& followed his path both with fetters & jails   175
But he kept both from fetters & locks
Yet somebody said wether joking or not
They had seen the strange crooked old man
So the majistrates instantly ordered a hall
To meet & consider a plan   180

& the hall it did meet & the meeting agreed
That knowledge was leading astray
But a voice from the crowd it might be from the sky
Muttered deeply & awfully 'nay'
– & those that had no wit at all in their heads   185
Begged advice from their neighbours that had
But a whisper was muttered no body knew where
That their reasons were idle & bad

So the hall it broke up & the crooked old man
Was as brief in all tales as before 190
& mischief as tho it a liscence had taen
Laid them all at the old fellows door
But rumour determined the tables should turn
As hed have no more laid on his back
So he faced his pursuers – the tale had it so 195
& they all fled away in a pack

The tyrants that rose like a storm in the night
With their terrors did nothing avail
Like cobwebs chains fell from the hands of the slave
& truths fetters broke in the jail 200
Tho mischief raged loud like a tempest at sea
Of war to the hilt & the haft
A shadow passed bye it might be the old man
& where was wars tyranny left

Its glory was huddled in velvet & pall 205
Its sword fell to rust in the sheath
Its warfield a coffin of lead in the wall
Its throne dust & rubbish beneath
& the terrible cloud that its tempest had spread
Oer the peace & the glory of day 210
The old man he turned up a smile to the sky
& like majic all vanished away

The people all marvelled & smiled at the sight
Feeling rapture they couldnt tell how
& the old man was heard of all tales & in sight 215
& his enemys dreaded him now
& they that were closest to track him today
Where they ever so selfish or brave
On the morrow the all that was left of his foes
Was an old rusty sword & a grave 220

So the crooked old man where it suited him went
Seas or mountains were nought in his way
Victors conquored not him – & the laurels of kings
By his look in an instant grew grey
He wandered thro citys by pallaces past   225
& where was their ornaments then
The ivy grew green upon desolate walls
Far away from the dwellings of men

Once again the spear glittered – the gun it was primed
& the tempest of warfare began   230
But thro whole files of muskets unwounded or hurt
Wonder marvelled – 'there goes the old man'
& he conquored & past like a child at his play
& petitions grew thicker & faster
For hatred it grew into fear every day   235
When they saw the old fellow was master

For rumour declared that the crooked old man
Had eyes that could see thro a wall
& could read all the thoughts of a man as a book
In a book he had written them all   240
Nay some said his eyes tho so old were so good
They could een see the very winds blow
& his ears if folks didnt tell lies they could hear
The noise the flowers make when they grow
& when they heard this the folks trembled out right   245
& couldnt tell wither to go

& prophecys written some hundred years back
Seemed now as if written today
& the crooked old man like the beast full of eyes
Looked the powers of the strongest away   250
The lion a shepherds dog grew & would cringe
From the feeble attacks of the ram
The tiger was scarce a cats paw of himself
& the wolf sneaked away from the lamb

So the prophets had wrote & their writings are true 255
Tho they turned not on tyrannys side
Whose abettors made out that truths learning was bad
& they wanted her writings to hide
But they might as well shut out the sun at noon day
For truth it had spread far & wide 260
So proudest of beings grew humble as men
& the tyrants of millions one hour
Grew as still in the next as a tomb in a church
& grasped but a shadow for power

The war sword was beat into shares for the plough 265
& the thunder of cannon all ceased
The slave looked about him he couldnt tell how
When he felt from his fetters released
So the crooked old man he a prophet became
Daniel scarcely was greater then he 270
& good & bad stirred at the sound of his name
As the winds stir the waves of the sea
For those who beheld him a prophet one hour
Couldnt dream what the next he might be

So up rumour hallooed & good & bad rose 275
While candour declared to her sorrow
Altho she was strong in professions today
She might be a cripple tomorrow
& trades & professions turned round with the news
Like a 'second edition' of men 280
Old things & old manners such new fashions took
That acquaintance scarce knew them agen

Yet none gave his reasons for changing his dress
Or for why he took up the new plan
But looks told it all when enquirey was made 285
If theyd heard of the crooked old man
For he came at all knowledge none couldnt tell how
If a heart aught of evil had in it

He wouldnt be flattered by title & bow
But smelt out a knave in a minute   290

No thought in a corner a moment could hide
He turned them all out in a mass
& the crooked old man knew all meaning as plain
As you would your own face in a glass
So his name & his fame like the sun in the sky   295
Startled darkness at once into day
& cunning who modeled truths face for a mask
Forced to break it or put it away

In an office of law there he kickt up a row
Tho the lawyer declared on his honour   300
He never did wrong all the days in his life
Still he quaked like the conscience of Bonner
& rummaged his desks where some things were turned out
That dare not see daylight for shame
So he made up a fire & he burnt them out right   305
– But he wished the old man in the flame

A gentleman worth a whole county in wealth
Spread his table to please the old man
But the old man he wanted no victuals nor drink
& fast oer the county he ran   310
But the crooked old man fell a telling a tale
How a spider was gulling a flye
& the gentlemans visage as ashes turned pale
& he looked as if ready to die
For a chancery suit like a nail in his boot   315
Pricked him deep – & his ruin was nigh

& he searched into hearts that had never been tried
Into locks that had never been moved
& there he found writings knaves wanted to hide
& wills that had never been proved   320
& they who owned fortunes no fortunes had got

& they who owned none had got all
& the bribes they were cooked to be ready & hot
When the crooked old man gave a call

He saw a reviewer reviewing a work   325
& the book was most wretchedly bad
But the writer declared – hed been paid for his praise
& the crooked man thought he was mad
For an excellent work had excited his wrath
– Here his wrath it was minus of pelf   330
So the cunning review thro the crooked old man
Lay unsold on the booksellers shelf

Then a writer he saw like a spider at work
Trying mischievous tricks with his pen
Who plundered all volumes that fell in his way   335
To make up a volume agen
& the crooked old man grew a critic in wrath
& he clapt a whasps nest on the head
Of the knave for a night cap & tortured his brains
To dream about more then he read   340

He was one day a preacher – a critic the next
& thumping down facts to his text
He was one day a prophet disclosing events
& a death hunted rebel the next
Then a will o whisps light he was up in a blaze   345
Then gone – as if sunk in the earth
& the people had scarce shut their doors on amaze
When up he sprang like a new birth

Blazing all unexpected in places remote
Where he near was expected to come   350
Twas as idle to say where his house it was not
As it was to say where was his home
He was one day a pleader upsetting bad laws
& the next he was of the excise
& at all times & seasons a terror & strife   355

182

As he made such good use of his eyes
Disguise – like a cloak in the summer he made
Burning hot tho himself a disguise

The tricks he found out were too many to tell
& more then a volume could hold   360
Yet he found that the root of all evils was fed
In a climate of silver & gold
So the rich who knew well what their meaning was at
& the poor who knew nothing at all
Bawled aloud for reform & the crooked old man   365
Seemed to mix himself up in the call

But as the petitions got written & signed
For which some reformers would pray
The taxes they marked as oppressive & bad
Where the taxes themselves had to pay   370
& want found himself just as far from relief
As the earth itself seems from the sky
So up goes the haloo – as after a thief
& the crooked old mans in the cry

Twas honesty now that was put to the rout   375
& the full weight & measure of men
For the crooked old man came at once at the fact
& hue & cry started agen
So his yard band the draper put out of the way
Tho pretention once made it an ell   380
& the grocer who made thumping weight yesterday
Threw his thumping weights into a well

The huswife again had her butter to weigh
As her pounds were two ounces too light
& honestys face had you seen it today   385
You'd have called him a villian out right
The publican who since the duty was off
Had put his full measures aside –

Now broke [his] short pints & his dandy laced quarts
To be all upon honestys side   390

The miller he ran straight away to his mill
For hed ta'en too much toll from a grist
The lawyer to clients gave back half the fee
Tho hed hard work to open his fist
The debtor to pay what he never had paid   395
Went straight away home to his till
& the creditor who had charged more then his due
Burnt the old one – & made a new bill

The baker had got a hot loaf on his peal
& he put all the baking away   400
To give in the water he sought for new meal
For hed charged for the water today
The butcher he talked about raising his price
As he couldnt get profits at all
But the moment he heard of the crooked old man   405
He said he intended to fall

The tailor who almost sold cloathing for nought
As his newspaper puffs would express
With the clothier looked out better goods then hed got
& when hed got better – took less   410
Masters unstrung their purses & said to their men
Twas all their intentions before
To give better wages – tho nine out of ten
Only gave it till danger was oer

Old plausible errors that lay in their nests   415
Lapt up like political tracts
Were turned in the storm with such terror & haste
Reason scarce left a rag on their backs
They couldnt bear cold & they couldnt bear heat
So they fled away into a mist   420
Some said they were turned into meteors at night
– They were no longer stars on the list

He even went church for so rumour declared
& murmurs grew audible then
To think that the devil should eer be alowed   425
To trouble such good living men
Yet they looked on their dress & they smoothed their heads
down
Fearing failings might get into sight
They were all unprepared for the crooked old man
& wished he had waited till night   430

The maid pinned her kerchief more close to her breast
Lest her heart should be blushing for shame
& the old man should see it had harboured a guest
That would certainly forfeit her name
& the fop with a kerchief hung out of his coat   435
Thrust it into his pocket again
Lest the crooked old man should discover a note
Where that maiden had written her pain
For he promised her marriage in seasons remote
& never went near her again   440

The preacher he stirred up his wits for a text
Thinking sin had occasioned the past
& he did as much good when hed written the next
As he did while a preaching the last
Yet he preached it aloud that twas nothing but sin   445
& the folks fled away from their pews
For one & all said twas the crooked old man
So rumour went off with the news

& the rumour went east & the rumour went west
Twas all oer the world in a trice   450
That the crooked old man had got into the church
& was preaching of nothing but vice
& falshood she sat with her head in her hand
& her visage as ashes was pale
For she dreaded the church & the tales of the priest   455

As bad as thieves dreaded a jail
So empty pews only he preached at – at last
& still he went on with his tale

& thus they were all frightened out of their wits
Till wits came again as it where   460
& they found that their conscience was all that was bit
As the old man had never been near
– They paused & where fluttered a minute or so
& again their pretentions began
To church they all went as good people should do   465
& denied all they'd done to a man

Some turned short about & believed it a lye
& instantly left the new plan
Till rumour again raised the tale in full cry
& away went the crooked old man   470
Twas in vain some declared the old villian was dead
& some that he'd never been born
His name was as bad as a voice from the dead
& they quaked who pretended to scorn

Some said the old man had a sword in his hand   475
& some that he carried a knife
One called him the very best man in the land
One swore that he wanted his life
& fresh rumours still from the east & the west
Rose up like a storm in an hour   480
That instead of a sword he'd a book in his hand
With the motto of 'Knowledge is power'

& now a Philosopher put it about
That he saw him peep out of a tomb
Where he lay all the day like a fox in his den   485
Till the gloom of the even was come
& the constable shouldered his staff in high glee
& the yeoman he up with his sword

Marching off for the tomb to secure the old man
All in hopes of the promised reward   490

Their hopes they were many but more their supprise
When they saw nought but shadow & gloom
& as writ with the mists half conscealing disguise
The word 'Time' rudely scrawled on the tomb
Like the breath on a looking glass left by a sigh   495
If the old man had been he was gone
Like a meteor that flashes at night from the sky
The tomb in its darkness lived on

Till writers they made quite a rout of the word
& stirred themselves into a name   500
For many declared that the crooked old man
Was no other being than fame
& one wrote to prove how he got in the tomb
& one to prove how he got out
& one wrote to show that hed never been in   505
& so his name travelled about

Then they unbraced the blood hound to follow his track
& the blood hound barked loud in the cry
Hark – away for the thief – cried the ill judging pack
& the thief hunters raptures got high   510
& their oaths were all ready to swear black or white
& the human dogs howled for the gains
Who ran all about – just to run back again
& they got but the run for their pains

So the mossy old monument got into fame   515
With that little word written thereon
Like the writing Belshazzar beheld on the wall
Waking fears when its writer was gone
Some dreaded its shade as a spirits at night
Some on sundays the church couldnt reach   520
Lest rumour should find that the crooked old man
Had mounted the pulpit to preach

Folks all met to talk of the wonderfull man
& to marvel as who could it be
When a 'Wise man' at last turned his books till he found   525
Time conscience & truth they were three
That kicked up the noise with the crooked old man
& the funds rose as fast as they fell
Tho the Monk hid his face in his cowl for awhile
& each snail popt his head in his shell   530
But the king on his throne was a true honest man
So the world it went on very well

But from that day to this all the books in the world
Which the wisest of men ever wrote
Never cleared up the truth of the crooked old man   535
Tho some swore to the cut of his coat
& from that hour to this let 'em talk as they would
In spite of each treatise & plan
The hardest to swear they were just at his heels
Only swore to the crooked old man   540

THE FALLEN ELM

Old elm that murmured in our chimney top
The sweetest anthem autumn ever made
& into mellow whispering calms would drop
When showers fell on thy many coloured shade
& when dark tempests mimic thunder made   5
While darkness came as it would strangle light
With the black tempest of a winter night
That rocked thee like a cradle to thy root
How did I love to hear the winds upbraid
Thy strength without – while all within was mute   10
It seasoned comfort to our hearts desire
We felt thy kind protection like a friend
& edged our chairs up closer to the fire

Enjoying comforts that was never penned
Old favourite tree thoust seen times changes lower   15
Though change till now did never injure thee
For time beheld thee as her sacred dower
& nature claimed thee her domestic tree
Storms came & shook thee many a weary hour
Yet stedfast to thy home thy roots hath been   20
Summers of thirst parched round thy homely bower
Till earth grew iron – still thy leaves was green
The childern sought thee in thy summer shade
& made their play house rings of sticks & stone
The mavis sang & felt himself alone   25
While in thy leaves his early nest was made
& I did feel his happiness mine own
Nought heeding that our friendship was betrayed
Friend not inanimate – though stocks & stones
There are & many formed of flesh & bones   30
Thou owned a language by which hearts are stirred
Deeper then by a feeling cloathed in words
& speakest now whats known of every tongue
Language of pity & the force of wrong
What cant assumes what hypocrites will dare   35
Speaks home to truth & shows it what they are
I see a picture which thy fate displays
& learn a lesson from thy destiny
Self interest saw thee stand in freedoms ways
So thy old shadow must a tyrant be   40
Thoust heard the knave abusing those in power
Bawl freedom loud & then opress the free
Thoust sheltered hypocrites in many a shower
That when in power would never shelter thee
Thoust heard the knave supply his canting powers   45
With wrongs illusions when he wanted friends
That bawled for shelter when he lived in showers
& when clouds vanished made thy shade amends
With axe at root he felled thee to the ground
& barked of freedom – O I hate the sound   50

Time hears its visions speak & age sublime
Had made thee a deciple unto time
– It grows the cant term of enslaving tools
To wrong another by the name of right
It grows the liscence of oerbearing fools   55
To cheat plain honesty by force of might
Thus came enclosure – ruin was its guide
But freedoms clapping hands enjoyed the sight
Though comforts cottage soon was thrust aside
& work house prisons raised upon the scite   60
Een natures dwellings far away from men
The common heath became the spoilers prey
The rabbit had not where to make his den
& labours only cow was drove away
No matter – wrong was right & right was wrong   65
& freedoms bawl was sanction to the song
– Such was thy ruin music making elm
The rights of freedom was to injure thine
As thou wert served so would they overwhelm
In freedoms name the little that is mine   70
& there are knaves that brawl for better laws
& cant of tyranny in stronger powers
Who glut their vile unsatiated maws
& freedoms birthright from the weak devours

THE REFORMERS HYMN

Reformers of old England support a kingdoms claim
Nor leagued with cunning knavery grow infamous in fame
Dishonour not the land where proud freedoms rights was born
Nor let your boast of knowledge now be lost in utter scorn
Stand up & with the honest few a noble cause pursue   5
The sun itself doth blush at deeds that some reformers do
Our king he hoists his standard & the lion is his sign
& who would shame his colours in a mutiny to join

Hail ye no tempting trickerys by tyrant hands unfurled
Who while they rave for liberty forge chains for all the world   10
Our king is freedoms pilot then muster at the helm
& stand against all wrongs that all rights would overwhelm
Prepare ye for the danger & the danger will be past
Though interest leaguing mutineers are watching at the mast
Our nationall reform of red white & blue   15
Is unfurled to the breeze & its motto is 'the true'

Our kings insulting enemies – are they the peoples friends
Do we think that freedoms tyrants will make her sons amends
Do we look or hope for any good that such reformers do
No no they hate the symbol whose motto is 'the true'   20
Our hearts are all for peace & our lion is at lair
But knaves who would rouse him had better beware
While the king is on our side all his enemies we scorn
For the tares & the thistles will be weeded from the corn

Our union shall baffle all our foes in the end   25
& our honesty erase all suspicions in a friend
Our freedom is our birth right & shall each pleading knave
Blind our enlightened reason that freedom to enslave
No – firesides shall be parliments our cottages be towers
Ere wrong shall cheat us of the rights our king declares as ours 30
Appealing to the people he makes their cause his own
& honesty & loyalty will rally round the throne

Self interest may plunge into dark mutiny
But thats no example for you or for me
We'll do no wrong to enemies to make ourselves amends   35
Deeds that disgrace our loyalty would injure all our friends
For honour is their pledge & if least their number be
The brook will run to rivers & the rivers flow a sea
& so reform shall flourish into oceans at the end
So heres success to england & every honest friend   40

& heres a health to ministers for noble men they be
& to our king the sailor though the bumper flowed a sea
If our thirst could match our loyalty that ocean we would drain
& when reform is past & won we'll fill the bowl again
Our flag is englands union thats weathered wind & storm   45
So up & join the banner & your victorys 'Reform'
For never did a king before such noble rights mentain
Then fill the bumper flowing oer – & heres his health again

[UP HONESTY A VOTE OF THANKS]

Up honesty a vote of thanks
Oft bounces in thy name
So many draws upon thy banks
Thou'lt be the looseing game
Then up & give the world its due   5
& take thy own conscerns
Leave cheats a beggars road to go
& labour all it earns

Theres some may pity want of course
& shake their heads to see't   10
Because wealth journeys on his horse
& labours on his feet
But labour caring not a jot
Would rather walk then ride
Pitys the whining beggars lot   15
& toil his honest pride

Though hard & stubborn is his toil
Want is as stubborn too
Though he but gathers from the soil
Small gains he makes it do   20
He sings old ballads oer his gains
& if his earning's scant
He works in silence nor complains
Of want untill he wants

See yonder stubborn lump of flesh   25
That sings behind his spade
His joys are ever new & fresh
As soon as labours paid
He wears his house upon his head
For so he calls his hat   30
& wether straw or feather bed
It never matters what

193

& thou'rt a feather in his cap
He neither begs or steals
But oftentimes to stop a gap   35
A ragged garb consceals
Credit with him will keep no kin
& toils his only brother
& luck is sure to sing & win
While one day keeps another   40

The ditcher squashes in the dyke
But p[i]ty keep thy grief
Some begs & pride thinks both alike
But toil wants no relief
Come honesty with open heart   45
The hate of cant & pride
& take with toil his humble part
& he wants nought beside

His tale although a tale of facts
None heeds save common sense   50
Cant steals behind its godly tacks
To pick up pitys pence
Stand honesty on labours side
He'll toil from morn till night
Sooner then beg the scorn of pride   55
If he got guineas by't

Knaves may their beggars wages give
& thrive on knaverys plan
Up honesty let labour live
On wages like a man   60
Up & if knaves will be the knave
To cheat thee to thy face
Then making freemen of the slave
Leave such to take their place

For great dogs they will beat the small   65
By main strength any day
His hungry tooth lays claim to all
That falls in t'others way
He picks & may be drops the bone
The t'other creeps to steal   70
But dare not use it as his own
& crouching to consceal
Himself in hedge or dyke alone
He grinds his offal meal

Theres law that ought to be thy own   75
Half brother sticks to gain
So close he's even lawless grown
& justice pleads in vain
If but a pound beyond his purse
Debt gets on credits list   80
Then up he bounces & by force
Takes both the toll & grist

Theres some that run a score of pounds
Nigh bothered out of breath
Credit & cant those public hounds   85
Will bark his wants to death
While some will run to thousands long
& still get credits vote
& then agen give sale the song
& change it like a coat   90

Consciet keeps young with tricks of gold
Like wind pufft feather struts
While poverty infirm & old
Stands pecking in the ruts
One on a fine horse sits that kicks   95
With o'er fed heaps of corn
The other bending oer his sticks
Puts up with every scorn

At whom the dogs bolts out to bark
& grins with jealous eye 100
But knows his manners in the dark
& lets consciet go bye
But let us hope to see the day
When thou'lt thy friends protect
Nor go a beggar by the way 105
With sneering disrespect

It hurts my heart to see thee go
The jest of every way
For bye & bye there'll cunning crow
Thy very name away 110
He'll treat thee just as interests suit
To be for gain the guide
& thou wilt wander lone & mute
A shadow by his side

He'll clad thee in his cast off rags 115
& thy own dress preserve
To win his tricks & fill his bags
& leave thy self to starve
Where debt may owe a little sum
He'll soon increase the lot 120
& keep thy name beneath his thumb
For what it owes thee not

Knaves cheat oerburthend debts & pack
For things he never saw
A load of charges on his back 125
& famish him with law
Tis oft a game at pitch & toss
Where doubt stands by to win
But debt is sure of meeting loss
& hardly keeps his skin 130

Deception bears upon thy track
To get thee into thrall
& hunts thee with a mouthing pack
That makes thee pay for all
But should those turn ought out for proof 135
To make accounts for pelf
Lord how the rascal keeps aloof
& tryes to eat himself

He turns his text another way
To pull his cunning through 140
But proof thou bull dog lug away
& bite him black & blue
If thou art weak bad luck's for thee
If strong thoult blunder bye
The web that keeps the spider free 145
Is sure to catch the flie

It grieves me oft to see thee wear
Old garments out at knee
& lord how cunning turns to stare
Thy ragged lot to see 150
Well clad himself in favour high
With all to eat & wear
Theres not a thing to profit bye
But he will have a share

Up honesty on cunnings track 155
Nor leave him room to win
He'll sell thy coat from off thy back
& strip thee to thy skin
So up & stir thy honest shanks
Theres cunnings got thy name 160
& draws his bills on all thy banks
& poaches on thy game

Theres reeling noise goes brawling bye
A knave & drunkard both
Who neer thinks honour stands so high   165
As when it swears an oath
But honesty thou'rt not the man
To kick the burthened ass
He gets spends shuffles as he can
But little knaves may pass   170

& poverty to keep alive
May limp an harmless leg
& though religion whiles she thrives
May care not who may beg
Yet keep thou hard on cunnings heels   175
& when they would purloin
Toils gains – see who the trick consceals
& pay him in his coin

For honesty I tell thee plain
A secret in a crowd   180
Knaves have a sort of liscence ta'en
& brag it out aloud
& business with his chinking fob
Ne'er goes to buy or sell
But thou art sworn to strike the job   185
& make the bargain well

He brings thee in to back a lie
& swear truth into drill
& barefaced profit higgles bye
Till both can have their will   190
Honour now jest of cunning wit
Is glad to keep unknown
For cunnings cloaths so well can fit
She swears the dress her own

198

Then up that falshood mayn't be true   195
Nor wrong be taen for right
That honest toil may have its due
& honour keep its right
Then up nor let the case grow worse
But take thy throne agen   200
Give cunnings self the empty purse
& thou be king of men

There was & is & still will be
The world that bustles bye
The rich the poor enslaved & free   205
To hope enjoy & die
But honesty thy humble mind
& peace thy quiet friend
Thy own reward of joy shall find
& live where these shall end   210

[THOU POVERTY WHEN PAST THY HELP]

Thou poverty when past thy help
Thy school's a bitter school
Chelpt at by every cocking whelp
& scorned by every fool
The scorn that pride intends should sting   5
Thy helpless eye must see
The stone that folly dares to fling
Is sure to aim at thee

Birds find a bush to build a nest
& weeds find room to flower   10
Where beast find peace to feed & rest
In sunshine & in shower
But poverty of lot severe
The meeanest knave can harm
Shoved here & there & every where   15
& always in the storm

Theres politics a brawling jade
Claps hope upon the back
& make[s] with mobs a mort of trade
Who listen to her clack   20
Theres daring animosity
Vents words of strife & mock
& blustering anger bullys bye
With pistol on the cock

But soon as tax unclasps his clutch   25
& right from wrong is won
Promise that paid thy ears so much
Now sees as little done
The strife to get & strife to keep
Made all the fight & fray   30
– When plenty has her corn to reap
Thourt never in the way

Her sermons speeches & protests
From texts as various rung
Are but so many earnest jests   35
Or interests said or sung
Peace harping plenty loud & long
& brawling hopes about
Left honesty an undersong
Scarce whispered in the rout   40

Poor honours on a dirty road
Where small knaves run him down
Cunning claims pounds he never owed
& rings it through the town
Mock honesty to gild the pill   45
With dates each claim surrounds
& farthings oath the rascals bill
To answer for the pounds

The world looks on him & his care
As nobody was near   50
& every rogue with mocks to spare
In passing leaves a sneer
But hard enough his back bears all
That scorn or pride lays on
He feels somtimes that they may fall   55
In ways that he has gone

[GOOD MORNING TO YE HONEST SWAIN]

Good morning to ye honest swain
Said one in garb of grey
Good morning tother said again
& journeyed on the way
One dropt opinions on the times   5
Stray words that suited well
Till both talked more then any ryhmes
Can go the length to tell

One had a budget at his back
That kept the world in awe   10
Oer bakers scales & farmers sack
He had the honest law
The alehouse mugs & grocers weights
He often finds em scant
& could he keep knaves tallys streight   15
Theyred many thrive that want

The other on his shoulder bore
A pecker & a spade
& shabby was the coat he wore
For labour was his trade   20
His coat was buttoned oer to hide
Holes which the thorns had rent

For he had still a spark of pride
To make the best of want

The wind blew oer the naked lands   25
Where paths led oer the farm
One in his pockets hid his hands
& tother knocked 'em warm
One bent a broad brimmed hat beneath
Nor feared the winds that blew   30
Though it lay full in tothers teeth
& seemed to nip him through

I think I surely know your face
You may the tother said
Though years have gone since in this place   35
I ever put my head
The king he bids God speed me well
To search in all complaints
& where I go I cannot tell
Whats come of all the saints   40

God bless you Sir nor more can I
Its all at pitch & toss
Ye may be poor as well as I
& living by the loss
Why neighbour as to that its true   45
Im banged by many a clutch
I would th[r]ive on an honest due
But some they want too much

& if I bid them hold their hand
They call me morts of names   50
But Im at I spy round the land
& up to all their games
& if I get them under hand
As sure as Im alive
I'll let the honest understand   55
That they alone shall thrive

God bless your name Ive not the pelf
In ale your healths to greet
But if its honesty himself
I een could dance to see't   60
They give me eigh[t] pence by the day
& make it up at night
With six pence more of parish pay
& can ye call it right

Im going to justice just to see   65
What she will have to say
& feth I doubt I shall not see
Your honour there today
No friend I am a faithful mate
To justice but ye mean   70
Whats may be named the majistrate
& there Im never seen

God bless your greeting g'i's your hand
I little thought to see
Your honour at my elbow stand   75
To break the ice for me
For do you see my name is toil
Im looked on by the knaves
As loss or profit on the soil
& treated next to slaves   80

& as for me your honour sees
I have no chance to thrive
Knaves for my debts charge what they please
I scar[c]e can keep alive
Theyll conjure shillings into pounds   85
Where credit runs a bill
& hunt ye like a pack of hounds
To get it – that they will

Shillings grow pounds where debts are due
Your honest blood would chill 90
To hear 'em swear em farthings true
When Im to pay the bill

Sure as these tools are what they are
Thats peckers & a spade
An honest man has not a share 95
To thrive in any trade
& as for me Im what they like
Some days shoved in a barn
& some times squashing in a dyke
& have not half I earn 100

I go to din[n]er with the lark
Behind a stubble shock
Just when the sun gets by the mark
That tells me twelve oclock
A bit of bread & little meat 105
Keeps life & soul together
But long as I get bread to eat
I never mind the weather

& jogging home when day is oer
Ive nothing much to crack 110
When tools are put behind the door
& baskets off my back
Goody my dish of paridge crumbs
Besure its wheaten bread
Yet I for meat may gnaw my thumbs 115
& so we go to bed

Theres cunning shall go any length
To hide her tricks for pelf
& rails at rogues with all her strength
As hearty as your self 120
& soon as 'eer she sees your face

She puts light weights aside
& takes your own thats no disgrace
& doesn't want to hide

She'll fill your eyes with morts of clack   125
& talk of honest gain
But the moment ye but turn your back
She'll nip & pinch again
& greedy debt if I but run
Five shillings on her slates   130
She'll make it pounds before she's done
& swear it right by dates

& as to law in any case
Ye'd better let em rob
They'll charge ye'r nose from off ye'r face   135
In profit for a job
They'd strip ye'r skin into a jail
& write away yer house
Aye sir & drain the water pail
Upon a drownded mouse   140

Aye bless ye sir so much surrounds
This laws decietful dance
A hare among a pack of hounds
May stan a better chance
For they have stopt me when Ive gone   145
To see what weights are light
& backed deceptions every one
That robs ye of your right

Why do ye say't I s[c]arce could think
Such tricks so near a jail   150
Could e'er be done – & dare they wink
To hear your honours tale
To pay the king for meat & drink
In tax is quite enough

But God defend your honour long 155
For good intents & I
Could wish ye'd go & sing your song
For such to profit bye
Theres some would have their shoes too tight
& grin with more then gout 160
If once ye brought your name to light
& blobed your errand out

Im fit to go beside myself
To hear your honour speak
For if your honour gets the pelf 165
Im sure of more a week
Ill surely gi the knaves a brush
Old man – so be at ease
For I dont care one single rush
Who I offend or please 170

Where trades they cheat the poor of weight
I owe them all a grudge
Ill set their selfish interest stra[i]ght
& leave the world to judge

Well as to me Im what I am 175
A poor oer burthened man
But honesty Ill never sham
To thrive on trickerys plan
I own yer honour we are led
To truckle when we can 180
This world would starve the king to dead
To be an honest man

So now & then Ill may be take
When going home at night
From out the hedge a rotten stake 185
The mornings fire to light
Aye bless your honour we may mourn

& ye may shake your head
But long as God sends sticks to burn
We cant be starved to dead   190

How long Ive had this coat of brown
Your honour cannot guess
Tis forty years & goodys gown
Is still her wedding dress
& what with taxes & draw backs   195
Of this & that & tother
We starve ourselves to cloath our backs
& yet cant get another

Theres straddling thrift with strouting leg
Chinks guineas in his fob   200
I know they'd force the poor to beg
& honest men to rob

But then the poor theres some indeed
I'm not a going to say't
That all are honest like their creed   205
Theres many aged mate
Who cant turn downright rogues for wealth
Who yet are often known
To use a neighbours things by stealth
As friendly as their own   210

Well bless your honour so they will
& many grows a debtor
Who never mean to pay the bill
&'s looked on all the better
We're scorned & pined & weekly teache'd   215
But your honour let me tell ye
The finest sermon ever preach[ed]
Neer filled a hungry belly

Lord if they do but smell ye out
Soon as ye get in town   220
How honest folks will brush about
To cover trickery down
In honest shops theyrell be a fray
Where weights been often dockt
There'll weights & measures run away   225
& cupboard doors get lockt

Yet surely some will by ye stand
Though mobs will cry em up
The lords & nobles of the land
Would think it scorn to stoop   230
& cheat the honest of their due
By tricks so much in vogue
If what your honour knows they knew
They'd may be smell the rogue

Theyre not the men to grind the poor   235
Or deal in cheating games
Though pedlars brawl from door to door
& call them morts of names
Theyre not the knaves a mouthing pack
Who rave in every place   240

Such overwartling angling work
As parlimental speeching
Such thrusts & cuts like turk with turk
Such praying & beseeching
Hope jumps to see the row begin   245
How he shall be befriended
But not a farthing does he win
All's nothing when he's ended

Its doused hard to tax the malt
But if ye wor to drop it 250
(Although they could catch the salt)
They'd may be scheme to stop it

Take taxes off of what they will
I never find em free
The grist gets tolled at every mill 255
Till none is left for me
Our shoes for which were foild to pay
& all upon our backs
Are just as dear in every way
As when they paid the tax 260

Theres some [will run] & make a fuss
In politics & debt
But bless ye sir whats that to us
Who've got our bread to get
Though parliment fills every week 265
The papers with their chat
We whove got bread & work to seek
Fare bad by reading that

The cows lap comes at early spring
Behind a bunch of rushes 270
& then the linnet prunes her wing
Among the leafy bushes
& Ive a hut to keep me dry
& so Gods will be done
If money tumbled from the sky 275
The poor would get at none

[KING WILLIAM YE'RE AN HONEST MAN]

King William ye're an honest man
Your Healths waste morts of drink
That speak ye all the good they can
& may be as they think
Though Ive no laureate tales to bring 5
Or radical addresses
But common wants Im fain to hing
Upon your garlands verses

Your parliment my liege may tell
Your heart we live in clover 10
But since the war cocks crowed & fell
The books but lost the covers
Tax has'nt lost a single leaf
& if ones ta'en away
Gain please your honour's such a thief 15
We've just the same to pay

These shoes that want the upper leather
Cost as much without the tax
& cloaths are doubled though the weather
Bleach the old ones off our backs 20
For what comes through ye're royal riddle
Theres many a lifted sieve
The poor mans luck they sorely diddle
That every trade may live

Theres poor oerburthened folks as me 25
With natures only teaching
Stands underneath an hedge or tree
Your majesty beseeching
To do the thing thats fair & right
So you would I never fear it 30
But talking to ones self till night
Will never make you hear it

Pride here looks on us as but muck
Scarce fit to blow its nose on
But knaves may meet with better luck   35
& get some better cloaths on
Your majesty would utter pish
Nor would I worth disparrage
But some would Sir a wooden dish
For the sake of water porridge   40

Tis not that I your worth respect
Just for the sake of riches
But that I know you'd want protect
From oerdevouring clutches
But then your highness be it known   45
That we're in such a plight
We scarce dare say our soul's our own
Much less to claim our right

We stand with tongues within our heads
& darent so much as use em   50
Theres those with whom we toil for bread
Would fancy we abuse 'em
Theres plentys harvest when it comes
That many hands engages
We dare as well go eat our thumbs   55
As stick for better wages

Theres young consciet so high & saucy
Twould turn you sick to see't
Prances his gelding down the causey
& frights folks down the street   60

Your majesty near saw the weather
That brings that stormy hussy care
That bangs poor folks for years together
& makes them worser then they are
O shes the worst tongue banging blether   65

Nor cares for gospel nor for law
& tye her to the strongest tether
She'll break it like a single straw

Ive had her jaw for years together
& at her elbow many a storm   70
Has made me grate my teeth together
She trod my toes as on a worm
& yet bin forced to gern & bide it
Anger & insults any how
Theres little joy for toil provided   75
Care drives & trouble holds the plough

But could I once get level handed
& whipe old scores from book & slate
& see the taxes all disbanded
We shouldnt starve at any rate   80
Theres debt I'd turn a saucey nose on't
& pray wherever he may range
He'd cares bad shilling so dispose on't
That cheats may get her in their change

God help poor creatures reckoned slaves   85
Thats dosed with i[n]dian syrrup
Those living horsing blocks for knaves
To step in fortunes stirrup
Theres flattery that common prayer
That kneels to wor[l]dly riches   90
Where ever wealth has much to spare
She thrives like clumps of twitches

Youd think they would [not] take such pains
The poor to cheat & cuff
Theres summot comes of honest gains   95
But that i'n't half enough
Such as your honour doesnt go
To even take the trouble

To see who cheats you but we know
Our wants are cheated double   100

& then with better times to sham us
Your highness as a many think
They opened beer shops that would cram us
With any bad excuse for drink
So bad that many think the trick   105
Would benefit the more
If you on taxes tally stick
Would knotch it as before

& much I fear that honest day
'll never get to come   110
When what a poor man has to say
Will find the king at home
& if it should I fear so long
Ere want picks up her crumbs
She'll be worn out with morts of wrong   115
& dead before it comes

[THE LAMENT OF SWORDY WELL]

Peti[ti]oners are full of prayers
To fall in pitys way
But if her hand the gift forbears
Theyll sooner swear then pray
They're not the worst to want who lurch 5
On plenty with complaints
No more then those who go to church
Are eer the better saints

I hold no hat to beg a mite
Nor pick it up when thrown 10
No limping leg I hold in sight
But pray to keep my own
Where profit gets his clutches in
Theres little he will leave
Gain stooping for a single pin 15
Will stick it on his sleeve

For passers bye I never pin
No troubles to my breast
Nor carry round some names to win
More money from the rest 20
Im swordy well a piece of land
Thats fell upon the town
Who worked me till I couldnt stand
& crush me now Im down

In parish bonds I well may wail 25
Reduced to every shift
Pity may grieve at troubles tale
But cunning shares the gift
Harvests with plenty on his brow
Leaves losses taunts with me 30
Yet gain comes yearly with the plough
& will not let me be

Alas dependance thou'rt a brute
Want only understands
His feelings wither branch & root   35
That falls in parish hands
The muck that clouts the ploughmans shoe
The moss that hides the stone
Now Im become the parish due
Is more then I can own   40

Though Im no man yet any wrong
Some sort of right may seek
& I am glad if een a song
Gives me the room to speak
Ive got among such grubbling geer   45
& such a hungry pack
If I brought harvests twice a year
They'd bring me nothing back

When war their tyrant prices got
I trembled with alarms   50
They fell & saved my little spot
Or towns had turned to farms
Let profit keep an humble place
That gentry may be known
Let pedigrees their honours trace   55
& toil enjoy its own

The silver springs grown naked dykes
Scarce own a bunch of rushes
When grain got high the tasteless tykes
Grubbed up trees banks & bushes   60
& me they turned me inside out
For sand & grit & stones
& turned my old green hills about
& pickt my very bones

These things that claim my own as theirs　　　　65
Where born but yesterday
But ere I fell to town affairs
I were as proud as they
I kept my horses cows & sheep
& built the town below　　　　70
Ere they had cat or dog to keep
& then to use me so

Parish allowance gaunt & dread
Had it the earth to keep
Would even pine the bees to dead　　　　75
To save an extra keep
Prides workhouse is a place that yields
From poverty its gains
& mines a workhouse for the fields
A starving the remains　　　　80

The bees flye round in feeble rings
& find no blossom bye
Then thrum their almost weary wings
Upon the moss & die
Rabbits that find my hills turned oer　　　　85
Forsake my poor abode
They dread a workhouse like the poor
& nibble on the road

If with a clover bottle now
Spring dares to lift her head　　　　90
The next day brings the hasty plough
& makes me miserys bed
The butterflyes may wir & come
I cannot keep em now
Nor can they bear my parish home　　　　95
That withers on my brow

No now not een a stone can lie
Im just what eer they like
My hedges like the winter flye
& leave me but the dyke   100
My gates are thrown from off the hooks
The parish thorough fare
Lord he thats in the parish books
Has little wealth to spare

I couldnt keep a dust of grit   105
Nor scarce a grain of sand
But bags & carts claimed every bit
& now theyve got the land
I used to bring the summers life
To many a butterflye   110
But in oppressions iron strife
Dead tussocks bow & sigh

Ive scarce a nook to call my own
For things that creep or flye
The beetle hiding neath a stone   115
Does well to hurry bye
Stock eats my struggles every day
As bare as any road
He's sure to be in somthings way
If eer he stirs abroad   120

I am no man to whine & beg
But fond of freedom still
I hang no lies on pitys peg
To bring a gris[t] to mill
On pitys back I neednt jump   125
My looks speak loud alone
My only tree they've left a stump
& nought remains my own

My mossy hills gains greedy hand
& more then greedy mind 130
Levels into a russet land
Nor leaves a bent behind
In summers gone I bloomed in pride
Folks came for miles to prize
My flowers that blo[o]med no where beside 135
& scarce believed their eyes

Yet worried with a greedy pack
They rend & delve & tear
The very grass from off my back
Ive scarce a rag to wear 140
Gain takes my freedom all away
Since its dull suit I wore
& yet scorn vows I never pay
& hurts me more & more

Who ever pays me rent or takes it 145
Ive neither words or dates
One makes the law & others break it
& stop my mouth with rates

& should the price of grain get high
Lord help & keep it low 150
I shant possess a single flye
Or get a weed to grow
I shant possess a yard of ground
To bid a mouse to thrive
For gain has put me in a pound 155
I scarce can keep alive

Im not a man as some may think
Peti[ti]oning for loss
Of cow that dyed of ages drink
& spavin foundered horse 160
For which some beg a list of pelf
& seem on loss to thrive

But I petition for my self
& beg to keep alive

Theres folks that make a mort of bother 165
& oer lost gainings whine
But lord of me Im this & tother
Theres no one cares for mine
They strip the grass from off my back
& take my things away 170
Im robbed by every outlaw pack
& nones to say em nay

I own Im poor like many more
But then the poor mun live
& many came for miles before 175
For what I had to give
But since I fell upon the town
They pass me with a sigh
Ive scarce the room to say sit down
& so they wander bye 180

The town that brought me in disgrace
Have got their tales to say
I ha'n't a friend in all the place
Save one & he's away
A grubbling man with much to keep 185
& nought to keep em on
Found me a bargain offered cheap
& so my peace was gone

But when a poor man is allowed
So to enslave another 190
Well may the worlds tongue prate aloud
How brother uses brother
I couldnt keep a bush to stand
For years but what was gone
& now I hant a foot of land 195
To keep a rabbit on

They used to come & feed at night
When dangers day was gone
& in the morning out of sight
Hide underneath a stone   200

Im fain to shun the greedy pack
That now so tear & brag
They strip my coat from off my back
& scarcely leave a rag
That like the parish hurt & hurt   205
While gains new suit I wear
Then swear I never pay 'em for't
& add to my despair

Though now I seem so full of clack
Yet when yer' riding bye   210
The very birds upon my back
Are not more fain to flye
I feel so lorn in this disgrace
God send the grains to fall
I am the oldest in the place   215
& the worst served of all

Lord bless ye I was kind to all
& poverty in me
Could always find a humble stall
A rest & lodging free   220
Poor bodys with an hungry ass
I welcomed many a day
& gave him tether room & grass
& never said him nay

There was a time my bit of ground   225
Made freemen of the slave
The ass no pindard dare to pound
When I his supper gave
The gipseys camp was not affraid

I made his dwelling free   230
Till vile enclosure came & made
A parish slave of me

The gipseys further on sojourn
No parish bonds they like
No sticks I own & would earth burn   235
I shouldnt own a dyke
I am no friend to lawless work
Nor would a rebel be
& why I call a christian turk
Is they are turks to me   240

& if I could but find a friend
With no deciet to sham
Who'd send me some few sheep to tend
& leave me as I am
To keep my hills from cart & plough   245
& strife of mongerel men
& as spring found me find me now
I should look up agen

& save his Lordships woods that past
The day of danger dwell   250
Of all the fields I am the last
That my own face can tell
Yet what with stone pits delving holes
& strife to buy & sell
My name will quickly be the whole   255
Thats left of swordy well

[THOU KING OF HALF A SCORE DOMINIONS]

Thou king of half a score dominions
With laurel plaited on thy brow
How outoway are pomps opinions
Thy picture speaks it plainly now
For though I bend to pick thee up   5
I hear a proverb mutter near
That tells me any fool may stoop
& pick up nothing every where

& yet your majesty the thing
Sets me some inches higher   10
To think Im talking to a king
E'en sets my heart on fire
For do you know tis somthing grand
So poor a lot as mine
Should hold your portrait in my hand   15
Though but a copper coin

For do ye know Ive felt a pride
& stood in many a place
When I'd a shilling in my fob
To gaze upon thy face   20
& thought & told ye many things
Though treason may be such
What common people think of kings
When taxed about so much

& somtimes feeling for the slave   25
Ive got a speech by heart
How I'd shop off each cunning knave
That took the taxes part
& honesty to drink & eat
I'd have as cheap as muck   30
That every honest man might meet
With nothing else but luck

That is if I was you your self
The king upon the coin
& all the world & all the pelf   35
Your majestys & mine
But I have not a power to pledge
To drive tax from the land
I'm pleading underneath a hedge
With your copper in my hand   40

& ye're so far from pomp & strife
I fear your powers like mine
If a pint of swipes would save my life
Theres none would take the coin
& many that did so respect   45
Your name have had their day
They'd treat ye with as much neglect
& prate for better pay

Ive often seen your rosey face
Inviting passers bye   50
To enter Inns with royal grace
But now its all my eye
Theres Williams arms have ta'en your place
Oer beer shops selling swipes
Where the lion wears as sad a face   55
As if he'd got the gripes

There where laureats buckram fine addresses
With royal Js & Ts & Ds
Labelling scores of birthday verses
To thee & to thy pedigrees   60
But now this squad has sunk to mutes
That marched as in thy days of glory
I scarcely think ye've two recruits
Would even care a button for ye

& now the regiment of letters 65
This awkard squad of odds & ends
Are off & after fareing better
Left only cypher with thy friends
Theres some in odes & other metal
To Williams praises cutting capers 70
& some on frying pans & kettles
Drumming like heroes in the papers

& all to Williams praise & glory
May him nor's money never see
The sad & lamentable story 75
That fashions follys leave with thee
But Ive heard say't & mores the pity
Thou art not in that loyal town
Ye'd pass as well in london city
As any coin beneath the crown 80

Shame on the wholesale twenty four
A splawfoot bowlegged awkard pack
That once beset thy royal door
With laurel faggots on their backs
To stick thy birthdays full with praise 85
In pomp heroics strutting odes
In epigrams & laureate lays
& fulsom stuff by waggon loads

Lud could thy bit of copper speak
& answer for their taunts & mocks 90
Twould wish theyd all their bread to seek
& strip the laurel from its locks
Thou'd let the supple hussy pass
With all her chelping hollow crews
& treat her as a bunch of grass 95
Whereon to whipe your dirty shoes

[ADDRESS TO AN OLD HALFPENNY]

1
Knaves for every purpose seize on
Thy copper face tho once twas treason
Thee to disfigure but thy season
        Of grace is past
& now theres neither ryhme nor reason   5
        Can make it last

2
Tho Lords would once as comrades rank thee
& in their velvet pockets clank ye
So low have times new fashions sank ye
        Thou fortunes ghost   10
Thourt now not worth a beggars thank ye
        To say the most

3
The loyal knaves thy worth deserting
Tis all my eye & peggy Martin
Thourt an old halfpenny that[s] certain   15
        & nothing more
I couldnt pass thee for a farthing
        Thy reign is oer

4
When thou wert new each canting thing
Pretended like a wedding ring   20
To prize this head where la[u]rels hing
        Knaves would caress him
& cheats toss up & cry the king
        God bless him

5

But now my poor old copper croney   25
Thou shadow of a shade tho money
& native of wealths hive of honey
    Tho dead nor rotten
Thourt stranded where the meanest shun ye
    A wreck forgotten   30

6

The gipsey tinker man with lawless fettle
May bruise thee into brods o metal
Theres none his lawless tricks to settle
    P[eel]l G[urney]ys jiant
Though thou wert clouting C[ob]b[e]ts kettle   35
    Would not say fye ont

7

God knows the hollow sounding praises
That clamour round the country raises
The milk & water canting phrases
    Like mizers prayers   40
Are all for pensions pence & places
    Self kin & heirs

8

For where self inter[e]st seems to lag
Tho kings themselves rides flatterys nag
What once was blessings all & brag   45
    The king god bless him
Did he but wear a beggars bag
    Thered few carress him

9
Praises isnt worth een apple pareings
Where praise is looking out for fairings   50
Such as the G[ur]n[ey]s P[eel]s & B[arin]gs
    As wasps for honey
Like conjurors tricks – & such comparings
    They work for money

10
Truth as cooks dish it – boil or bake it   55
Is but an oath – how ere they make it
& wether it be clothed or naked
    A lies a lie
Self interest she can loose or brake it
    Untie or tie   60

11
The Gordian knot was like a fiddle
Where wonder gapes at diddle diddle
Till what seemed music in the middle
    To farces grow up
Self interest soon finds out the riddle   65
    & breaks the show up

[BLESS THY OLD FASHIONED COPPER FACE]

Bless thy old fashioned copper face
Tho knaves have left thee in disgrace
Who fawned for pension & for place
  While thou wert living
Tis so with all 5
  While aught is given

Feth who would trust them now adays
With honours that vain flattery pays
With saintish cant & devilish praise
  For een devotion 10
Self interests brazen face displays
  In every motion

As gods my judge tis down right pity
That that same canting brawling city
Where prayers & many a godly ditty 15
  Are sung & said
Should like Jerusalem be
  <   >

There thou wert born & met behaviour
As tho thou wert a very saviour 20
From Stemphens hatch to honest paviour
  Who cleaned the street
But now thourt like a beggar
  Im shockt to seet

But now behold my copper croney 25
New kings must een new mint their money
& thourt an out cast <   >
  & like us all
Canst find at last that flattery
  Is nought but gall 30

228

When thou wert in thy gilded <season>
To call thee aught but royal money
Were nothing else but down right treason
  & now to call the[e] any money
Would show ones head bereft of reason   35
  Naught but copper

Old knaves that could have got new places
& as new fashions find new graces
Old masks that will not suit new face[s]
  Are thrown away   40
& thoust has had thy Ascot races
  <   >

The very head of G   3rd
Wont pass for coin amid the herd
Of money mongrels – but intered   45
  With other fames
Tis scouted like a very <turd>
  Of fouler name

Well tis no wonder such the case is
Our dearest friends will get new faces   50
& what wi pensions & wi places
  <   >
Thy power is changed old copper croney
Thy power was once the hive for honey
& food for worshiphers of money   55
  <   >

DON JUAN A POEM

'Poets are born' – & so are whores – the trade is
Grown universal – in these canting days
Women of fashion must of course be ladies
& whoreing is the business – that still pays
Playhouses Ball rooms – there the masquerade is   5
– To do what was of old – & now adays
Their maids – nay wives so innocent & blooming
Cuckold their spouses to seem honest women

Milton sung Eden & the fall of man
Not woman for the name implies a wh—e   10
& they would make a ruin of his plan
Falling so often they can fall no lower
Tell me a worse delusion if you can
For innoscence – & I will sing no more
Wherever mischief is tis womans brewing   15
Created from manself – to be mans ruin

The flower in bud hides from the fading sun
& keeps the hue of beauty on its cheek
But when full blown they into riot run
The hue turns pale & lost each ruddy streak   20
So 't'is with woman who pretends to shun
Immodest actions which they inly seek
Night hides the wh—e – cupboards tart & pasty
Flora was p—x—d – & womans quite as nasty

Marriage is nothing but a driveling hoax   25
To please old codgers when they're turned of forty
I wed & left my wife like other folks
But not untill I found her false & faulty
O woman fair – the man must pay thy jokes
Such makes a husband very often naughty   30
Who falls in love will seek his own undoing
The road to marriage is – 'the road to ruin'

Love worse then debt or drink or any fate
It is the damnest smart of matrimony
A hell incarnate is a woman-mate   35
The knot is tied – & then we loose the honey
A wife is just the protetype to hate
Commons for stock & warrens for the coney
Are not more tresspassed over in rights plan
Then this incumberance on the rights of man   40

There's much said about love & more of women
I wish they were as modest as they seem
Some borrow husbands till their cheeks are blooming
Not like the red rose blush – but yellow cream
Lord what a while those good days are in coming –   45
Routs Masques & Balls – I wish they were a dream
– I wish for poor men luck – an honest praxis
Cheap food & cloathing – no corn laws or taxes

I wish – but there is little got bye wishing
I wish that bread & great coats ne'er had risen   50
I wish that there was some such word as 'pishun
For ryhme sake for my verses must be dizen
With dresses fine – as hooks with baits for fishing
I wish all honest men were out of prison
I wish M.P's. would spin less yarn – nor doubt   55
But burn false bills & cross bad taxes out

I wish young married dames were not so frisky
Nor hide the ring to make believe they're single
I wish small beer was half as good as whiskey
& married dames with buggers would not mingle   60
There's some too cunning far & some too frisky
& here I want a ryhme – so write down 'jingle'
& there's such putting in – in whores crim con
Some mouths would eat forever & eat on

Childern are fond of sucking sugar candy   65
& maids of sausages – larger the better
Shopmen are fond of good sigars & brandy
& I of blunt – & if you change the letter
To C or K it would be quite as handy
& throw the next away – but I'm your debtor   70
For modesty – yet wishing nought between us
I'd hawl close to a she as vulcan did to venus

I really cant tell what this poem will be
About – nor yet what trade I am to follow
I thought to buy old wigs – but that will kill me   75
With cold starvation – as they're beaten hollow
Long speeches in a famine will not fill me
& madhouse traps still take me by the collar
So old wig bargains now must be forgotten
The oil that dressed them fine has made them rotten   80

I wish old wigs were done with ere they're mouldy
I wish – but heres the papers large & lusty
With speeches that full fifty times they've told ye
– Noble Lord John to sweet Miss Fanny Fusty
Is wed – a lie good reader I ne'er sold ye   85
– Prince Albert goes to Germany & must he
Leave the queens snuff box where all fools are strumming
From addled eggs no chickens can be coming

Whigs strum state fiddle strings untill they snap
With cuckoo cuckold cuckoo year by year   90
The razor plays it on the barbers strap
– The sissars grinder thinks it rather quere
That labour wont afford him 'one wee drap'
Of ale or gin or half & half or beer
– I wish prince Albert & the noble dastards   95
Who wed the wives – would get the noble bastards

232

I wish prince Albert on his german journey
I wish the Whigs were out of office &
Pickled in law books of some good atorney
For ways & speeches few can understand   100
They'll bless ye when in power – in prison scorn ye
& make a man rent his own house & land –
I wish prince Alberts queen was undefiled
– & every man could get his wife with child

I wish the devil luck with all my heart   105
As I would any other honest body
His bad name passes bye me like a f—t
Stinking of brimstone – then like whisky toddy
We swallow sin which seems to warm the heart
– There's no imputing any sin to God – he   110
Fills hell with work – & is'n't it a hard case
To leave old whigs & give to hell the carcass

Me—b—ne may throw his wig to little Vicky
& so resign his humbug & his power
& she with the young princess mount the dickey   115
On ass milk diet for her german tour
Asses like ministers are rather tricky
I & the country proves it every hour
W—ll—gt—n & Me—b—ne in their station
Coblers to queens – are phisic to the nation   120

These batch of toadstools on this rotten tree
Shall be the cabinet of any queen
Though not such coblers as her servants be
They're of Gods making – that is plainly seen
Nor red nor green nor orange – they are free   125
To thrive & flourish as the Whigs have been
But come tomorrow – like the Whigs forgotten
You'll find them withered stinking dead & rotten

Death is an awfull thing it is by God
I've said so often & I think so now   130
Tis rather droll to see an old wig nod
Then doze & die the devil don't know how
Odd things are wearisome & this is odd –
Tis better work then kicking up a row
I'm weary of old Whigs & old whigs heirs   135
& long been sick of teazing God with prayers

I've never seen the cow turn to a bull
I've never seen the horse become an ass
I've never seen an old brawn cloathed in whool –
But I have seen full many a bonny lass   140
& wish I had one now beneath the cool
Of these high elms – Muse tell me where I was
O – talk of turning I've seen Whig & Tory
Turn imps of hell – & all for Englands glory

I love good fellowship & wit & punning   145
I love 'true love' & God my taste defend
I hate most damnably all sorts of cunning –
I love the Moor & Marsh & Ponders end –
I do not like the song of 'cease your funning'
I love a modest wife & trusty friend   150
– Bricklayers want lime as I want ryhme for fillups
– So here's a health to sweet Eliza Phillips

Song

Eliza now the summer tells
Of spots where love & beauty dwells
Come & spend a day with me 155
Underneath the forest tree
Where the restless water flushes
Over mosses mounds & rushes
& where love & freedom dwells
With orchis flowers & fox glove bells 160
Come dear Eliza set me free
& oer the forest roam with me

Here I see the morning sun
Among the beachtree's shadows run
That into gold the short sward turns 165
Where each bright yellow blossom burns
With hues that would his beams out shine
Yet nought can match those smiles of thine
I try to find them all the day
But none are nigh when thou'rt away 170
Though flowers bloom now on every hill
Eliza is the fairest still

The sun wakes up the pleasant morn
& finds me lonely & forlorn
Then wears away to sunny noon 175
The flowers in bloom the birds in tune
While dull & dowie all the year
No smiles to see no voice to hear
I in this forest prison lie
With none to heed my silent sigh 180
& underneath this beachen tree
With none to sigh for Love but thee

Now this new poem is entirely new
As wedding gowns or money from the mint
For all I know it is entirely true   185
For I would scorn to put a lie in print
– I scorn to lie for princes – so would you
& ere I shoot I try my pistol flint
– The cattle salesman – knows the way in trying
& feels his bullocks ere he thinks of buying   190

Lord bless me now the day is in the gloaming
& every evil thought is out of sight
How I should like to purchase some sweet woman
Or else creep in with my two wives to night –
Surely that wedding day is on the comeing   195
Abscence like phisic poisons all delight –
Mary & Martha both an evil omen
Though both my own – they still belong to no man

But to our text again – & pray where is it
Begin as parsons do at the beginning   200
Take the first line friend & you cannot miss it
'Poets are born' & so are whores for sinning
– Here's the court circular – o Lord is this it
Court cards like lists of – not the naked meaning
Here's Albert going to germany they tell us   205
& the young queen down in the dumps & jealous

Now have you seen a tramper on race courses
Seeking an honest penny as his trade is
Crying a list of all the running horses
& showing handbills of the sporting ladies   210
– In bills of fare you'll find a many courses
Yet all are innoscent as any maid is
Put these two dishes into one & dress it
& if there is a meaning – you may guess it

Don Juan was Ambassador from russia   215
But had no hand in any sort of tax
His orders hung like blossoms of the fushia
& made the ladies hearts to melt like wax
He knew Napoleon & the king of prusia
& blowed a cloud oer spirits wine or max   220
But all his profits turned out losses rather
To save one orphan which he forced to father

Theres Docter Bottle imp who deals in urine
A keeper of state prisons for the queen
As great a man as is the Doge of Turin   225
& save in London is but seldom seen
Yclep'd old All—n – mad brained ladies curing
Some p—x—d like Flora & but seldom clean
The new road oer the forest is the right one
To see red hell & further on the white one   230

Earth hells or b—gg—r sh—ps or what you please
Where men close prisoners are & women ravished
I've often seen such dirty sights as these
I've often seen good money spent & lavished
To keep bad houses up for docters fees   235
& I have known a b—gg—rs tally travers'd
Till all his good intents began to falter
– When death brought in his bill & left the halter

O glorious constitution what a picking
Ye've had from your tax harvest & your tythe   240
Old hens which cluck about that fair young chicken
– Cocks without spurs that yet can crow so blythe
Truth is shut up in prison while ye're licking
The gold from off the gingerbread – be lythe
In winding that patched broken old state clock up   245
Playhouses open – but mad houses lock up

237

Give toil more pay where rank starvation lurches
& pay your debts & put your books to rights
Leave whores & playhouses & fill your churches
Old clovenfoot your dirty victory fights   250
Like theft he still on natures manor poaches
& holds his feasting on anothers rights
To show plain truth you act in bawdy farces
Men show their tools – & maids expose their arses

Now this day is the eleventh of July   255
& being sunday I will seek no flaw
In man or woman – but prepare to die
In two days more I may that ticket draw
& so may thousands more as well as I
To day is here – the next who ever saw   260
& In a madhouse I can find no mirth pay
– Next tuesday used to be Lord Byrons birthday

Lord Byron poh – the man wot rites the werses
& is just what he is & nothing more
Who with his pen lies like the mist disperses   265
& makes all nothing as it was before
Who wed two wives & oft the truth rehearses
& might have had some twenty thousand more
Who has been dead so fools their lies are giving
& still in Allens madhouse caged & living   270

If I do wickedness to day being sunday
Can I by hearing prayers or singing psalms
Clear off all debts twixt god & man on monday
& lie like an old hull that dotage calms
& is there such a word as Abergundy   275
I've read that poem called the 'Isle of Palms'
– But singing sense pray tell me if I can
Live an old rogue & die an honest man

I wish I had a quire of foolscap paper
Hot pressed – & crowpens – how I could endite   280
A silver candlestick & green wax taper
Lord bless me what fine poems I would write
The very tailors they would read & caper
& mantua makers would be all delight
Though laurel wreaths my brows did ne'er environ   285
I think myself as great a bard as Byron

I have two wives & I should like to see them
Both by my side before another hour
If both are honest I should like to be them
For both are fair & bonny as a flower   290
& one o Lord – now do bring in the tea mem
Were bards pens steamers each of ten horse power
I could not bring her beautys fair to weather
So I've towed both in harbour blest together

Now i'n't this canto worth a single pound   295
From anybodys pocket who will buy
As thieves are worth a halter I'll be bound
Now honest reader take the book & try
& if as I have said it is not found
I'll write a better canto bye & bye   300
So reader now the money till unlock it
& buy the book & help to fill my pocket

LONDON *VERSUS* EPPING FOREST

The brakes, like young stag's horns, come up in Spring,
And hide the rabbit holes and fox's den;
They crowd about the forest everywhere;
The ling and holly-bush, and woods of beach,
With room enough to walk and search for flowers;   5
Then look away and see the Kentish heights.
Nature is lofty in her better mood,
She leaves the world and greatness all behind;
Thus London, like a shrub among the hills,
Lies hid and lower than the bushes here.   10
I could not bear to see the tearing plough
Root up and steal the Forest from the poor,
But leave to freedom all she loves, untamed,
The Forest walk enjoyed and loved by all !

[LAND OF PERPETUAL SUMMER ITALY]

Land of perpetual summer Italy
Land of the golden City of the sun
Cradle of Europes Empire – but for thee
The rest were darkness & perpetual dun
Celestial clime & garden of the sun   5
Country of Virgil Hessiod – once the free
Latium & Greece both kingdoms of the sun
Their infant cradles rocked by Liberty
& still the sunniest Land is Italy

Greece Land of Homer & the muses fire   10
How nations read & kindle at thy name
The freemans sword the poets native lyre
Have filled thy history with a classic fame
& is not Greece that Land of Isles the same

The sun shines oer its freedom & wars cease   15
The despots chains near made it stoop to shame
Its hills & classic sky's repose in peace
& freedom owns it as the soil of Greece

TO LIBERTY

1
O spirit of the wind and sky;
Where doth thy harp neglected lie ?
Is there no heart thy bard to be,
To wake that soul of melody;
Is liberty herself a slave ?   5
No God forbids it, On ye brave;

2
I've loved thee, as the common air,
And paid thee worship every where;
In every soil beneath the sun,
Thy simple song, my heart has won;   10
And art thou silent ! still a slave ?
And thy son's living; On ye brave.

3
Gather on mountain, and on plain,
Make gossamer the iron chain,
Make prison walls as paper screen,   15
That tyrant maskers may be seen;
Let earth, as well as heaven be free,
So, on ye brave for liberty.

4
I've loved thy being from a boy,
The highland hills was once my joy;   20
Then morning mists did round them lie,
Like sunshine in the happiest sky.
Her hills, and valleys, seemed my own,
When Scottish land was freedom's throne.

5
And Scottish land is freedom's still;   25
Her beacon fires on every hill,
Have told in characters of flame,
Her ancient birthright, and her fame;
A thousand hills will speak again,
In fire, that language ever plain.   30

6
To sychop[h]ants, and fawning knaves,
That Scotland, ne'er was made for slaves. –
Her fruitful vales, her mountain thrones,
Are ruled by natures laws alone:
And nought but falshoods poisoned breath,   35
Will urge the Claymore from its sheath.

7
O spirit of the wind and sky,
Where doth thy harp neglected lie;
Is there no heart thy bard to be,
To wake that soul of melody;   40
Is liberty herself a slave,
No God forbids it – on ye brave !

July 9th 1844

LOVE OF LIBERTY

1
Bless't is the man with mind erect –
That seeks no rise that fears no fall
For freedoms love shall him protect
And having nothing leaves him all
There liberty is ever free   5
Knowing that such a love must be

2
'Tis Adam's love for Adam's kin
That Eden of earths Liberty
That triumphs over death and sin
And will in natures love be free   10
'Twas so when this our world begun
Love – bright and lasting as the sun

3
Free bonds that knit the son and sire
The daughter and the mother too
The links of heavens eternal fire   15
Which death and hell can ne'er undo
The love of Liberty is free
Feeling that such a love must be

4
I bear my fate – but no misdeeds
Has ever been my minds disgrace   20
But like the corn above the weeds
I make earths home my dwelling place
Love Liberty and think I'm free
For Freedom's love is all to me –

Feby 14th/47

243

THE THISTLE

1
I love the thistle with its ruddy flowers
It cheers me on the waste in lonely hours
It cheers me in lone sunshine out of doors
When seeking solitude on rushy moores
It cheers me resting on the way-side stones 5
Where tears of morning glitter on the thorns
I love the thistle 'tis an ill used flower
And bees are singing round for many an hour

2
I love the thistle and its prickles too
Cobwebs are round it with a veil of dew 10
I love the thistle where it bravely stands
For rights of Liberty in many lands
Simply defying every rogueish eye
With 'wha dare meddle wi me' that passes bye
My right is simple, blooming 'mong the flowers 15
That God's hand scatters on this land of ours

3
So I love the thistles spread round Scottish bowers
Better than any other of the wildling flowers
I love the warrior thistle where it stands
Though often wounded in the legs and hands 20
On Bannockburn its bloom undaunted stood
Dy'd deeper in the streams of human blood

Feby 13th/47

THE SONGS OF OUR LAND

The Songs of our land are they not worth reviving
To sing o'er brown stout by the English fire side
They are national links 'gainst deception contriving
That spread over oceans & lands far and wide
They sing of our homes which great heroe's have bled for   5
And the child o'er its horn book doth well understand
That its birth's not a slavery which it learns to abhor
Thro reading & singing the songs of his land

The Songs of the land sing of Englishmans freedom
The songs of our land cheer the hearts that are true   10
While they've voices to sing or fond hearts to read em
And heroes to guard them in scarlet or blue
The songs of our land are made for our comfort
While on settles or chairs by our cottage fireside
A fig for your priestcraft I'd give not a crumb for't   15
A priest-ridden nation I ne'er could abide

The Songs of our land are like ancient landmarks
And curs'd be the traitor who takes one away
Would man sell his birthright to literal land sharks
And leave home & friends to the stranger a prey   20
We'll have nought o' the kind brace the nerves & be steady
The one in bright scarlet the other true blue
Let the foe come & welcome we're all waiting ready
Rose, Thistle and Shamrock united are true

HERES A HEALTH TO SCOTLAND

Heres a health to bonny Scotland and the land o the west
Heres a health to bonny Scotland as the land I loo the best
I've a love for the mountain and the freedom o the flood
And the bonny sight o Highland hills it does my spirits good
Heres a love for bonny lasses and a health for honest men 5
The dwellers on the mountains and the tenants o' the glen
I've drank old Scotlands health and I mean to do it still
And my own hearts bluid for liberty is left upon yon hill –

Where the boldest men have conquered and freedom truly won
Upon the Scottish mountains beneath a glorious sun 10
I've done it ance or twice for that highly favored land
And I'll do it ance agen wi my claymore in my hand
And charge wi all her chivalry the flower o Highlan men
And the bonnet and the Thistle shall cross the Tweed agen
Shall cross the Tweed for liberty and leave the English free 15
For her union is the roses & I'll never spoil the tree

So here's a health to Scotland o' the whiskey gill
And may her claymore ne'er be drawn for honest body's ill
When the bayonets on the musket and the claymore from the
    sheath
Let each stroke be for Liberty for guilty tyrants death 20
His bluid shall stain the heather who our Scottish right defames
And Bannockburn is living still that tyrant felon shames
So here's a health to Scotland the freest of the free
Her ain laws are the bible which speaks of Liberty

Notes

Helpstone

This was the first poem in Clare's first collection, *Poems Descriptive of Rural Life and Scenery* (1820). The introduction to that volume declared that it was written 'before he was seventeen', i.e. before July 1810, though as one reader pointed out this is not consistent with the reference in line 52 to 'twenty lingering years'. It is likely that Clare worked on the poem over a number of years.

Lines 125–34. These lines were omitted from the fourth edition of *Poems Descriptive*; they had been much disliked by Clare's patrons Lord Radstock and Mrs Emmerson as expressing 'Radical and ungrateful sentiments' (Mark Storey (ed.), *Clare: The Critical Heritage* [London and Boston: Routledge & Kegan Paul, 1973], p. 61). Stephen Colclough notes the use of the plural in these lines ('our loss ...') and argues that they 'directly echo the voices of alienation found in the early fragmentary poems, such as 'labour and luxury', because they speak from the collective position of labour' (Colclough, p. 36).

Waterloo

The battle of Waterloo occurred on 18 June 1815; there is no evidence for the date of this poem, not published in Clare's lifetime, but presumably it was written soon after the event.

Lines 1, 6. As Poet Laureate, Robert Southey (1774–1843) could be expected to commemorate the victory in verse, as he did in *The Poet's Pilgrimage to Waterloo* (1816). Robert Bloomfield (1766–1823), whom Clare regarded as an important predecessor in what he considered true pastoral poetry, is a less likely celebrant of triumphant nationalism.

On seeing a Lost Greyhound in winter lying upon the snow in the fields

This exercise in fashionable sentiment, published in *Poems Descriptive of Rural Life and Scenery* (1820), allows Clare to register a protest about the treatment that labourers could expect.

Line 18: The comparison between English labourers and negro slaves is a common theme in protest at this period; see 'One monday morning sour & loath' (p. 17), 'Thy eye can witness more then others', lines 19–20 (p. 15). For Clare's view of slavery see his letter to [Thomas Pringle], [after 8 Feb. 1832] (p. 323).

Lines 25–32: Clare uses the traditional language of the Great Chain of Being.

Elegy ... In the Ruins of Pickworth Rutland

This poem, dated by Clare to 1818 and included in *Poems Descriptive of Rural Life and Scenery* (1820), is an early exercise (on a consciously small scale) on the theme of 'Triumphs of Time', explicitly invoked here as a response to social inequality.

Lines 25–8: These lines appeared from the second edition of *Poems Descriptive* onward.

[Labour and Luxury]

In his autobiographical notes Clare wrote: 'I only regret the loss of one of my early poems a sort of Pastoral the title was 'labour and luxury' the plan was a labourers going to his work one morning overheard a lean figure [accosted] in a taunting manner by a bloated stranger the phantom of luxury whence the dialogue ensues labour makes its complaints and the other taunts and jeers him till the lean figure turns away in dispair' (*JCBH*, p. 64). This is followed by what Clare's editors call two alternative endings: 'when the phantom of liberty in[s]tantly appears to cheer the lean figure with prophetic' and 'when the bloated pha[n]tom shrinks from its presence and fades away' (p. 297, n. 60), though this is probably a single ending in which the phantom of Luxury is abashed by the appearance of the phantom of Liberty. Despite Clare's regret, this fragment of his eclogue does survive, containing part of the address of Labour (Clare's 'lean figure'), addressed either to the phantom of Liberty or to the labourer who witnesses the scene. It is written on a sheet that contains a draft for 'Elegy ... In the Ruins of Pickworth Rutland', which Clare dated to 1818, the probable date for this fragment too. In content, form and style this early poem is a striking anticipation of poems that Clare was to write over a decade later in Pet. MS A59, particularly 'Good morning to ye honest swain' (see pp. 201–9).

Line 21: parsons

Lobin Clouts Satirical Sollilouquy on the Times

The heavy dialect of this poem is probably intended to distance Clare as author from the opinions expressed by 'Lobin Clout'; it was not published in Clare's lifetime. Stephen Colclough observes: 'Clare does not often use dialect as the main voice of a text, and when it appears in other texts it forms a kind of double voice used to mark the speaker as other. ... Because this voice is at one remove from that of the author ... the poem is recording the voice of the labourer, rather than speaking it. Through this strategy the poem is able to inhabit the official language and culture and explore the possibility of using dialect to give voice to the alienated labourer' (Colclough, p. 17).

Line 9: Damn carcass god soul
Line 12: devil
Line 14: wooden jacket, i.e. coffin
Line 15: maggots humour suck
Line 16: podgey swilling tub
Line 27: Clare has written 'gamlely'.

Line 33: damned rogues beggar
Line 35: scabbed-arsed-sheep
Line 39: damned roguish

[One monday morning sour & loath]
This epigram or fragment, unpublished in Clare's lifetime, cannot be dated with any certainty. It reflects the point made by radicals like Cobbett that English labourers were treated worse than slaves in the colonies, and that the sympathy of middle-class abolitionists would be better directed nearer home.

[O thrice lucky town (the more lucky poor creatu'rs)]
The occasion and date of this squib, unpublished in Clare's lifetime, is not known. The town is probably Stamford and the great Lord mentioned the Marquis of Essex; since 1809 the Tory Marquis's electoral interest had been challenged by an independent party, and the ostentatious charity that Clare satirises may have been intended to bolster his political influence in the town. The organ of the independent party was *Drakard's Stamford News*, whose first editor was Octavius Gilchrist, a friend of Clare who may have passed on Stamford political gossip to him.

[O freedom freedom sacred name]
The date of this early epigram, unpublished in Clare's lifetime, is not known; it anticipates Clare's scepticism about radical rhetoric in *The Parish* and 'The Fallen Elm'.

The Lamentations of Round-Oak Waters
This poem, dated '1818' by Clare in the manuscript and not published in his lifetime, anticipates interestingly the poem known as 'The Lament of Swordy Well' (see pp. 214–21). The title suggests an allusion to the lamentations of Jeremiah and implies that, like the Old Testament prophets, Clare is trying to articulate a grief that is both personal and that of a community.

A Familliar Epistle To a Friend
This poem, dated by Clare '1819', was published in *Poems Descriptive of Rural Life and Scenery* (1820), with the omission of lines 61–78.

Helpston Green
This poem, described as 'early' by Clare, was published in his second collection, *The Village Minstrel* (1821). Like 'Helpstone' and the excerpt from 'The Village Minstrel' it is an early example of Clare's 'enclosure elegies'.

The Village Minstrel, lines 924–1281
According to Northampton MS 3, the title poem of Clare's second collec-

tion was written between October 1819 and January 1820. The lines dealing with the siege of Woodrcroft Castle and Michael Hudson (not published in 1821) followed by those about the effects of the enclosure and the gypsies are extracted here. Clare's treatment of enclosure drew forth the comment 'This is radical slang' from Lord Radstock, but Clare was unrepentant: 'never mind Lord R[adstock]'s pencelings in the 'Peasant Boy' [the original title of 'The Village Minstrel'] what he dont like he must lump as the dog did his dumpling I woud not have 'There once were lanes' &c left out for all the Lord Rs in Europe' (Clare to Taylor, 9 Jan. 1821; *Letters*, p. 139).

England
Clare included this poem in a letter of 19 April 1820 to John Taylor, with the comment: 'what think you by 'England' I think I shall stand a chance for the Laureat Vacancy next time it turns out!!!!' (*Letters*, p. 51). The anxiety Clare expresses is in response to the political crisis following Peterloo in August 1819 and more specifically to the Cato Street conspiracy, an abortive radical plot to assassinate the Cabinet whose members were either executed or transported. While it is clear that Clare shares radical scepticism concerning English 'freedom' he is concerned to discountenance the kind of direct action attempted by Thistlewood and the other Cato Street conspirators (see John Lucas, *John Clare* [Plymouth: Northcote House, 1994], pp. 16–17, and P.M.S. Dawson, 'Common Sense or Radicalism? Some Reflections on Clare's Politics', *Romanticism*, 2.1 [1996], 84–5). The poem was not published in Clare's lifetime.
Epigraph: From William Cowper, *The Task* (1785), II. 206–9.

Langley Bush
This poem, published in *The Village Minstrel*, celebrates one of Clare's favourite landmarks. See also 'A Walk in the fields', lines 467–80 (*MP*, III. 392).
Line 7: 'Lord Exeter's steward ... keeps also a court-leet, at Michaelmas and Lady-day. This court, corruptly called Langley-court, was formerly kept at Langdyke-bush: and within the memory of man hath been summoned there, and adjourned to the Lord Exeter's house at Helpston' (Peter Whalley, *The History and Antiquities of Northamptonshire. Compiled from the Manuscript Collections of the late Learned Antiquary John Bridges, Esq.* [2 vols., Oxford: Sold by T. Payne, London; D. Prince and J. Cooke, Oxford; and Mr. Lacy, Northampton, 1791], II. 489).

The Mores
This poem refers to the enclosure of the common land, previously waste and open to all, but subsequently divided among the landowners in the enclosed parishes. It was never published during Clare's lifetime.
Lines 79–80: The landowners who dreamed of 'plunder' in their 'rebel

schemes' of enclosure (rebellious against the laws of nature) were disillusioned when the price of agricultural produce fell after the end of the war.

The Parish

In correcting the text of *The Parish* we have altered the numbering of the lines. The Oxford English Text's lines 1220–1241 now follow lines 1241–75 and 12 lines omitted between lines 1333 and 1334 have been added; the OET line numbers are given in square brackets.

Line 701: 'tools' in the manuscript is written through 'fools', which makes better sense.

Lines 1412ff.: Clergymen who were also Justices of the Peace were generally unpopular both with farmers and with labourers (see G.E. Mingay, *Land and Society in England 1750–1980* [London and New York: Longman, 1994], pp. 26–7, 79); the radical loathing of them is commemorated in the famous Janus-faced caricature by Cruikshank of 'The Clerical Magistrate' (see illustration p.89). Clare's treatment is in fact remarkably indulgent, perhaps because his Justice Terror stands for an old, paternalist order that, for all its faults, is preferable to what he sees as replacing it.

Lines 2140–94: The figure of Puff is clearly intended as a portrait of Henry Ryde (see *Letters*, pp. 427, 428–9); these lines were evidently intended for 'The Parish' but were not included in Clare's latest extant version and were inserted at this point by the editors of the Oxford English Texts edition.

Death

This was one of the poems that Clare attempted to pass off as the work of an earlier poet. On 23 June 1825 Clare recorded sending this poem 'which I fatherd on Andrew Marvel' to William Hone's *Every-Day Book*, where it appeared (attributed to Marvell) on 28 June 1826 (*JCBH*, p. 235; *Letters*, pp. 335–7). He later explained to H.F. Cary why he had chosen Marvell: 'I had read that Marvel was a great advocate for liberty & as Death is a great leveller I thought it would add to the disguise to father upon him that subject' (3 Jan. 1829; *Letters*, p. 453). The theme of death as leveller anticipates 'The Summons'.

Greece

In 1825 Clare sent a poem entitled 'Freedom' (see *Poems of the Middle Period*, IV. 402–3) to Thomas Pringle, who commented on 4 August, 'the 'Song' and 'Freedom' are somewhat unfinished & unequal, and may I think be improved when you have leisure to revise them' (BL MS Egerton 2248, f. 21r). It may be in consequence of this comment that Clare revised 'Freedom' to form lines 49–64 and 73–80 of 'Greece', which was published in *Spirit and Manners of the Age* for 1828. As early as 12 May 1823 Joseph Henderson had urged Clare to write something on the Greek struggle for independence (BL MS Egerton 2246, fol. 197r). The Greek struggle for independence from Turkey was a popular cause with the English, particularly liberals, especially after the death of Byron at Missolonghi in April 1824, though the government's policy (influenced by a desire to prevent the growth of Russian power in the Mediterranean) was less favourable to the Greek cause than public opinion generally.

Line 19: Scio is the modern name of Chios, in the Aegean Sea, one of the 'seven cities' that claimed the honour of being Homer's birthplace. It was laid waste by the Athenians in 412 BC and was famous for its wine and figs.

The Gipseys Song

This poem was published in the *European Magazine* for November 1825 and included in the *Midsummer Cushion* manuscript but in a form which lacks lines 77–84, which stress the antagonism of the authorities to the gypsies. Mrs Emmerson was responsible for the cut, with the approval of Van Dyk, explaining 'by such means we avoid repetitions of words' (30 Sept. 1825; BL MS Egerton 2247, f. 79v), including the repetition of 'free' as a rhyme word in lines 80 and 86.

The Poachers

This seems to be Clare's version of a popular song usually known as 'The Lincolnshire Poacher', 'although as Kennedy points out in his *Folk Songs of Britain and Ireland* many of the collected versions of the song were known to the source singers as 'The Northamptonshire Poacher'' (George Deacon, *John Clare and the Folk Tradition* [London: Sinclair Browne, 1983], pp. 58–9). Despite the disapproval of the propertied classes poachers were often viewed with popular approval (see Harry Hopkins, *The Long Affray: The Poaching Wars in Britain* [London: Macmillan, 1986]), though the final stanza of Clare's poem suggests that he does not view illegal violence with complacency. The poem was included in Clare's fair copy book Pet. MS A40 but not published in his lifetime.

Ballad: Boys bring the booty from the cave
Robin Hood & the Gamekeepers

Clare wrote several poems about Robin Hood, whose role as a 'social bandit' aligns him with other marginal or excluded groups, such as gypsies or poachers. For the politicization of the figure of Robin Hood and his treatment in the poetry of Keats, Leigh Hunt and Clare's friend Reynolds, see Stephen Knight, *Robin Hood: A Complete Study of the English Outlaw* (Oxford: Blackwell, 1994), pp. 153–71. Taylor wrote to Clare on 20 May 1826: 'You could make, I think, another Robin Hoods Garland, if it were worth while. The Old Songs are valuable for their antiquity & simplicity, but they are not very highly poetical. ... Why should not you give us an improved Robin Hood ? – You might imagine new Subjects for your Songs, or recompose the Old Songs, or write New Songs on the Old Subjects' (BL MS Egerton 2247, f. 176v). While one of Clare's poems, 'As bold Hood he was marching along' (see *Poems of the Middle Period*, II.

259–61), is Clare's version of a traditional ballad known in other versions (it is in [Joseph Ritson], *Robin Hood: A Collection Of all the Ancient Poems, Songs, and Ballads, Now Extant, Relative to that Celebrated English Outlaw: To which are prefixed Historical Anecdotes of His Life* [1795; London: C. Stocking, 1823], pp. 210–14), George Deacon argues that the other two Hood poems are entirely Clare's own work (see Deacon, pp. 132–4, 138–40, 164–9), perhaps in obedience to Taylor's suggestion. Clare included these two in his fair copy book Pet. MS A40, but none of the poems were published in his lifetime.

[Honesty though kings revile thee]

This poem was copied into one of Clare's fair copy notebooks (Pet. MS A50), but not published in his lifetime.

On seeing a Skull on Cowper Green

This poem was published in the *Amulet* for 1829, which suggests a composition date of 1828 (albums were usually published in the November before their date). It probably relates to an incident mentioned in a note with the date '1813 May': 'Some men digging stone on Copper [i.e., Cowper] green found several bones of the human species lying all their length in one grave –' (*JCBH*, p. 244, correcting 'along' to 'stone'). In MS A40 and the *Amulet* publication the poem has an epigraph deriving from lines 42–3 of Byron's 'Churchill's Grave' (1816):

In which there was Obscurity and Fame, –
The Glory and the Nothing of a Name.

Clare was always much concerned about his own fame and in 1828–29 he was also preoccupied with illness and death. In 1825 he had sent William Hone his forgery of 'Death' (see above, pp. 113–14) and on 3 Jan. 1829 he sent a copy of it to the Rev. H.F. Cary (*Letters*, pp. 453–6). On 13 Jan. 1828 he wrote to James Montgomery: 'I believe but always doubt that I shall ever be good enough to meet with heaven & under these feelings when ill I am often miserable' (*Letters*, p. 414). Later in the same year, on 21 Dec., he told John Taylor: 'I had some desire to try one [a poem] on 'The last judgment' but expecting I shall be on the wrong side in this world as well as the next by so doing I dare not –' (*Letters*, pp. 446–7). On 19 Oct. 1829 he wrote to Marianne Marsh concerning epitaphs (*Letters*, pp. 467–9).

Nelson & the Nile

Nelson's first great victory, that made him a national hero, was in Aboukir Bay, at one of the mouths of the Nile, on 1 August 1798. This poem may be connected with Clare's project of producing 'some imitations of the Provincial Poets in Sea Songs Love Ballads &c &c &c' in late 1826 (to Taylor, 1 Dec. 1826; *Letters*, p.387). It was sent to Thomas Hood on 3 Aug. 1828 (*Letters*, p. 436), and published in the Stamford *Champion* on 5 Jan. 1830.

The Cottager

This poem, published in the *Stamford Bee* on 31 December 1830, may have
been originally intended as part of the expansion of 'The Parish'. This
portrait of the conservative, old-fashioned farmer (identified in one draft
as 'Old farmer Ling') defines Clare's ideal as against the new, gentrified,
progressive tenant farmer. The same or a very similar figure is the subject
of Clare's prose sketch 'The "Old Farmer" & his neighbour the Vicar'(Pet.
MS A18, pp. 236–7; Oxford Authors *John Clare*, ed. Eric Robinson and
David Powell [Oxford: Oxford University Press, 1984], pp. 438–44).

The Monarchy of Nature

This poem was included in the *Midsummer Cushion* manuscript but not
published in Clare's lifetime. The title 'the Political government or
commonwealth of Ants & Bees' figures in a list of essays that Clare had
written or contemplated writing (Pet. MS A46, p. 61).

Honesty

'Honesty' is a key term in Clare's moral and political vocabulary. This pair
of sonnets was published in *The Rural Muse* (1835).

The Summons

This first appeared in *Drakard's Stamford News* for 25 September 1829,
following an announcement in the previous week's issue: '"The
Summons", a poem, is in type, and will appear in our next. We regret that
the diffidence of its ingenious author will not allow us to attach his name
to a production which honours alike his head and his heart.' Lines 149–72,
in which Clare makes his most direct reference to contemporary politics,
were not in this first publication. In November 1830 Clare wrote to John
Drakard: 'In the Summons which appeard in your News some time ago I
minced the matter by the omission of three verses & spoiled the Poem
which I was sorry for & I here send you them for your own reading'
(*Letters*, p. 521). The poem was reprinted in the *Stamford Champion* of 30
November 1830 with the extra verses. The fact that they are added to the
fair copy in Pet. MS A40 suggests that they were actually an afterthought
on Clare's part.

The epigraph which appears in MS A51 and three printed versions is from
'The Soul's Errand' by Joshua Sylvester (c.1563–1618), which is included
in George Ellis, *Specimens of the Early English Poets* (1811), II. 333–6
(Northampton Collection, item 196). The first verse reads:

> Go, soul, the body's guest,
> Upon a thankless errand!
> Fear not to touch the best,
> The truth shall be thy warrant;
> Go, since I needs must die,
> And give the world the lie.

Lines 155–6: 'the tory is always at an excuse with his speeches – he hates tyranny & to show it puts freedom into prison for speaking & calls that liberty' (Pet. MS A45, p. 31; see below, p. 293). Clare seems to be referring to the prosecutions of radical journalists for seditious or blasphemous libel of the 1810s and early 1820s; at least three of the newspaper editors with whom he corresponded (James Montgomery, John Drakard and William Hone) were imprisoned or prosecuted by the government or its Tory sympathisers. 'The prosecutions had been counter-productive for they were very much identified with the Tories and brought to the victims the support of Whigs and middle-class reformers' (Edward Royle and James Walvin, *English Radicals and Reformers 1760–1848* [Brighton: The Harvester Press, 1982)], p. 129). 'Prosecution dropped off substantially by the mid-1820s, under a growing perception that they were counter-productive. ... The government implicitly acknowledged the failure of the law of libel as an instrument of political repression when it stopped pros-ecuting after the middle of the 1820s' (Kevin Gilmartin, *Print Politics: The press and radical opposition in early nineteenth-century England* [Cambridge: Cambridge University Press, 1996], pp. 123, 143).

Triumphs of Time
Clare mentioned having written this to Mrs Emmerson before 17 August 1829 (BL MS Egerton 2248, f. 165v). It was submitted to the *Iris*, edited by Thomas Dale and L.T. Ventouillac, but was not accepted, as Ventouillac explained to Clare on 5 November 1829, on account of 'partly the length of your poem, & partly the nature of some of the religious sentiments expressed in it, which my friend, M[r]. D[ale] thought, I believe, hardly *orthodox* enough. He intends with your permission, making the necessary curtailments & alterations in it, so as to insert it next year ...' (BL MS Egerton 2248, f. 186r). In the event it was published in the *Stamford Champion* on 1, 8 and 15 June 1830.
Line 136: A note in the *Stamford Champion* reads 'Roman encampment, Helpstone'.
Lines 164 and 168: A note to l. 163 in the *Stamford Champion* reads 'Dog's Monument, Walcot Park.' The reference is to the Dolphin monument in Walcot Park, near Barnack, which Clare also mentions in lines 157–68 of 'Walcott Hall & Surounding Scenery' (*MP*, II. 39–40).

Familiar Epistle to a Friend
An early version of this poem (consisting of the first nine stanzas plus an extra stanza) was completed by 1823 or 1824 when Taylor had it tran-scribed. Its revision and completion in the present form probably dates from 1830, shortly before its publication in the *Stamford Champion* on 14 December 1830. In November 1830 Clare wrote to John Drakard: 'I have another shoot at follys as they flye in the shape of a long poem in a Familiar Epistle to a friend which you may insert if you please' (*Letters*,

p. 521). There is no evidence to identify the original addressee of this poem, if Clare actually intended one, but a reference in the 1830 drafts to 'Friend Hal' suggests that Clare then had Henry Behnes in mind.

Line 46: Henry Brougham (1778–1868), Whig politician who supported liberal measures and law reform, and later Lord Chancellor.

Line 48: 'Corporal Cazy'. Tune in MS 12 (see Deacon, p. 312).

Line 54: cf. Samuel Butler, *Hudibras*, part 1, canto 2, lines 866–1022, where the Knight 'routs the Bear, and takes the Fiddler prisoner'.

Line 79: 'patriot' was the current, slightly derisive term for those in opposition. Although the line should be read as 'The patriot gives lesson of union', the collocation of 'patriot unions' might imply a reference to the Political Unions formed to agitate for Reform.

Line 118: 'canaans milk & honey'. Exodus 3: 8.

Lines 129–44: 'pride sees a great & a degrading difference between the pewter badge of a workhouse & the silver star of a court but reason only marks it in the metal for what difference can there be in the men if their situations only denote it for why is the poor honest dependant on a workhouse less honourable then the dependant on a court is it beggarly to be beholden for a few shillings weekly to the parish which every little hamlet is called & honourable to be penshioned for thousands a year on the overburthened parish of the country – where is the honour or where is the beggary –' ('On Honour'; Pet. MS A43, pp. 43–4). The degrading practice of making the recipients of poor relief wear badges infuriated Cobbett (see Ian Dyck, *William Cobbett and Rural Popular Culture* [Cambridge: Cambridge University Press, 1992], p. 37).

Line 130: 'a second Daniel'. Cf. *The Merchant of Venice*, IV. i. 334.

Line 157: George IV died on 26 June 1830.

Line 161: 'King William is now all the cry'. A Whig up to his succession, then turned Tory, but the Reform Act of 1832 and other reform measures were carried without obstruction from him.

Line 182: 'At next years coronation'. The coronation of William IV did not take place until 8 Sept. 1831.

[Just like the lion in alarms]

For the background to this unpublished party squib, written in early 1830, see the Introduction (above, p. xxxviii).

Line 8: The implication is that Thorpe's allies are clergymen.

Lines 21, 45: Thorpe's concluding letter to John Bedford was dated '*Hanthorpe House*, Jan. 30th, 1830' (*Stamford Mercury*, 5 Feb. 1830). The concluding 'Caw thorp' of Clare's poem may be a mock address, implying that Clare had 'cawed' (clawed) his opponent.

[Och by jasus hes a irish lad]

This poem is written in praise (possibly ironic) of the Duke of Wellington, born Arthur Wellesley in Dublin. It celebrates the abolition of the Beer Tax

by Wellington's government in February 1830.
Line 12: Wellington, along with Sir Robert Peel, was mainly responsible for the Catholic Emancipation Act of 1829, to the fury of their Tory supporters.

1830

This was first published under the title 'St. Stephen's' in *Drakard's Stamford News* on 5 March 1830. At the Reformation, under the Chantries Act of 1547, the Royal Chapel of St Stephen, like all other private chapels, was secularised, and by 1550 had become the meeting place of the Commons. Until its destruction by fire in 1834 shortly after Clare was writing, St Stephen's was in fact the House of Commons, and it can hardly be by accident that Drakard printed the poem immediately above the report of parliamentary proceedings!

[George 4th Death]

This fragmentary poem was not published in Clare's lifetime; the title is taken from a manuscript note by Clare.

The Blues & the Sailors

This poem, not published in Clare's lifetime, was sent to Frank Simpson with the following comments: 'I have been ruminating over "A scene in the Election" & the Song on the other side is a part of it – I thought of introducing 3 old women singing a song under the tricolour which they had made jointly by tearing up their petticoats & I thought of heading them & the mob by a serjant in a blue sash who figured in the Election & who after being defeated by the constables commences with an harangue – & joins with the Mob in {advising} tempting the sailors who are passing by accident to join them – if you think any thing of it I will go on with it for the pomposity of such scenes is cursed rediculous – be as it will *burn* this scrawl after you have read it' (*Letters*, p. 580). Charles Tennyson (line 37) stood as a candidate in Stamford in 1830 and 1831. The reference to the revolutions in France and Belgium suggests the earlier date and allows us to correct Storey's date of [May? 1832] to July 1830. Joshua Jepson Oddy, who came forward as an independent candidate to challenge the political interest of the Marquis of Exeter in Stamford in 1809, 'declared that all flags, ribbons and favours for his supporters must be blue. This was his chief legacy to later generations. For the next fifty years any opponents of the Burghley interest were labelled "the Blues"', forcing the Exeter party to retaliate by choosing red, and becoming known as "the Reds"' (J.M. Lee, *Stamford and the Cecils: A Study in Political Control 1700–1885* [B.Litt. thesis, Oxford, 1957], pp. 104–5).

The Hue & Cry

Clare told Frank Simpson in late December 1830: 'I am now writing the

"Devils Drive"' (*Letters*, p. 523), almost certainly this poem (cf. line 58). Clare may have been modelling his work on Byron's poem 'The Devil's Drive', written in 1813 but not published until 1830 in Thomas Moore's *The Life, Letters, and Journals of Lord Byron* (and then only partially). On 28 December Clare told H.B. Burlowe: 'I have scribbled a poem of 50 verses detailing the alarms & as it is just finished my vanitys fancy that it might as a trifle make me a trifle – & all I want is the opinion of George Cruikshanks in the matter' (*Letters*, p. 524). Clare hoped that Cruikshank might be induced to illustrate this poem and 'The Summons'. He sent it to Burlowe after 4 Jan. 1831 (*Letters*, p. 528). Hue and Cry was an early system for apprehending suspected criminals. Neighbours were required by common law to join in a hue and cry and to pursue a suspect to the bounds of the manor. It became the common law process of pursuing 'with horn and with voice' (O.Fr. *huer*, to shout). The poem was preceded on its publication in the *Stamford Champion* on 11 January 1831 by an editor's note: 'We insert the following stanzas, notwithstanding their great length, from the genius and taste they evince, and from our deep respect for their author, whose name we cannot mention, but whose name will be mentioned among the few sterling poets of this age, long after the hand that is now offering a feeble homage to one of Nature's own bards, shall have mouldered in the dust'.

Introductory couplet: Possibly misquoted from lines 25–6 of Pope's imitation of the first satire of the second book of Horace: 'Rend with tremendous Sound your ears asunder, / With Gun, Drum, Trumpet, Blunderbuss & Thunder'. Byron had adapted line 26 as the epigraph to *The Siege of Corinth* (1816).

Line 15: Incendiarism was one of the most alarming manifestations of the Swing disturbances. In Clare's own neighbourhood the stacks of Mr Clarke of Deeping St James were fired on 19 Dec. 1830 (*Stamford Mercury*, 24 Dec. 1830). See Appendix.

Lines 17ff.: The yeomanry – in rural districts consisting largely of tenant farmers – were the usual first response to serious disorder. 'Many of the corps of yeomanry cavalry had been disbanded since the Napoleonic Wars – to the regret, it was said, of many farmers. 'It is vain now,' wrote a Berkshire magistrate, 'to lament the dismissal of the Yeomanry force in this county. If it had existed, all these insurrectionary movements would have been easily controlled.' Possibly. But in Wiltshire, where the yeomanry rode round the county with great zeal, and received the right to call themselves 'royal' for their efforts, it would seem that they made the rioters more embittered, if anything' (Eric Hobsbawm and George Rudé, *Captain Swing* [1969: Harmondsworth: Penguin Books, 1973], p. 215).

Lines 42, 165: The Stamford *Bee* carried reports of the aurora borealis on 24 December 1830 and 7 January 1831 and of recent occurrences of the aurora borealis, a comet, and zodiacal lights, which were thought to precede 'great wars' on 21 Juary 1831.

Line 53: 'I have made a few more enquiries respecting those strangers whom the "Hue & Cry" leads me to suspect are the creators of those horrid mysterys that darkness envelops & day light discovers – The Gig was very light & apparently small for two men to occupy one was dressed in a light great coat & the other in a dark one they came in at a end of the town no strangers ever enters as it is a bye road leading no where but to bye places' (*Letters*, p. 522). Part of the popular mythology surrounding Swing was 'the constantly repeated tale that 'gentlemen' or 'strangers' were travelling round the countryside in 'green gigs', making mysterious inquiries about wage-rates and threshing machines, distributing money and firing stacks with incendiary bullets, rockets, fire balls or other devilish devices' (Hobsbawm and Rudé, p. 166). Clare's mockery of these tales in the poem is more justified than his alarmist credulity in the letter.

Lines 77–92: Cf. 'Thus in the time of war a general fast was so generally the introduction of a new tax & a public thankgiving so publicly the finale of a "victory" that was the universal tho not the acknowledged cause of such taxes that the lower orders always looked upon the anouncement of these religious rites as the bad omens of new oppression & dreaded them both as they would the anouncement of a pestilence' ('The Bone & Cleaver Club'; see below, p. 287).

Line 101: Foreign, especially French, agitators were often (quite wrongly) blamed for instigating Swing disturbances (see Hobsbawm and Rudé, pp. 182–3).

Lines 117 and 127: William Cobbett (1763–1835), author of *Rural Rides* (1830), popular radical journalist, and champion of the poor. Henry 'Orator' Hunt (1773–1835) was a good speaker before large audiences, but too vain, self-centred and quick-tempered to work with any party. He spent much of his life advocating parliamentary reform and the repeal of the corn-laws . In 1819 he presided over the demonstration that ended in the Peterloo Massacre, and made a speech which cost him nearly three years in Ilchester gaol, where he solaced himself by composing his wordy and egotistical memoirs (cf. line 155, 'Orator Hunt in his quiet retreat'). 'Cobbett's and Hunt's activities were viewed with particular suspicion. Cobbett, as we have seen, lectured at Maidstone and Battle in mid-October, and it was noted that riots and arson followed in both districts shortly after; moreover, Thomas Goodman, an East Sussex incendiary actually saved his life by 'confessing' that Cobbett's lectures had virtually 'turned his head'. Meanwhile, the worst possible construction was being put on Hunt's West Country travels. It seemed all the more credible that he was up to no good when it was learned that Cooper had borrowed Hunt's name at Fordingbridge and that a Dorset rioter had testified that 'there was a gentleman rode through [the village] a few days before who said his name was Hunt and who told us that the Government wished people to break threshing-machines, and that they should be paid for their trouble.' It was even suggested by a magistrate at Fordingbridge that

Cooper had been a fellow-prisoner of Hunt's at Ilchester, and had become his servant and followed him to London' (Hobsbawm and Rudé, pp. 183–4). For Clare's comments on Cobbett see pp. 299–300, 332.

Lines 117–18: Thomas Paine (1737–1809), author of *Rights of Man* (1791) and *The Age of Reason* (1793), greatly influenced the working-class radical movement in England (see p. 294). Voltaire (1694–1778), French philosopher and writer, was frequently blamed by conservatives for the French Revolution and for Radical atheism. Clare's reference to possible intellectual sources of inspiration for the Swing disturbances suggests that he saw them as a result of the intellectual progress of the age.

Line 127: For Hunt see note to line 117. Daniel O'Connell (1775–1847), Irish political leader, called 'the liberator'. Elected M.P. for Clare in 1828, he was prevented as a Catholic from taking his seat, but was reselected in 1830, the Catholic Emancipation legislation then being in place. Also in 1830 the potato crop had been very poor, and under his advice the people declined to pay tithes, and that winter disorder was rampant.

Lines 130–2: When Cobbett returned from America in 1819 he brought with him the bones of Paine, to the glee of conservative satirists (see illustration p. 175). Paine was frequently burnt in effigy by loyalists.

Line 165: See note to line 42.

Line 249: Probably an allusion to 'four beasts full of eyes before and behind' of Revelation 4:6; see also Revelation 4:8 and Ezekiel 10:12.

Lines 251–4: Cf. Isaiah 11:6 and 65:25 (one of the 'prophets' mentioned in line 255).

Line 265: Cf. Isaiah 2:4.

Line 302: Edmund Bonner (c.1500–1569), English prelate and bishop of London from 1540. In 1533 he was sent to Rome to appeal on behalf of Henry VIII, who had been excommunicated after his marriage to Anne Boleyn. His language at the general council was said to have prompted the pope to suggest that he should be burnt alive, or thrown into a cauldron of molten lead. Not surprisingly Bonner judged it prudent to depart. In May 1559 he refused the oath of supremacy, so was deposed and imprisoned in the Marshalsea, where he died.

Lines 333–40: Clare seems to be referring to a poem published by 'The Lowland Peasant' under the title 'The Better Land' in the Stamford *Bee* (3 December 1830), which, according to 'Philo-Veritas', was plagiarized from a poem by Felicia Hemans published in the *Literary Souvenir* for 1827 (*Bee*, 7 January 1831). A note on the affair (evidently intended for newspaper publication) uses similar imagery: 'We copy the following from the Souvenir of 1827 as the Poem which an asumption of falshood grossly mutilated & sent to the 'Bee' as his own writing himself down as a Peasant & as the Editor of the Bee neglected to 'write him down an ass' we write him down a fool clap a whasps nest on his head for a night cap & leave him to rest as he can' (Pet. MS A20, p. R28) Cf.: 'In Watts Souvenir for 1827 at page 65 you will find Old Doubles Better Land – does he not deserve a swarm of Bees for a Nightcap [Ill put] I should feel pleasure in putting it on him' (Pet. MS A20, p. 53). As a consequence of the controversy 'The Lowland Peasant' issued a challenge to which Clare responded in his 'The Challange' (see *Poems of the Middle Period*, ii, 151).

Line 482: From 14 May 1830 *Drakard's Stamford News* carried the slogan 'Knowledge is Power' as a masthead motto, attributing it to Bacon (4 Jan. 1833). The probable source is Bacon's aphorism 'Nam et ipsa scientia potestas est' in 'Of Heresies' in *Meditationes Sacrae* (1597).

Line 517: Cf. Daniel 5:22–31.

The Fallen Elm

Mrs Emmerson to Clare, 21 February 1831: 'Your lamentation for the loss of your "Old Elm" – the Siren of your Cottage is no less natural than *touching* . . .' (BL MS Egerton 2248, fol. 331r). Clare to Taylor, October 1831: '. . . they have insulted my feelings latterly very much & cut down the last Elm next the street' (*Letters*, p.551). These references and the evidence of the manuscripts suggest late 1830 as a likely date of composition for this poem, which was included in the *Midsummer Cushion* MS but not published in Clare's lifetime.

The reformers hymn

Not published in Clare's lifetime. An earlier draft was entitled 'The Labourers Hymn' (see *EP*, II. 590–3). The fact that 'The reformers hymn' was copied into his fair copy book Pet. MS A40 suggests that it is the later and definitive version.

Line 42: Prince William Henry was sent to sea on board the *Prince George* in 1779 when he was only 14. He became a competent naval officer. This explains the nautical imagery throughout the poem. A poem in the *Champion* entitled 'King William the Tar' praised him as 'an Englishman born and bred' and noted that 'his jacket was BLUE' – the usual dress of sailors in the Royal Navy and also the colour of the Whig party in Stamford (21 Sept. 1830; p. 304). The navy tended to command greater patriotic appeal than the army, even among opposition parties.

[Up honesty a vote of thanks]

This and the next five poems are from Pet. MS A59; none of them were published in Clare's lifetime. 'Up honesty' reflects Clare's preoccupation with the cheating of the poor through the use of false weights and measures, referred to in the 'bakers scales & farmers sack', as well as in the alehouse 'mugs', and by the failure to pay the poor man a living wage. He condemns the 'cash nexus' by which the labourer is turned into an item of profit or loss as well as the usurious interest charged by tradesmen on the poor man's debts.

[King William ye'r an honest man]

King William IV 1830–7.

Line 5: Throughout the eighteenth and nineteenth centuries it was common for poets to write a congratulatory poem on the monarch's birthday. Clare's poem, however, is very different from such productions, though loyal in tone. As in 'Apology for the Poor', Clare complains that the removal of taxes has not benefited the poor man. His shoes, his clothes and his bread are just as dear as ever they were and only the prosperous classes have benefited from so-called 'tax reforms': 'If money tumbled from the sky / The poor would get at none'. In these lines the concealed reference to manna falling from heaven reminds us of Clare's preoccupation with scriptural imagery.

[The Lament of Swordy Well]
Although this poem is widely known as 'The Lament of Swordy Well' it must be remembered that Clare himself rarely supplied titles during this period and this is no exception.
Lines 21, 256: Usually known as Swaddy Well, an ancient stone quarry used by the Romans, famed in Clare's childhood for wild flowers, white lizards, and a fine species of copper-hued butterfly. It was also a traditional camping site for gypsies.

[Thou king of half a score dominions]
Line 54: Probably an allusion to 'the unlimited number of low Alehouses created by the late Beer Act' complained about by 'A Constant Reader' in the *Stamford Mercury* ('To the Landlords of England', 28 Jan. 1831).
Line 53: King George IV (1820–30), King William IV (1830–7). This poem seems to have been written sometime after William IV's coronation on 8 Sept. 1831.
Line 92: 'the simple hussey' is the muse of the poets who write birthday odes (line 86).

[Address to an old Halfpenny]
[Bless thy old fashioned copper face]
These two poems were left unfinished and not published in Clare's lifetime. The title for the first poem occurs in a manuscript note by Clare. Another fragmentary poem, 'On finding a Silver coin of Cromwells while at work in the Field', also addresses coinage for a political purpose (see *MP*, II. 327).

Don Juan
In May 1841 Clare, then a patient at Dr Allen's asylum at High Beach, Epping Forest, was composing 'Don Juan', written in his *persona* as Byron, in which he mentioned both Mary Joyce, who had already died in 1838, and Eliza Phillips, who has never been identified (see *Letters*, pp.646–8). The poem is highly charged with Clare's disillusionment with women, with marriage, and with women's hypocrisy. A wife is described as 'this

incumberance on the rights of man' and equated with the commons and the rabbit-warrens that had been 'trespassed' over by enclosers. Thus his resentment at woman's infidelity is interwoven with his hatred of the hypocrisy of the nation, which he recognises in the false imprisonment of honest men (for debt or for offences against the Game laws), the corruption of parliament, the falsehoods of Whig and Tory party-politics, the impositions of tax and tithe, and the failure to pay the labouring man an honest wage. His suggestion of the prevalence of sexual dishonesty extends to Queen Victoria and Prince Albert and to Lord John Russell's marriage to Lady Fanny Elliott on 26 July 1841, announced in the *Northampton Mercury* for 12 June and 17 July 1841. Though the poem is sometimes fantastic in its eroticism, it is infused with a raw energy unequalled in Clare's poetry. 'Don Juan' reflects Clare's hatred of cant, both in sex and politics, hypocrisy, self-interest and fashion. C. V. Fletcher in his M. Phil. Thesis, University of Nottingham, 1973, entitled *The Poetry of John Clare, with particular reference to poems written between 1837 and 1864*, also showed the importance of 'Don Juan' in reflecting Clare's visits with Rippingille to the Royal West Theatre, London (known as the 'French Theatre') and what E.V. Rippingille, in his letter to Clare, Sept. 1824, referred to as its 'atmosphere of smoke, smocks, smirks, smells, and smutty doings'. Tim Chilcott published with the Trent Press his edition and evaluation of Clare's Byronic poems in 1999.

Line 32: Possibly an allusion to Thomas Holcroft's celebrated play *The Road to Ruin* (1792).

Line 40: An echo of the title of Thomas Paine's *Rights of Man!* (1791–92). Cf. Clare's letter to his wife of 1849–50 in which he alludes to the titles of Paine's three most celebrated works (p. 324).

Line 48: Introduced at the end of the Napoleonic Wars to protect the agricultural interest by keeping the price of corn high, the Corn Laws were opposed by working-class radicals and by Lord Milton.

Line 63: 'crim con'=criminal conversation, a legal term for adultery; cf. Byron, *Don Juan*, XV. lxxxiv: 'crim. con. with the married'.

Line 68: 'blunt', slang for money (cf. *Dictionary of the Vulgar Tongue: A Dictionary of Buckish Slang, University Wit, and Pickpocket Eloquence* [London: C. Chappel, 1811; reprinted Chicago: Follett Publishing Company, 1971]).

Line 75: a pun on Whigs.

Line 78: 'traps', warders ('Constables and thief-takers', according to the *Dictionary of the Vulgar Tongue*).

Line 80: To oil someone's wig=to make them drunk.

Line 84: The wedding of Lord John Russell to Lady Fanny Elliott, second daughter of the Earl and Countess of Minto, took place on 26 July 1841 and was announced in the *Northampton Mercury* on 12 June and 17 July 1841.

Line 86: Albert's first absence from England was in fact in March 1844.

Line 87: 'snuff box'=female pudendum. To strum='To have carnal knowl-

edge of a woman' (*Dictionary of the Vulgar Tongue*).
Line 113: Melbourne resigned as Prime Minister 28 Aug. 1841.
Line 121: 'toadstools': a reference to new peers or ministers?
Line 197: 'Mary & Martha': cf. Luke 10: 38–42.
Line 203: 'the court circular', official announcement of the activities of the royal family, reprinted in newspapers.
Line 215: Cf. Byron, *Don Juan*, X. xliv–xlvi.
Line 220: 'max', gin (*Dictionary of the Vulgar Tongue*). Cf. Byron, *Don Juan*, XI. xvi: 'Oh! for a glass of max!'
Line 222: Cf. Byron, *Don Juan*, X. li ff.
Lines 255–6: 11 July fell on Sunday in 1841.
Line 262: Clare's own birthday was on 13 July, Byron's was on 22 January.
Line 274: *The Isle of Palms* (1812) by 'Christopher North' (John Wilson); it is in vol. 1 of John Wilson, *Poems* (2 vols., 1825), item 402 in Clare's library.

London versus Epping Forest
Published in the *English Journal* for 29 May 1841.

To Liberty
The association in Clare's mind between liberty and Scotland, particularly in the later poetry, is illuminated by the discussion in John Goodridge and Kelsey Thornton, 'John Clare: the trespasser', in Hugh Haughton, Adam Phillips and Geoffrey Summerfield (eds.), *John Clare in Context* (Cambridge: Cambridge University Press, 1994), pp.108–13.

Love of Liberty
Dated 14 Feb. 1847, in the Knight Transcripts; the opening two lines are reminiscent of Bunyan's hymn: 'He that is down needs fear no fall, / He that is lost no pride'.

The Songs of our Land
Dated 12 Feb. 1847, another in a group of seven poems written within a few days of each other.

PROSE

" Portentous, unexampled, unexplain'd !
————————— What man seeing this,
And having human feelings, does not blush,
And hang his head, to think himself a man ?
————————— I cannot rest
A silent witness of the headlong rage,
Or heedless folly, by which thousands die——
Bleed gold for Ministers to sport away."

THESE ARE

THE PEOPLE

all tatter'd and torn,

Who curse the day

wherein they were born,

On account of Taxation

too great to be borne,

And pray for relief,

from night to morn ;

Who, in vain, Petition

in every form,

Apology for the Poor

Clare's essay entitled 'Apology for the poor' was evidently intended for newspaper publication and there is evidence that it was published, although the published version has not yet been located. The version given is the draft from Clare's manuscripts.

Mr Editor

In this suprising stir of patrioutism & wonderful change in the ways & opinions of men when your paper is weekly loaded with the free speechs of countys meetings[1] can you find room for mine – or will you hear the voice of a poor man – I only wish to ask you a few plain questions

Amidst all this stir about taxation & tythes & agricultural distress – are the poor to recieve corresponding benefits they have been told so I know but it is not the first time they have heard that & been dissapointed – when the tax was taken from leather they was told they should have shoes almost for nothing & they heard the parliment speeches of patriots as the forthcoming prop[h]echys of a political millenium but their hopes were soon frost bitten – for the tax has long vanished & the price of shoes remains just were it did nay I believe they are a trifle dearer then they was then – thats the only difference then there was a hue & cry about taking off the duty on Sp[i]ritous liquors & the best Gin was to be little more in price then small beer – the poor man shook his head over such speeches & looking at his shoes had no faith to believe {again} any more of these cheap wonders so he was not dissapointed in finding gin as dear as ever – for which he had little to regret for he prefered good ale to any spirits & now the Malt & beer tax is in full cry what is the poor man to expect – it may benefit the farmers a little & the common brewers a good deal & there [no] doubt the matter will end the poor man will not find the refuse of any more use to him then a dry bone to a hungry dog – excuse the simile reader for the poor have been likened unto dogs before now

& many other of these time serving hue & cries might be notised in which the poor man was promised as much benefit as the stork was in the fable for pulling out the bone from the Wolfs throat & who got just as much at last as the stalk [sic] did for his pains Some of the patriots of these meetings seem to consider the corns law [sic] as a bone sticking in the throat of the countrys distresses but I am sure that the poor man will be no better off in such a matter – he will only be 'burning his fingers' & not filling his belly by harbouring any notions of benefit from that quarter for he is so many degrees lower in the Thremometer [of] disstress that such benefits to others will not reach him & tho the Farmers should again be in their summer splendour of 'high prices' & 'better markerts' as they phrase it the poor man would still be found very little above freezing point – at least I very much fear so for I speak from experience & not from hearsay & hopes as some do – Some years back when grain sold at 5 & 6 guineas a quarter I can point out a many villages where the Farmers under a combination for each others inter[e]sts would give no more in winter then 10 Shillings per Week[2] – I will not say that all did so for in a many places & at that very time Farmers whose good intentions was 'to live & let live'[3] gave from 12 to 15 shillings per week & these men would again do the same thing but they could not compel others & there it is were the poor man looses the benefit that ought to fall to him from the farmers 'better markets' & 'high prices' for corn – I hope Mr Editor that I do not offend by my plain speaking for I wish only to be satisfied about these few particulars – & I am so little of a politician that I would rather keep out of the crowd than that my hobnails should trample on the gouty toes of any one[4]tho I cannot help thinking when I read your paper that there is a vast number of taxable advocates wearing barrack shoes or they would certainly not leave the {honest} advocates for reform to acchieve their triumphs without a struggle – I wish the good of the people may be found at the end & that in the general triumph the poor man may not be forgotten for the poor have many oppressors & no voice to speak his oppressions above them – he is a dumb burthen in the scorn of the worlds prosperity yet in its adversity they are found ever ready to aid & assist & tho that be but as the widows mite yet his honest feelings in the cause are as worthy as the orators proudest orations Being a poor man myself I am naturally wishing to see some one become the advocate & Champion for the poor not in his speeches but his actions for speeches are now adays nothing but words & sound Politicians are known to be exceedingly wise as far as regards themselves & we have heard of one who tho his whole thoughts seemd constantly professing the good of his country yet he was cunning enough to keep one thought to himself in the hour of danger when he luckily hit upon the thought of standing on his hat to keep himself from catching cold & to die for the good of their country as some others did & to be alive as he is at this moment[5] now if the poor mans chance at these meetings is any thing better then being a sort of foot cushion for the benefit of others I shall be exceedingly happy {to hear} but as it is I much fear it as the poor mans lot seems to have been so long remembered as to be entirely forgotten

I am sir your humble St

A Poom [sic] Man

The poor have many oppressors & no voice to be heard above them[6]

(Pet. MS A46, pp. 22–24)

The strongest evidence for the publication of 'Apology for the poor' is the existence in Clare's manuscripts of the following drafts apparently in reply to an answer to the letter above.

Apology for the poor

Is it right that an atom should prescribe bounds to infinity is it proper that one individual should consider his opinions the mouth piece for millions of humanitys is it common sense or radicalism when the many express their disapprobation of the tyranny & domineering of the few & they such mountebanks as this imposter – is it not very absurd when we hear a provincial orator a Tom Thumb politician whose name is never known but in a country newspaper & whose domains are not of consequence enough even to prot[r]ude their confined limits in a county atlas is it not absurd to hear such a person dictate his crabbed bigotry to the yeomanry of England – the very paper in which he intrudes seems to turn

blue[7] with the ridiculous consciet of the man & the audacious absurdity of the matter just as I had concluded this letter & the very sun [which] is seting upon the close of such orations for persecution against freedom blushes red with shame & hides his head in that shadow of oblivion & darkness as if purposly to show the fate of such orators & orations & speaking with the emblems of silence which is louder then the speaking trumpet of words that the finale of tyranny & oppression shall be oblivions forgetfullness & darkness eternal So I bid your eternal farewell Mr Manners[8]
(Pet. MS A46, pp. 14–15)

Pray who is this Mr – — has stept from under a coronet to attack a poor essayist has he laid aside his pedigree to enter the ring with a vulgar antagonist verily he wears all the ambition of a {little} great man & he looks down as scornfully with his bombastical simile strung sentences as if he possest 'all the blood of all the Howards' in his veins – who is he – clear the stage – & let me listen this mountebank
(Pet. MS A46, p. 25)

I think you are [*blank*] or you would not have addressed me & most assuredly you are one of those tyrannical persecutors of the poor or you would not have been offended at what I have written so far your bark betrays you as none others [*sic*] then the identical Sir Oracle[9]
(Pet. MS A46, p. 25)

You seem to know all about the history of the rebellious hat that prevented its owner from dying the death of a patriot but as you think it was a very loyal hat I have no objections to argue against it – your memory is very retentive of such matters aye indeed it is excellent & your learning & parts & wit & alltogether are as great as your memory is excellent you are undoubt[ed]ly a great man aye a very great man in your parish & its a pity that no other parishes will share the glory of your own parish by thinking so – pray as your memory is so excellent can you tell me wether the loyal hat which you consider as such from the goodness of its owner & the rebellious hat as I consider it from not letting its owner die for the good of others will you I repeat have the goodness to tell me wether it was a long nap or short nap or no nap at all for that it was a remarkable hat you & I are both of opinion therefore have the kindness to set me right in that great matter as the people who cannot get hats to put on their heads much less to put under their feet are of such minor considerations as to be unworthy any place or mention in this oration of yours that defends the situation of that remarkable hat which plainly shows that your opinion of them still is that they ought to [be] nothing more then foot cushions for such mountebanks as you to tumble your tricks upon until you get into power – & gain your remedy & that they ought to be thankful even tho they have no share in the gain I am Mr Mountebank far from being among the number of your foot cushions for your gouty great toe of expiring tyranny & very far from believing that your pretentions are any other then the evil ones of a petty tyrant to enslave & pauperize the poor

tho at the same time I have the misfortune to be

A poo[r] Man

(Pet. MS A46, pp. 25–26)

Mr Editor

Your bumptious orator who signs himself ———— swaggers like a bantum when he finds the dung[h]ill all his own & thinks himself master because his master is absent – he crows over the silence of former antoginists who set too against the set whose place he occupys & arogates that silence into signs of fear it is not the first time that an ass imagined him self a lion when dressed in its skin or a daw blusterd like a peacock when decked in its feathers but it would be the first time that any body but them selves mistook such things for either the one or the other if any body but him self imagined him either of these metamorphoses – the fact is his arguments & his [blank] are too contemptible to notice – I shall not think it worth while to throw astone [sic] when I am only pelted with feathers – it is the neighbourhood for goose quills but while they are handled by a goose only I have given a

271

suff[i]cient reply

Aye what the goose again – he has been moulting into new feathers & tho asuming the name of a swan his cackle betrays him

Goosey goosey gander
Where would you wander
Up the fen & down the fen
To cackle & to slander

(Pet. MS A46, p. 33)

The following fragments were evidently intended for the 'Apology for the poor', which Clare seems to have intended to expand beyond its original newspaper publication.

Apology for the Poor

There are many great speech makers who rave much about liberty but the good of their country seem as a carpet for their oratory to trample on when in power & it may be averred that her welfare never reaches so high as their hearts tho it flows from their mouths with the common occurrences of fine words & other pretentions [*gap of about three lines*] a step ladder to get in to power with as Jacobs ladder assisted the angels to remount into heaven[10] [*gap of about two lines*] I think every man of common sense must easily percieve that a man who earnestly wishes & endeavours to make others believe as proselites what he himself fancys to be right & threatens his audience with ruin in this world or dam[n]ation in the next if they cannot believe so wether he be called a divine or an orator no matter for I say I think it is very percievable to common sense that such men only want power to be equal to the greatest tyrants that ever existed & that the basest deeds would not be blushed over to attain their ends tho burnings & bloodshed were the price of its attainment

(Pet. MS A46, pp. 16–17)

Apology for the poor

The poor man is obliged to buy every thing at the highest possible rate his poverty compels him to purchase his quart of common b[r]ewhouse stuff because he cannot purchase a bushel of malt & has no credit with the seller therefore he is obliged to support knaves in their luxury while he himself is starving he has a many burthens worse the[n] public taxes he is taxed by a numerous fry that the rich man never knows or dreams of for his modicums of nessesary food he goes to the petty village retailer who sells him the very worst articles at the highest price to be sure he could get better at the market & low prices but he has not the money & who will credit strangers & these poor men the wealthy talk of opressions but they only have a tythe of the oppressions felt by the poor – they only complain in the loss of high prices for their merchandise by which they quickly amassed large fortunes to be as quickly converted into [*blank*] for their familys – but at the same time the poor man was starving amidst his family with not even sufficient food to give them – thus it is justly said that while England was increasing in wealth she was increasing in poverty[11] (Pet. MS A46, pp. 20–21)

If the nessesitys of the poor are always to be left to the mercy of anothers prosperity – their oppressions in a general way will always be permanant & their benefits ever precarious thousands of poor will be left as destitute of comfort under the high prices of the Farmers interests as thousands of the poor are now – I wish to see some one become the champion of the poor so far in disinterested honesty as to forget his own interests & partial[i]tys {in the anxiety} of bettering himself & his class by attempting some simple plan for bettering the community at large for any thing universally attempted for the benefit of all will benefit the poor man partial blessings to those above him will be no use to him – the manna must be scattered in the wilderness for the poor to claim as a right & not left in the power of anothers charity alone for them to solicit as a blessing for then thousands will be sent empty away

As to taking off the malt tax {& Beer tax} that will benefit the poor next to nothing for if he could have malt at even the price that corn makes now the poor man who has a family could not get it & if the Malt & beer tax are all taken off together the poor mans general good will be a minus in the matter tho to be sure a pint of beer will be cheaper & tho he can purchase that when he cannot get a bushel of malt to brew good ale yet he must give so much interest out of his money to the publican & brewer & what he buys as cheap ale is nothing better then slow poison or at best table beer under a new name – for let times be as they will common brewers & pot house retailers will have their profits or they will not sell A general reduction of taxes in general & a total abolishment of such that press so hard on the nessesitys of life & like pharoahs lean kine[12] swallow up the fatness of the earth making a famine where we might enjoy plenty – I repeat the abolition of these taxes that would confer benefit to all would {I alow} in the end benefit the poor – like a sun burst from a cloud it would smile upon them in time for I dare say they would be the last that struggled out of the shadow of poverty

(Pet. MS A46, pp. 27–28)

Apology for the Poor

I say what good has been yet done by the partial reduction of particular taxes why as yet nothing but a cheese paring of comfort for the poor & that was the removal of the tax on salt – & the Malt & beer duty will I fear be nothing but another morsel for a came-lion & the worst is the poor cannot feed on air – the common brewer & the pot house retailers so long as their respective monop-olies are sanctioned & reserved in [*blank*] so long will they recieve every benefit from the deducting of these taxes & the trifleing refuse that[13] falls to the poor will be as much benefit to them as throwing dishwas[h]ings to a hungry dog – to benefit the poor would be to take off the tax on beer & the power from the brewing Magistrates disovling [*sic*] the spell of the liscencing system alto-gether & leaving every body to sell ale as chose to do so & then the poor would be benefited & not till then

(Pet. MS A46, pp. R45–R44)

these are strange times

Every farmer is growing into an orator & every village into a Forum of speech making & political squabbles – the general good is the universal out cry of these speakers & peti[ti]oners but self interest is the undoubted spirit that puts all in motion – the poor

cottager & the little freeholder is called upon to back their inten-
tions that good may come – & yet I am as full of doubt respecting
the good of the poor man by this bustle & bother of helping him as
I was when he sank alone in his poverty & not a hand was raised
to help him or a voice was heard in his favour – there was a time
when the prosperity of other[s] was universaly popular yet at that
very time the poor man was as an alien in a strange land[14] – he was
not suffered even to open his mouth about his distresses for if [he]
had he would have been instantly thrust into jail as a raiser of mobs
& seditions & who were the lords & tyrants of every village that
treated the rights of the poor with such contempt as not even to let
the murmurs of sorrow to go unpunished – why these very
farmers who are now raising up mobs themselves – they were
metamorphosed into special constables[15] & paraded the dirty
streets with shouldered muskets in all the swaggering awkward-
ness of the raw lobsters that now infest the metropolis[16] – & if a
poor man only smiled upon the ridiculous groups of armed
animals when it was almost impossible to resist laughter he was
instantly seized & guarded to prison by these files of reduculous
assumptions these treasons upon honour & libels on courage who
would have retreated from the bray of a jackass as the cannon of
the emeneny [*sic*] & turned their backs on a scare crow if it had
been infested[17] with a red jacket as from a file of soldiers they seem
now to wish to make the same use of the poor as a noble lord did
of his beaver in the chapple of Windsor by treading upon them to
save themselves from danger[18] – but the poor are quiet spectators
of [*blank*] & seem to have no dispositions to meddle with the diffi-
cultys of others & they are right in so doing when they know they
are not alowed to speak of their own distresses which have been
permanant they would be foolish to have any conscern in the
distresses of others that have only just began & that by accident
(Pet. MS A46, pp. 28–30)

Apology for the poor
Here are people turning round as determined radicals outlaw &
abusive radicals who somtime back would have transported
people for even attempting to urge what they themselves now

swear avowedly to be right[19] & the strange apologys they make for their former bigotry is not less ridiculous then Donquixottes encounter with the windmills for janants [sic] & the very reason that makes them so wise now is that they cannot get the people to be fools any longer to back them & so they find themselves left alone in their frothy eddies of old notions & therefore they struggle on into bubbles to ride with the stream

I fear these tory radicals these out of place patriots (or parrots) who are so loud in their insults against the present minestry only want to make paddles of the people to sail into their harbours of old sinecures & then to be again themselves they will be as silent of suffering people & all such alusions – as an old maid is of her age or an old borough monger of common honesty
(Pet. MS A46, p. 113)

Apology for the poor
These out o place patriots have grown into as fierce a perception of the countrys wrongs & grievances as the boy in the Tales of the fa[i]ries had of the secrets of nature who could hear the flowers grow & see the wind – yet a twelvemonth is scarcely past sinces [sic] these perceptible neverous [sic] ambitionists in the countrys welfare where as silent & as ignorant of all but their own interests as a deaf man is of the distinction between noise & silence & a blind man of that of light & darkness
(Pet. MS A46, p. 101)

Apology for the Poor
To talk of libelling every individual in a body by speaking the truth about one individual in that body of people or urging general observations on practices very common in that body of people wether of the clergy or ministry were as absurd as to acuse a man of libeling his neigbour with unjust suspicions of thieving because he closeses the shutters of his shop on an evening & locks up his doors onights ere he goes to bed in protection of himself & prop-erty telling truth ought always to be far from libellous & suspi-cions of [blank] if not true ought in many instances to be far from being harshly dealt with – for a public character who is placed in

any office by the suffrages of a people to act for the good of that people – ought always to feel that they have as much right to the use of freedom in speaking of his actions wether honest or dishonest as he in his own discretion has of using [*blank*]

If a man follows any sect or party for gain that man sacrifices a good cause to a cunning deception in making use of a present principle & therebye loosing a lasting interest

no man ever cared about the publicity of a good action (we should not have so many subscription lists in the papers if they were) & he ought never to take unjust means in his public capasity of detering people to speak the truth of him for the moment he does that the people justly conclude that[20] he & the party he aspouses are ashamed of their actions & the suspicions of others are confirmed into facts by them selves & in a most humiliating manner become their own accusers
(Pet. MS A46, p. 102)

Apology for the poor

Death as often lurks in the remedy of an unskilful phisician as in the disease & so it is with the conserns of a people left in the hands of an unskilful person his plans for their protection & safety often becomes the means of their misfortunes & calamitys thereby ilustrating the old proverb that the remedy is worse then the disease
(Pet. MS A46, p. 103)

Apology for the Poor

It is not at all nessesary that the laws of nations should be conformable to the creeds & opinions of their several religions in every point because then the laws would be partialy favourable to the clergy & they would grow as its power when others would often be left in oppression so it is always nessesary that the laws of nations be conformable to the equality of all having a just & equal equilibirum to the liberty of the community – Justice should keep the scal[e]s in even suspension – & the poor mans rights ought to be defended & protected with the same earnestness & deliberation as his delinqu[e]ncys are punished – while the rich mans evil doings ought to recieve correction with the same degree of power

& partiallity that the law alows him in the defence of his rights & station – but alas when will that be

Our present laws defend the propertys of the great but they often leave the propertys of the poor man to the care of providence alone

(Pet. MS A46, p. 109)

Apology for the Poor

If an acorn be dropt in [a] wood it may grow in the protection of the under wood to a great timber in the strength of time but if an acorn be dropt on an unfenced common be the soil ever so rich it never rises higher then a shrub from the oppressing [*blank*] of the cattle who eat off the spring shoot & midsummer shoot yearly as they put forth – it is just so with the industrious individual who has to begin the world for himself unassisted by heirships or places or pensions & with no other interest but his own industry if such a one happens to begin his career in a free country no doubt but he grows into a rich great man & becomes the predecessor of a race of nobility but if such a man in every respect happens unfortunately to start in a country oppressed with taxes & overloaded with ambitions [*blank*] he plods on anxiously & unweried & saves nothing but leaves a large family not to the heirship of large estates or to the pensions of [*blank*] but to the protection of providence in their youth & the dread of a workhouse in their old age such are the chances of industry in a goverment where money & not knowledge is power

Where goverment in the first instance is made subse[r]vient to the advantage of all & where money & not knowledge is made the power of the second where idleness grows rich by dishonestly [*sic*] & labour remains poor by oppression

(Pet. MS A46, p. 110)

Apology for the poor

How strange a thing it is to turn round for a moment & see the changes in the times – self – is the only motto that sticks to its own

(Pet. MS A46, p. 113)

Every restraint now adays is laid on poverty & every liberty is given to luxury burthens are constantly laid upon the weak & the strong are left without them – with the weak they are called usefull & nessesary laws & with the rich they are considerd as mean & incommod[i]ous matters never intended for them thus every nessesary article with the poor is taxed & every luxury with the rich goes scot free as far as is possible with the descency of parsiality to participate
(Pet. MS A42, p. 46)

Every discontented man who is not poor declares the poor peasants lot to be the happiest in the world & the hardest labour as the best exersise for health – yet he himself would sooner chuse any lot then that of a poor man & any labour but that of hard work
(Pet. MS A45, p. 34)

They are like the showman tho less honest they cheat the public for thousands – he gulled them for a penny – Walk in gentlemen & ladies walk in here is the most wonderful sight you ever beheld an outlandish animal whose head is where its tail should be – walk in gentlemen walk in – & what did they see – why humbug in miniature an asses foal with its tail tied to a manger – where was the candidate he had pocketed the copper & was gone – making as gentlemanly an exit as if he had been a candidate for a burrough or a representative for a county
(Pet. MS A51, fol. 32r)

The rage of party was every thing & reason & common sense stood for nothing like cyphers on the left hand of numbers – but these days are nearly over
(Pet. MS A51, fol. 32v)

to those macaroney[21] listeners who take the greatest share of impudence as the most profound learning – & nonsense as excessive reasoning merely because they cannot understand it – thus a blustering declaimer or a political prize fighter in party becomes a philosopher – while reason cannot be heard & when she shows her

self she is instantly cried down like an interfering majistrate who spoils the sport – illustrating the old proverb of none are so blind as those who wont see – & such meetings as these were regular prologues to the Bristol Tragedy[22] & tho it ended one act we have only providence to thank that it did not proceed to the
(Pet. MS A51, fol. 39r)

There is a great out cry against the taxes & I for one thought these great burthens on my class the poor & common people – but I find I am mistaken – for since I thought so taxes have been taken of[f] of articles that may be said to be lifes nessesitys rather than comforts of the poor & yet these nessesitys are almost aye even to a fraction as dear as they were before
(Pet. MS A51, fol. 39v; written on a letter dated 10 Jan. 1832)

So that taxes which the government takes off to better the poor are kept on in high prices by those very people have been declaiming against them & the gov[ern]ment to the poor as their common enemys & oppressors
(Pet. MS A51, fol. 41r)

the complaints of the poor have been long seen but they have seldom been utterd while the complaints of others have been loud but not seen their appearances are as usual
(Pet. MS A51, fol. 59r)

I am not a member of parliment but I am the representative of an increasing number of constituents who look up to me to represent their wants & protect their interests & welfare because they are unable to do it themselves – I must therefore begin to act in their interests as well as speak for them
(Pet. MS A53, fol. 17r, cancelled)

Essay on Political Religion

Clare intended to write an 'Essay on Political Religion', for which the following passage and another reprinted in the footnotes to the material from Pet. MS A45 (see below, p. 303, note 45) survive; we have added three further passages that seem to relate to this project.

For Essay on Political Religion

Religion hath little need to be connected with an oppressive government to force or secure either protection to the one or power to the other if stability is wished for in the matter for precepts however good or just no longer appear so when forced down the throats of the people to teach them patience only to bear unjust burthens the better in the shape of taxes &c for the sole benefit of luxury & extravagance such precepts of religion turn pretexts of oppression in the eyes of the oppressed & instead of reconsiling the subject to his lot make him stubborn for his right thus in bringing religion which is considered justice that cannot err to support power which is most commonly injustice in the end only serves to add power to the weakness of the subject & tends [to] deminish the power or tyranny of government in the end
(Pet. MS A18, p. R253, cancelled)

The government religion of a state or empire is properly speaking a political religion – framed to suit the demands or nessesitys of governments as well as the conversion of souls where the church like a standing army seems ready at any time to maintain her opinions & join her banners with their voices if not their conscience – self convenience & not honest opinions weigh most in these matters
(Pforz. Misc MS 198, p. 48)

Any superstition that is perfectly harmless however incredulous[23] may be tollerated & any supersti[ti]on that renders good to individuals so far as to deter its believers from the commiting of

bad actions by terror & the encouragment of doing good ones by hopes of reward ought to be reverencd as the especial revelation[24] of providence who works by unknown means for the advancement of the earthly welfare & eternal happiness of mankind – giving to every human being an instinct of faith & a tallisman of futurity according to his possesion of natural knowledge & powers of intellect – & every sect whose aim is in unison with such desires – ought not only too be tollerated (call them by what names they may) but placed on an equality of rights & laws with the other subjects of a free country & every thing that leads man to do contrary to such principles is unworthy the name of a religion if it obtains one & utterly worthless to the purposes of eternity if it unluckily obtains any desciples to believe in the errors of such principles
(Pet. MS A46, p. 108)

Pity hath often been an excuse for the excersise of cruelty – how many a savage under the mask of religion in pity as he pretended for the soul of the object of his hatred hath put the body into the greatest tortures thus pity is a plausible excuse for the excersise of hatred or revenge or self interest which latter spirit ignited more fires in Smithfield & brought more Martyrs to the stake in one century then the love of creeds hath done throughout all the world
(Pet. MS A46, p. 109)

The Bone and Cleaver Club

'Friendly societies' at this period were a kind of mutual insurance society, but they were often criticised as being 'mere haunts for drunkenness and irregularity. ... In the first place, the members profess to unite and assemble together to promote brotherly love, and to assist each other in sickness and distress; but in effect it is only to benefit the alehouse-keeper (who is the Father of the Club,) by his providing a supply of liquor once a month for the members, who reside in the neighbourhood of the place of meeting' (Letter to the editor from 'A Member', Lincoln, in the Stamford Mercury, *11 January 1828). Clare's skit seems to endorse such criticisms, but the satire in this piece is double-edged, for while it appears to ridicule the radicalism and anti-clericalism of popular debating societies the opinions expressed and the songs sung have significant parallels elsewhere in Clare's work, particularly with his essay 'On False Appearances' (see Pet. MS A43, pp. 26–34). Bones and cleavers were traditionally used to make 'rough music', and were particularly associated with mob participation in elections.*

Hearing a great deal about a notorious club at the Butchers Arms I felt anxious to fall in by accident to spend my glass of liquor & listen[25]some of their lucubrations which I understood was eloquent it[26] professed to be a friendly society but from the house it got the name of the 'Bone & cleaver club' & surely the bone of contention was never more stu[r]dily band[i]ed from mouth to mouth then there order & reason was talked off [*sic*] but if they were ever members they have been crossed out of the society (Pet. MS A46, pp. 63–64)

I found even here in the lowest attendants of one of the lowest clubs or benefit societys as they are generaly called – that self interest was a predominant feeling & that every member considered every body wrong but him self & all felt conscieted enough by fanc[y]ing they had the wisdom which others wanted & even the hedger & ditcher thought himself qualified to take the place of

Accordingly, these Moonites, full of rancour,
Met in a house, just like the

CROWN AND ANCHOR;

And there it was resolv'd, by this committee,
To hold a meeting, somewhere in the city,
To which all sorts of folks should be invited,
To see, as they declar'd, "the people righted;"
And therefore they did draw up an advertise-
        ment,
Which to the various papers straight was sent :—

a minister & give advice to the king whom they considered little
better then a tyrant while they looked upon laws as another name
for oppression & this seemed to be the general feeling of their
meeting & they seem to look upon these [*about twenty-five lines left
blank*]
(Pet. MS A49, p. 28)

For Essay on Bone & cleaver club
This man did nothing but swear   oaths oath oaths wear[27] all he
could get up he had not a sentence of common sense about him &
to bring him into law a little the president made him come down
the forfeit of a new hammer as he has worn the old one out with
knocking the oaths back agen down his throat
(Pet. MS A42, p. R150)

For Essay on 'Bone & cleaver club'
Nonsense Mr President down right nonsense I say Mr President
to talk of virtue Aye[28] virtue what is virtue who is virtue where is
virtue   virtue Mr President is nothing & all nonsense Mr
President no I say virtue is not nothing retorted a little didapper
[*sic*] sort of fellow with his arms at full spread like the wings of a
lapwing virtue is the 'Suppression of vice'[29] for so said the parson
in his sermon on sunday & they roared heartily round the table at
the joke that
   Song come push round the glass &c[30]
If manna was sent from heaven Mr P as in the days of Moses it
would be of little benefit to the poor Mr P for they would instantly
claim it in tythes & taxes[31]

For Essay on D°
A little spruce figure in a shovel hat & a black coat without a
collar now gave his toast 'Heres to the destruction of the black
locusts that eat up a tenth part of our land'[32] & it was recieved with
applause he seemed by his dress to be an autograph of the sect
called quakers which he resembled in every thing but christian
charity & meekness[33]

———

285

Morality Mr President whats that Sir its all fudge the best way to succeed in the world is to do as the world does Mr President every thing in the shape of a letter will slip thro the post office (applause) whats the use of the words virtue & morality I want to know that Mr President we cant live by religion Mr P thats truth its all hypocrisy in the saints to seem religious & to talk about character thats a pretty trick Mr P isnt it when they dont posses common honesty thats truth now to please every body Mr President we must act justly to nobody thats truth – we must praise the church to the parson Mr president & abuse it to the parishioners we must speak well of justice & belie it in our actions Mr P thats fact we must miscall magistrates wise men to their faces Mr P & knaves to our neighbours Mr P thats truth we must go to church with farmer folly to be good & get an hours sleep in the pew only contriving to waken to sing amen with the clerk in the prayer for the royal family only go to church Mr P thats all go to church wait in the porch to make a bow to the priest & praise his dull sermon Mr P thats truth then go home & drink to the abolition of english slavery (aplause) tythes ([applause]) parsons ([applause]) & taxes in the company of radicals & then we stand in the praise of all Mr P as good men good subjects & good every things thats truth Mr P Cant humbug & hypocrisy are the three in one grand principles of this age Mr P thats truth if you would be up right you must suffer buffets from one party or the other Mr P thats truth & whats the use if we decline opinions we are insinuators if we give opinions we are enemys to our country or infidels to religion if we decline to praise ministers we are traitors Mr P thats truth & whats the use if we fancy patriots bribe fishers the mob worrys us for government men Mr P thats fact & whats the use of it – if we say parsons have great salarys Mr P we are deists & devils & worse & whats the use Mr P but if we say these things as oppertunity offers we are saints Mr P aye every thing Mr P very Ceasars Mr P fit for one of the oracles of family devotion & public worship Mr P a very saint a down right saint & only inferior to a red letter saint in the almanack & a stone & mortar saint in the church thats fact Mr P Cant & hypocrisy are the grand nessesitys of the world & the salt of life[34] & theres no help for it Mr P that[s]

fact: & now for a song
  Topers Rant[35]
(Pet. MS A46, pp. 86–87)

For Essay on 'bone & cleaver club'
Whats all the fuss for religion Mr P who is she

Thus in the time of war a general fast was so generally the intro-
duction of a new tax & a public thankgiving so publicly the finale
of a 'victory' that was the universal tho not the acknowledged
cause of such taxes that the lower orders always looked upon the
anouncement of these religious rites as the bad omens of new
oppressions & dreaded them both as they would the anouncement
of a pestilence while the haters of religion held them up as farces
of penitence & rejoicing & turned the matter into ridicule by
declaring that religion was nothing more then a liscence to pick the
pockets of the people with impunity such are the evils of scacred
[*sic*] things being made to mingle with the intrigues of politics
where cunning to disguise their actions from the people is consid-
ered the highest stretch of political philosophy & skill to make the
basest actions appear plausible the greatest abilities of a
state[s]man
(Pet. MS A46, p. 90)

For the Bone & Cleaver Club

Well you see as I sed says I this is pretty work this ove our viker
baiting me about working my donkey on a sunday now you see
our viker dus duty at three chirches & rides one hoss to all three
now you see as I sed says I whose beest is the most woked the
vikers hoss what goes three jurneys of severel miles in a day or my
donkey that oney goes one & thet a few furlongs to the mill to fetch
a few stones of flower when the vikers hoss carreys sixteen stone
at the full in the bargen & they all laghed heertily you see as I sed
& as I sey now & swore it wor a good un – & even he when finished
his oration relighted his pipe & looked for applause & was not
dissapointed for the bone & cleaver club roared in a body

Practibility Mr President thats religion – cheat as cheat can –
thats the plan for hard times Mr P to live in the world we must live

287

by the world thats fact to be moral & virtuous is to be books & not
men it will take a wise man to bind me in calf skin Mʳ P we cannot
act as we read demure our matters as we will³⁶ lifes a rudish plant
& we cannot become a bunch of lavender pressed in a ladys band
box or a rose folded in a novel this is romance Mʳ P & deals with
enchantment & I dont want to be reckoned a wizzard Mʳ P & as to
religion why we cannot be folded in a sermon or lye in a parsons
pocket (immense cheering) we must do as others do or wheres the
living – & not as parsons tell us (tremendous cheering) we must
cheat to be cheated³⁷ thats fair (thunders of applause) we cant live
by religion thats truth (more cheering)
(Pet. MS A49, p. 25)

For Essay on Bone & cleaver club
    Now for the matter of that Mr President whats the use laws &
religions are all very well in their places Mr President but they
wont keep there (bravo) for when religion backs some matters Ive
a notion shes no better then a nother body who trys the 'by hook
or by crook' for a living & weres the good (bravo bravo) in our late
distressing wars she was bottle holder to the oppressing taxes &
the pulpits Mr President I say the pulpits ecchoed with the justice
of the war & the justice of the taxes when you & I Mr P & every
body else saw there was neither justic[e] nor honesty in them all
for Ive a notion Mr P they had their hands in my pocket pretty
deep tho I was not even alowed to say they were picking it so I sold
my horse & went on foot & fearing the claim of the tax might rest
in the saddle Mr P I sold that also but found afterwards that had I
sold the saddle & kept the horse I should have saved the taxes but
who can be deep enough for the game were every trick wins & fair
play looses you & I said so Mr P & where was the harm or the lie
but before we could say Jack Robinson were was we why at the
fag end of the six acts³⁸ [blank] an[d] [blank] in prison the blanks
contain only oaths & hiccups which are ommitted & what did we
say Mr P why here is the glorious page from our journal for which
we suffered martyrdom (bravo bravo bravo) & living yet Mr
P what did we say thats the matter why we said when a new tax
was proclamed³⁹we were phisiced with a public farce I mean fast

288

Mr P (roars of applause) to cool & temperate our tempers Mr P & when the nessesity of a new tax was discovered we was cherished with a public thanks giving for a victory the only apology for taxes so that the people Mr P I say the people dreaded the anouncement of Fasts & Thanks givings as they would the announcement of a famine or a pestilence & what I say is truth & I say it under the roof of our clubhouse Mr P & I help to pay for the liberty & thats the beauty & wheres the harm Ive done bravo bravo bravo hip hip hip three rounds & bumpers[40] to the year 18
    & now for a song
    'Self interest is a rude maschine' &c[41]
    every man who sets his glass down before he drinks it forfeits a shilling or drinks an extra glass said a blustering lump of a fellow as short & fat as the indian appollo[42] so that I had to forfiet a shilling to keep the peace & shun dangers he then drank me in a bumper & began his speech which containd too many oaths for repetit[i]on & too little of any thing else to be connected or understood without them the only good about it was that the president made him come down forfeit but not much above a penny a score & as they hung on his tongue like hissing serpents had he made him forfiet a guinea he could not have made him swallow them
(Pet. MS A46, pp. 62–63)

        For Essay on 'Bone & Cleaver club'
    Truth is always asserted with the fewest words & falshood with the most protestations Truth simply thinks you believe her & falshood wishes to make you believe her
(Pet. MS A18, p. R240, cancelled)

[Advice to his children]

A number of Clare's prose passages and fragments can be identified as intended for letters of advice that he meant to write, primarily for the benefit of his children. A list of essays he intended to write or complete includes 'Living in the world aright addressd to my two Daughters' (Pet. MS A46, p. 61). Many of the fragments copied into Pet. MS A45 (see below, pp. 291–4) probably belong to the same project.

In the first place set a resolution down & keep it as you would an oath never to mix or associate in bad company for if it ever is your lot to rise above their stations they will do their utmost to degrade you – of good & its estimate they have no more ideas then brutes but they are prolific in the invention of evil – consider your masters interests as your own & he will feel towards you as a friend – & above all things value common honesty it is a current coin all over the civilized world & will win you esteem in the end Look upon your inferiors in life with respect for that is your duty & upon the Clergy with reverence for they are Gods servants – untill you are able to chuse your own creeds I would advise you to hear every sunday the Prayers of the church for they are the best ever written or uttered & I think you will never grow weary of them by frequent hearing to me they have been comforts in illness hopes in trouble & a charm over every {ill} evil that surrounded me & I have had my share – consider that I who give you this advice would never injure you or wish to lead you wrong although false friends there are & many who would wish so to lead you that they might mock & revile you in the end – & to prove the value of this advice I have tried it tho not so early as I wish you to do & found it good & therefore I give it to you with the sincere assurance that if you *follow* it – it will be your best friend & altho it may not insure you wealth it will assuredly give you comfort which is much better – never meddle with political contentions for they are the battles of strife & interest & if it conserns not you leave them alone & if they should consern your interests you will find men allotted to defend

your party much better then you could defend it your self – whatever side your inclinations may lean you will find this as a universal & general rule to guide you – & if you value a quiet mind go by it – for there are many whose superior abilitys force them into that storm & strife of opinion who would give all the wealth they possess for that quiet which you may enjoy for nothing – when you read the flowery orations of great minds admiration[43] may win[44] you to praise but never let ambition urge you to become a partizan – for if you do farewell peace of mind for ever – if you can be impartial read the speeches & they will improve you – & if style or composition or purity of diction delight you there you will find it in perfection in the orations of both partys for to me they have been of great benefit although I never saw a book on grammer before I was 20 or knew any thing what ever of the proper construction of sentences – yet I was so far benefited from reading an old newspaper now & than as to write pretty correctly & never any other wise then to be intelligible although before this I could not scarcly write a common letter so as to understand it my self for it was my lot
(Pet. MS B5, pp. 90–1; on a sheet originally addressed: M^r E T Artis / Caistor)

Prose notes in Pet. MS A45

Clare used Pet. MS A45 to preserve a number of prose notes and fragments; we have here excerpted those that refer to politics and related issues.

By the hasty conclusions of mobs cunning is generally mistaken for wisdom they applaud its ready impudence of speech as the flowers of oratory & its unintellegible gargon as the only common sense of liberty & perfection – while the precepts of reason & wisdom are not alowed a hearing & hustled from their stations like so many noisey crows who interrupt the subtle songs of these audacious nightingales (p. 3)

That religion that becomes a cloak for political power is seldom the religion of common sense – texts are perverted to purposes for which they were never intended & the odd combinations are so easily discovered that instead of forcing conviction they excite contempt (p. 6)[45]

Tyranny may make obedient slaves but liberty & kindness only make willing subjects (p. 9)

With mobs freedom & plunder are synonymous (p. 21)

There is neither wisdom or reason in a mob its sole end & aim is mischief – they fall into degredation but they never do an action that raises them into esteem or renders them sacred in history – it took the genius of a Wren[46] much time & labour to rebuild St Pauls but the army of Jack Cade would without genius & in little time destroy it thus it is ever easier to descend into obscurity than to rise into fame (p. 26)

Never let vanity or passion (for lack of temper is a lack of knowledge) lead you to join the party quarrels of party writers – peace is only found by her own name & belongs to no party wig or tory or radical are not of her company ambition is a dead language to her & strife a cert[a]in death to her existance therefore she avoids it as a pestilence – to be continually quarreling & writing about the nusiance of error in this party & that party leaves the writer at last the greatest nuisance to be compla[i]ned of – he who dabbles in mood[47] injures his own cloaths (p. 28)

Party turmoils makes real enemys & doubtful friends therefore never interfere with conscerns that conscern not yourself but others – advice if requested should be conscil[ia]tory not vituperat[iv]e – when the turmoil is over you will have the satisfaction of offending nobody & of keeping old friends for every one feels a value for the quiet hearth that shelters him from the pelting storm (p. 30)

There are some partys or sects that are so tenacious of argument & so watchful after oppertunitys to cavil with the creeds of others that if all the world was to agree with them they would instantly for arguments sake – like a litter of vermin fall on & wrong each other (p. 30)

Politics may be said to be an art of money catching – the terms Wig & Tory & Radical are only distinctions between the actors in the play – their discourse is of their country but when their parts are done we see they only meant themselves – the wig clamours of liberty when out of the harvest but when amidst the lo[a]ves & fishes[48] he is silent making no noise at his meals – the tory is always at an excuse with his speeches – he hates tyranny & to show it puts freedom into prison for speaking & calls that liberty[49] – self interest supplies the definition – Radicals having no share in the harvest grow clamorous in mobs & raise a hue & cry against laws & propertys which prevents them from possesing it themselves these are the 'sea roamers' who are watching for storms & looking out for oppertunitys to share in the plunder[50] (pp. 31–2)

There are many laws to prevent people from making use of their tongues but there has as yet been no inventions of tyrany to hinder people from thinking (p. 32)

If we judge party intentions by party arguments it would show that they constantly oppose each other for this reason that one is in power & the other wants it & though it be said that the motives of the weaker are ever wrong it may as truly be said of the stronger by the latter that their reasonings are never right (p. 34)[51]

War has ever been the watch word of political intriguers & religion but too often as the professional bottle holders on each side to encourage the combat[52] (p. 34)

Politics may be defined as the struggles of opposition to act in unison where the greatest evils ever canvassed find some base enough to support them & the best good ever offered for the countrys benefit or the peoples happ[i]ness is never aimed at but there is some mean enough to oppose it – thus 'Party is the madness of many for the gain of a few'[53] (p. 37)

To live by one mans will would be the cause of many mens misery

Old Proverb (p. 38)

A crust with liberty is better than a feast in prison (p. 43, cancelled)

Miscellaneous notes and fragments

Pain[54] was a man of strong mind & great natural abilities added to these he shows an easily agitated temper & a restless ambition that led him to fancy his own extravagance of opinion as the highest wisdom & his subtelties of detecting seeming inconsistences as the labourous discoveri[e]s of reasoning & this pompous presumption of self confidence this led his acknowledged abilities into wrong channels where his strong temper made his dissapointed ambitions the foundation of a continued warfare against every thing that time had rendered sacred & the oldest of convictions had taken for truths – yet rem[em]ber this – this great enemy & far from contemptible – could not satisfy himself much less others that the Scriptures were falshoods – all he could was to make superficial readers doubt about some parts & common sense readers reflect upon them & trust that the whole was founded on truth thus Pains Attempt to under value the bible stird up an evidence in its favour it is only dangerous to people who take any thing for granted that others may tell them to save them the trouble of thinking for themselves
(Pet. MS B5, fol. 85r-v)

People who have little reflection look upon no remedy better than force – while peacable complainers offer them up in [*word omitted?*]

mobs strengthen their cause & then with riots & disorders peti-
tions then grow into dissati[s]fact[i]ons & become demands these
in time strengthen into force & become downrig[ht] robberies thus
mobs of any kind should be put down before any remedy is
proposed for any thing short of downright allowance to plunder
the peacable will be despised & rejected – what a time we live in –
one class have been complaining & from complaints I fear have
been encouraging the lower orders to break away for their own
intention this class complain of poverty but show no appearance
of it while the other is so destitute that one almost wonders they
should have been silent for so long[55]
(Pet. MS B5, p. 5)

Common sense would never covet the property that belongs to
another
  I could not feel happy with the wealth that I had no right too, &
therefore feel a greater happiness in peace & poverty then I should
do in the riches of lawless force & unchecked rebellion – I do not
know from what cause I inherit this feeling unless the little
wisdom I have gotten imbued me with it – but this I do think if I
had not been taught to read & write I should not have indulged in
such scruples tho I might not have joined the violence of mobs I
should not have seen the unlawful cupidity of their notions of
right & freedom as I do now & therefore I feel happy with the little
learning that my parents gave me as the best legacy fortune could
ever bestow
(Pet. MS B5, p. 74)

  I read history & am astonished at the lesson it gives of the
vanitys of pride pomp & power – mind alone is the sun of the earth
– it lives on when the clouds & paraphanalia of pretention are
forgotten – The life of a man & the life of a kingdom may be
compared to plants they have their infancy – their prime of
manhood their dotage of age & their death – kingdoms struggle
into existance – by industry they arive to power they then decline
into grandeur & indolence assuming strength to hide weaknessess
untill they can hide it no where but in the arms of eternity when

they fall into the ruins of other shadows & grandeurs that perished before them – where the levitys of time condences the pomps & pretentions of a world into the page of a history & settles the boasts of a kingdom with the single dash of a pen – 'if Troy was it is buried in oblivion'[56]
(Pet. MS A43, p. 35)[57]

Nothing can equal in history the fanatical cruelty & barbaritys of some of Charles 1[sts] enemys but Charles 2[nds] revenge – truth often finds king & tyrant synonimous – tho flattery {often} always keeps them seperate by the cant of the king can do no wrong – a fine apology for cruelty in a tyrant – & a needless falshood that adds no worth to the actions of a good man & no defence in times of danger & extremity to a tyrant
(Pet. MS B5, p. 86)

I should like to see the effect of schools established by govern-ment in every village – I should think they would put human life & commonsense into that dull & obdurate class from whence I struggled into light like one struggling from the night mare in his sleep & now I only see the wretched ignorance I have left behind me in more vivid lights – & that great desert of intelect the lowest of the people is darker then the long nights of greenland latitudes if vulgarity & want of human knowledge be considered darkness – assuredly it may be felt
(Pforz. Misc MS 198, p. 39)

They must not copy the french so far as to make the english nobility life annuals if they do danger is apparent – the modern creations of modern parliments let them model as they please – ornament is not strength – modern decorations perhaps are often more accordant with difference of taste then unison of perfection & therefore in some instances[58] the simplicity of the old building will rather be restored then injured – yet some of these moderns even are ancients from merit & deserve [word omitted?] & who but the brutish deeds of mobs would destroy the young pretentions of their pedigree but if those old distinctions which time has served

& seasoned are trampled on – let them beware if the building stands when the pillars are taken away it stands by[59] miracle & not by precedent & therefore destruction is more to be expected than preservation – let them draw callumny from commonsense & not from modern extravagance & popular delusions
(Pforz. Misc MS 198, p. 41)

Such restless spirits are not the poor mans friend tho they grow popular in that pretention – they use the poor as a 'cunning workman' uses his tools to accomplish their own ends & then they would leave them when not wanted or load them with tenfold oppressions
(Pforz. Misc. MS 197, item 4)

These political bottle holders defend their party with indis-criminate [blank] there is no medium with them for a man who would take to neether party but comend or condemn the actions of each as they deserved would 'between two stools come to the ground' & his self interest would be suspended over a presipice & in thinking on getting a footing on both sides he would drop & fall down plump into the crater either utterly ruined or eternally forgotten
(Pet. MS A42, p. 13)

The wigs & torys may be better classified perhaps by the terms of outs & ins for be they wigs or torys in those situations the outs are always vocivorators of 'liberty' 'cruelty of taxation' & 'good of the people' while the ins are inflexible tyrants & determined supporters of all that is oppressing & annoying to the people & benefitting to themselves & their connections
(Pet. MS A42, p. 94)

These sort of politicians seem as
'Steady patriots of the world alone
'The friends of every country – but their own'[60]
(Pet. MS A46,p. 3)

I never meddle with politics in fact you would laugh at my idea of
that branch of art for I consider it nothing more or less then a game
at hide & seek for self interest & the terms wig & tory are nothing
more in my mind then the left & right hand of that monster the
only difference being that the latter lyes nearer the windfalls of
wills for self interest then the other – that there are some & many
who have the good of the people at heart is not to be doubted but
with the others who have only the good of themselves in view
when balloted I fear that they will always be as the few
(Pet. MS A46, p. R43, cancelled)

In country[s] where the community are governed by men
instead of the laws people are oftener punished for good actions
then bad ones & instead of being rewarded for good deeds are as
often rewarded for bad ones & uncerta[i]nty pervades the [blank]
which at last ends in rebellion [blank] & cruelty
(Pet. MS A46, p. 74; pencil)

Religion is not only nessesary for the interests of the individual but
useful for the better order & government of the comunity at large
(Pet. MS A46, p. 74)

Party animosity always runs foulest among the dregs & filth of
human beings – these boaking taggs[61] delight in the storm where
they crouch brooding over their inventions to do evil like a toad in
a hotbed
(Pet. MS B5, p. 87)

A King is always better then no king
With no laws there would be no living
& the absence of these two principles would let loose a liberty
more savage then a Lion whose ravages would leave a waste too
desolate for reflection to dwell upon – a Tragedy in five Acts with
murders in every page would be but a comedy to such a picture[62]
(Pet. MS A48, p. R38)

common sense will teach you that a king is better then no king &

that to make up a government church & state are nessesary matters
– were there no religion there would be no law & were there no
law there would be no living – the nobility are the props of a
nation like the order of architecture too they const[it]ute the splen-
dour of the building equallity is an impossibility & the men who
rave about leveling distinctions & tickle the ears of their auditors
with the poor fancys of enriching you only mean the desire of
enriching them selves[63]
(MS Pet. MS A53, fol. 33v)

Slavery origionates with the luxury of tyranny & force only
submits to the crueltys of oppression untill the effeminance of its
oppressors grows into dotage it then rises & regains its liberty –
like as the lion in his strength overawes the lesser beasts into unjust
subjection but in the season of age when he looses his teeth &
needs friends they oppress him in turn with injustice & regain
their former freedom thus tyranny gennerally gets paid with its
own coin

Tyrants hate liberty & the reason is plain because they them-
selves can enjoy every thing but liberty they persecute their slaves
into obedience but never concilliate them into friends therefore
fear makes them the slave of slaves for as they are dreaded by
others yet it is only as one tyrant to many of the oppressed so they
more bitterly feel the dreaded vengance of the many enemys
which their cruelty have made recoiling upon themselves
(Pet. MS A49, p. 15, up to 'concilliate them into friends'; the
remaining text is taken from a cancelled parallel passage on an
unnumbered sheet preceding p. 1 of Pet. MS A49)

I must write to Miss [Mortlock] to tell her that I have read Mr
C[obbett]s tracts[64] & the more I know of him the more am I dissa-
pointed to think of what he might have written & what he might
have done – tallents that lifted him above every obstacle are sacri-
ficed to present grievances picques & self interested animositys –
when they might have handed his name down to ages as a great
phol[os]opher of domestic life instead of a timeserving polotician
& a restless adversary of what hangs about every lover of their

co[u]nt[r]y as constitu[tio]nal principles that seem as nessesary to its existance as the cir[c]ulation of the blood does to our own diseases it may have but the skill of a phisician is more nessesary then the hasty levelling of such changing & unreasonable opi[n]ions – that from their very want of stability show their want of truth – for one of two contradictory opinions must be wrong & therefore it is wrong from its very principle which is a foundation which right can never build upon – the the [*sic*] foolish man built his house upon the sand but the wise man chose the rock – & I am sure I feel the example & see no safety in the restless ambitions of Mr Cobbet
(Pet. MS B5, pp. 77–78)

When both sides are beaten the only way to know the fact is by hearing them both claim the victory
(Pet. MS A49, p. 20; cf. Pet. MS A42, p. 5, cancelled)

As it is the fashion in politics to dissemble & to appear what we are not to be fashionable therefore is to be an hypocrite successfully as the actor when he appears on the stage to do his part as successfully as possible hide[s] himself behind it as much as he can & the more he contrives to cheat his audiance in this way the more he is applauded Tis just so with the world at this time – if a man would live or be successfull in life he is told not to be honest at all times or speak the truth at all times but he must act just as chances but he must always have an appearance of religion in his acting wether he is so or not – no matter if he tryes to appear so little matters will be winked at & his character is unimpeachable but if ever he suffers his conscience or his honesty to stand in the way of his self interest he is considered nothing but a fool & instead of meriting praise will receive nothing but contempt for his pains – consistancy is not to be looked at in the way to preferment – for that is a merit & the only one that the stubbornly rebellious humour of the spirit of evil is alowed to posses – & it is not at all consistant to good living to take any pattern from him – little delinquencys will be looked over as
(Pet. MS A55, fol. 9, cancelled)

Notes

1   In early 1830 the *Champion* published reports of county meetings in Lincolnshire, Norfolk, Cambridgeshire, Devon, Cheshire, Wiltshire, Suffolk, Berkshire, Essex, Bedfordshire, Rutland, Northamptonshire, and Hertfordshire (12, 19, 26 Jan., 2, 16, 23 Feb., 2, 16, 23 March 1830).

2   'When grain sold at 5 guineas & 6 guineas the quarter poor men in hundreds of parishes worked for 10 shillings a week this is true Mr Editor for I my self was one of the [blank]' (Pet. MS A46, p. 21).

3   Cf. 'Whatever may have been the demerits of the farmer, 'live and let live' has been his motto; but when oppressed by high rents, tithes, and taxes, to a degree almost bordering on ruin, he has been reluctantly forced to recur to the alternative of exercising his influence over the poor in curtailing their wages, sending them to the roads for a pitiable allowance, and having his work done by the 'round' system: thus tampering with the poor man's rights, and debarring him who is the support of the nation, almost of the bare necessaries of life.' ('Agricultural Distress' by A True Patriot; *Champion*, 14 Dec. 1830, p. 395)

4   Cf. 'Would any man, who is walking along, tread as willingly on another's gouty toes, whom he has no quarrel with, as on the hard flint and pavement?' (David Hume, *Enquiries concerning Human Understanding and concerning the Principles of Morals* [1777], reprinted 1975, Section V, Part II, p. 226). We owe this reference to Mr Noël Staples.

5   Clare is alluding to the funeral of the Duke of York in 1827. 'On 20 January, ignoring the advice of his doctors, the King went down for the funeral to Windsor ... It was a bitterly cold day, and the congregation which included most members of the Cabinet and of the Royal Family stood shivering in the gloom. There was no matting or carpeting on the floor, and Canning presumed that whoever had filched it had had bets on the duration of their lives. Lord Eldon sensibly followed Canning's advice and stood on his cocked hat and then 'in a niche of carved work where he was able to stand on wood'. But the Duke of Wellington caught a severe cold; so did the Duke of Sussex; so did the Lord Chamberlain of the Household, the Duke of Montrose. Canning contracted rheumatic fever, the Bishop of Lincoln subsequently died, and it was alleged that the soldiers who had made up the guard of honour expired at the rate of half a dozen a day.' (Christopher Hibbert, *George IV: Regent and King, 1811–1830* [London: Allen Lane, 1973], p. 283)

6   Cf. 'Poverty has many oppressors & no voice to be heard above them' (Pet. MS A48, p. R39).

7   This may be an allusion to the colour of the paper on which the news-

paper in which Clare's unidentified antagonist published his comments was printed.

8   This word is hard to read (it may be 'Merriman'), but it could be a reference to Lord Charles Manners, brother of the Duke of Rutland, and like the Duke a noted Tory.

9   See *The Merchant of Venice*, I. i. 93–4:
> As who should say 'I am Sir Oracle
> And when I ope my mouth let no dog bark.

10   Genesis 28: 12.

11   Clare is evidently alluding to a remark by Robert Owen that had been reported in several newspapers. 'Mr. OWEN, the well-known philanthropist ... says, in one of the letters that he has lately addressed to a friend ... 'On returning to my native country, I found it increased in wealth and increased in poverty ...'' (*Champion*, 2 Feb. 1830, p. 36) Cf. 'Fellow Countrymen, – After having visited various countries, I find you on my return increased in wealth, and also in poverty and distress.' (Robert Owen, 'Address to the British Nation', 11 Jan. 1830; in the *Times*, 13 Jan. 1830)

12   Cf. Genesis 41: 1–36.

13   Clare wrote 'to' as a slip for 'that'.

14   See Exodus 18: 3. This is a favourite quotation with Clare, expressing, perhaps, for him his own condition.

15   'clubs &c six acts &c' is added in the margin at this point. The Six Acts, passed after Peterloo in 1819, were directed against the activities of the radical Reformers, by curtailing freedom of meeting and the publication of seditious material. See below, p. 303, n. 38.

16   Clare may be referring to regular soldiers, or he may mean the police officers appointed by Peel in 1822 to patrol central London who were known as 'redbreasts' because of the colour of their tunics (Eric J. Evans, *Britain Before the Reform Act: Politics and Society 1815–1832* [London and New York: Longman, 1989], p. 59).

17   Presumably a slip for 'invested'.

18   See footnote 5 above.

19   Cf. 'Five years ago, the very shibboleth of the Aristocrats, was the scorn with which they flung out the term Radical. What was he who groaned under distress ? – a Radical ! What was he who manifested "an ignorant impatience of taxation" – a Radical ! ... at the end of five years we find High Tories, Ministers, Country Gentlemen, Nobles, and all our former antagonists, occupying the positions which were at the commencement of that period allotted to the Radicals as their very pillories of contempt. ... Country Gentlemen, Magistrates, and even Clergymen, appear in the parts of demagogues ...' (*Examiner*, 24 Jan. 1830, p. 49).

20   Clare has written 'the' as a slip for 'that'.

21   This reading is tentative; 'macaroni' was a Regency term for a fop or

dandy.

22 Clare is referring to the riots in Bristol on 29–31 October 1831.

23 Presumably a slip for 'incredible'.

24 'mystery' is added over 'revelation' in the manuscript.

25 Clare regularly uses 'listen' as a transitive verb taking a direct object.

26 Clare has written 'I' for 'it', perhaps a significant slip.

27 'wear' for 'were'.

28 Clare has 'I' for 'Aye'.

29 A probable reference to the Society for the Suppression of Vice, of which Lord Radstock was Vice-President, and whose attempts to preserve the Sabbath are satirised in Thomas Love Peacock's poem 'Rich and Poor' (see above, p. lix, note 65).

30 The company are singing one of Clare's songs, of course (see *MP*, IV. 61–2).

31 Cf. 'Perhaps if manna was to fall from heaven as it did in the time of Moses & Aaron it would soon have a tythe & tax on it' (Pet. MS A46, p. 74, cancelled).

32 A reference to church tithes.

33 Cf. Nor. MS 17, p. 20, cancelled.

34 Cf. the cancelled parallel passage in Nor. MS 17, pp. 37–8, which concludes: 'If you turn critic you must be sure to flatter the living but abuse the dead as you please'. See also Pet. MS A46, p. 140, cancelled; Pet. MS B5, p. 87; Pet. MS A18, p. R241, cancelled; and Pet. MS A46, p. R34, cancelled.

35 Another of Clare's songs (see *MP*, IV. 75–7).

36 This means, perhaps, 'no matter how demurely we pretend to behave'.

37 It is possible that 'not' has been omitted before 'to be cheated'.

38 'at the fag end of the six acts' is an addition in the manuscript. The Six Acts, passed in the wake of Peterloo in 1819, were designed to prevent public meetings of reformers and to aid the repression of radical opinion.

39 At this point occur the words ' a public farce', which Clare probably forgot to delete; the meaning is certainly clearer if they are omitted.

40 Clare has actually written 'bumbers' for 'bumpers' (i.e., toasts with a full glass).

41 Clare is quoting his own works again, citing l. 33 of 'Familiar Epistle to a Friend' (see above, p. 166).

42 We have not been able to identify this reference.

43 'admiration' is written over 'ambition' which is deleted.

44 'win' is written over 'urge' which is deleted.

45 Cf. 'For Essay on Political Religion The religion of power is never the religion of common sense texts are perverted to purposes for which they were never intended & the odd combinations are so easily discovered that instead of forcing conviction they excite ridicule' (Pet.

MS A18, p. R253, cancelled).

46   Clare has written 'Wrey'.

47   I.e., 'mud'

48   'Loaves and fishes' was a proverbial phrase for the benefits of polit-
     ical office, presumably because party managers had to work miracles
     to satisfy all their supporters with the limited resources available.

49   Cf. 'The Summons', lines 155–6.

50   Cf. 'For Essay on Politics   Radicals are considered as embodying
     every species of party who differ from the court part[y] that are as
     erroniously considerd the constitutional party but radicals are only
     that mear [?mere *or* mean] class of clamourous mobs that raise a hue
     & cry against laws & propertys which prevents them from possesing
     it themselves   they are in fact 'sea roamers' who are watching for
     storms & looking out for oppertunitys to share in the plunder' (Pet.
     MS A42, p. 132, pencil, cancelled in ink). Richard Ayton, in his *Essays
     and Sketches of Character* (1825, item 100 in Clare's library; Powell, p.
     23) describes 'a class of lowly labourers, calling themselves *Sea-
     roamers*', whom he distinguishes from wreckers, saying 'the roamer is
     a never-failing attendant at the sea side, where he wanders about
     from morning till night, to pick up ... the refuse – the offal of the sea,
     native and extraneous, that is cast ashore by the tides' (pp. 217–18).
     Clare evidently uses the term in the same sense of opportunistic scav-
     engers.

51   Cf. 'For Essay on Politics   Both partys constantly oppose each other
     for this reason generally that one is in power & the other wants it &
     tho it is said by the stronger side that the motives of the weaker are
     ever wrong it may as truly be said of the former by the latter that their
     reasonings are never right' (Pet. MS A42, p. 147, cancelled)

52   'combat' replaces the deleted 'contest'

53   Cf. 'A great Poet who searched into human nature & human actions
     not only with the wit of a poet but with the truth of a philosopher
     designates Political matters as "Party" & defines it as "the madness of
     many for the gain of a few"' (Pet. MS A45, p. 40; a cancelled draft of
     this passage in Pet. MS A18, p. R259, is headed 'For Essay on
     Politics').This statement, used from 1808 as a motto by *The Examiner*,
     is cited in an article 'On War' in *The Literary Speculum* (1821, item 286
     in Clare's library; Powell, p. 30), which states: 'Swift has defined party
     to be "the madness of many, for the gain of a few"'. *The Examiner* also
     attributes it to Swift, although it was actually made by Alexander
     Pope, in a letter to Edward Blount, 27 Aug. 1714: 'Party-spirit, which
     at best is but the madness of many for the gain of a few' (*The
     Correspondence of Alexander Pope*, ed. George Sherburn [5 vols.,
     Oxford: Clarendon Press, 1956], I. 247).

54   In this note Clare refers to Paine's notorious Deist religious writings,
     particularly *Age of Reason* (1794–96). His interest in (though not neces-

sarily his knowledge of) Paine's political writings is indicated by a note 'Carlisles One Vol Edit of Paines Works Pt' (Pet. MS A61, p. 3). His first-hand knowledge of Paine evidently postdates the following comment: 'I have not read Tom Paine but I have always understood him to be a low blackguard', though he had read Bishop Watson's *An Apology for the Bible* (1796), which quoted extensively from Part II of *Age of Reason* (Journal, 17 March 1825; *JCBH*, p. 219). Watson's *Apology* is item 388 in Clare's library (Powell, p. 33).

55 See 'Apology for the Poor', above, p. 280.

56 We have been unable to trace this quotation.

57 Cf. Pet. MS A20, p. R76, cancelled.

58 'in some instances' is inserted to replace the deleted word 'perhaps'

59 'by' is inserted to replace the deleted words 'upon a'

60 Clare is paraphrasing lines 113–14 of 'New Morality' by George Canning and John Hookham Frere: 'A steady Patriot of the World alone / The Friend of every Country – but his own' (see Jonathan Wordsworth (ed.), *Poetry of the Anti-jacobin* [1799; Oxford and New York: Woodstock Books, 1991], p. 224).

61 'boak' is a dialect form of 'bolk', meaning to belch or vomit; 'tagg' is a collective term for the rabble.

62 Cf. Pet. MS B5, p. R78, deleted.

63 This fragment is preceded by the cancelled note 'Meddle very little with matters that consern not your selves – the reputation of a quiet man is much better then that of a meddler – therefore shun political contentions –', which is mainly copied in Pet. MS A48, p. R38 (see 'Advice to his children', above, pp. 290–1).

64 Mary Ann Mortlock was a friend of Herbert Marsh, Bishop of Peterborough, and his wife and often wrote letters for Mrs Marsh. On 24 Dec. 1831 Marianne Marsh sent Clare three of Cobbett's twopenny tracts (BL Egerton MS 2248, fol. 413v). This passage may be a draft for a letter to Mrs Marsh, with whom Clare corresponded about Cobbett (see *Letters*, pp. 556, 560).

LETTERS

Page references are given to Mark Storey's edition of The Letters of John Clare *(Oxford: Clarendon Press, 1985), but the text has occasionally been silently corrected by reference to the manuscripts. Deleted words are given in curly brackets; editorial additions in square brackets; and uncertain readings in square brackets with a question mark.*

I look not at Riches – tis Sense & Learning that gains my Esteem (To I.K. Holland, [early 1819?]; *Letters*, p. 6)

I ... shoud like Whites Life & Funeral of Lord Nelson[1] I feel a great Regard for that Saviour of his Country & shoud be happy to posses an account of him I once saw 'whites' & likd it much (To Markham E. Sherwill, 8 Apr. 1820; *Letters*, p. 45)

Being very much botherd latley I must trouble you to leave out the 8 lines in 'helpstone' beginning 'Accursed wealth' & two under 'When ease & plenty' – & one in 'Dawnings of Genius' 'That nessesary tool' leave it out & put ***** to fill up the blank this will let em see I do it as negligent as possible d——n that canting way of being forcd to please I say – I cant abide it & one day or other I will show my Independance more stron[g]ly then ever you know who's the promoter of the scheme I dare say – I have told you to order & therefore the fault rests not with me while you are left to act as you please (To Taylor, 16 May 1820; *Letters*, pp. 68–70)

'are you 'St Caroline' or 'George 4th'[2] I am as far as my politics reaches 'King & Country' no Inovations on Religion & government say I – this night is the grand illumination for our City in honour of St Caroline the woman that is to personate her majesty is a deformd object who is to be dressd in white & all the rest are to have 'white favours' the windows are to be illuminated but as the grand characteristic of an Englishman is liberty of consience I will for once sustain it – I am persuaded to light up in consequence of keeping the peace & my windows unbroken[3] – but they have their whims & jack will have his & I am now soon as your letter is done making preparations of defence a large oaken bludgeon & if the devil heads the mob let him head it so as he passes my door peacably but if his develship throws one stone at my window mind ye hostilitys begin & if his hide is not cudgel proof Ill feel for it & for once let him know I am as rebellious against his opinions as he was in old times against a superior adversary

Lord R. ask'd my opinion of the present matters & I bluntly told him that 'if the King of England was a madman I shoud love him as a brother of the soil' in preference to a foreigner who be as she be shows little interest or feeling for England when she lavishes such honours on the menials of another which Nelson has long characterizd as a set of 'whores scoundrels poets & fiddlers' still poor St Caroline she has seen much trouble & perplexity god forgive her – (To J.A. Hessey, 1 Dec. 1820; *Letters*, pp. 109–10)

I have seen 1 Vol of Crabb (last winter) called 'Tales' I lik'd here & there a touch but there is a d—d many affectations among them which seems to be the favourite play of the parson poet – in our 4 Vol I mean to have a good race with him & have consciet enough to have little fear in breaking his wind – ... whats he know of the distresses of the poor musing over a snug coal fire in his parsonage box – if I had an enemey I coud wish to torture I woud not wish him hung nor yet at the devil my worst wish shoud be a weeks confinment in some vicarage to hear an old parson & his wife lecture on the wants & wickedness of the poor & consult a remedy or a company of marketing farmers thrumming over politics in an alehouse or a visionary methodist arguing on points of religion either is bad enough & I know not which is the best – (To John Taylor, [7 Jan. 1821]; *Letters*, pp. 137–8)

Drakard the Editor of the 'Stamford News' has been severly beaten this week in a rather cowardly way by a person coming in with the excuse of buying a book who while D. turnd to look [for][4] it cudgeld him with a stick & rid off the stranger had a footman with him & is some one no doubt that the Paper has provokingly abused but who it is or for what cause he has beaten him I know not – perhaps this is News to you if you dont see Ds Paper for I expect it makes a flaming appeal there with its usual addition of a Lye –[5] (To Taylor, 24 Feb. 1821; *Letters*, pp. 159–60)

– my two favourite Elm trees at the back of the hut are condemned
to dye it shocks me to relate it but tis true the savage who owns
them thinks they have done their best & now he wants to make use
of the benefits he can get from selling them – O was this country
Egypt & was I but a caliph the owner shoud loose his ears for his
arragant presumption & the first wretch that buried his axe in their
roots shoud hang on their branches as a terror to the rest – I have
been several mornings to bid them farewell – had I £100 to spare I
woud buy their reprieves – but they must dye – yet this mourning
over trees is all foolishness they feel no pains they are but wood
cut up or not – a second thought tells me I am a fool was People
all to feel & think as I do the world coud not be carried on – a green
woud not be ploughd a tree or bush woud not be cut for firing or
furniture & every thing they found when boys would remain in
that state till they dyd – this is my indisposition & you will laugh
at it – (To Taylor, 7 March 1821; *Letters*, p. 161)

I am anxious of getting my book out & not only that let me tell you
but am as anxious of seeing you do justice to Keats by bringing him
out agen which I hope you will loose no time to do – excuse my
conscieted meddling advice – else I think the sooner you publish
a vol of his remains with an account of his Life &c the better while
the ashes of genius is warm the public look with a tender anxiety
for what it leaves behind – to let this get cold woud in my opinion
do him an injury – the ill treatment he has met will now be produc-
tive of more advantages – tho the warm heart that once felt it – is
cold & carless to praise or to censure now – still he left those hopes
behind him – which his friends cherish in remembrance that
justice woud be done him – is the cold hearted butchers of annony-
mous Critics to {blast a} cut up everything that escapes their
bribery or thinks contrary to them is polotics to rule genius – if it
is – honesty & worth may turn swindlers & liberty be thrown to
the dogs & worried out of existance – & that she has been long ago
– (To Taylor, [5 May 1821]; *Letters*, pp. 188–9)

'Critisism may do her worst' – & be d——d when shes done it – to
escape the hell of party-political critisism is impossible – so I am

prepared – (To Hessey, 17 May 1821; *Letters*, p. 190)

I have nearly finished another its 'a tale of other days' I call it 'the Vicar'[6] the man whom I copy has been gone nearly a century – long before hunting parsons had existance – his character floats in the memory of the village – & from that my rescorces are gleaned – I think I have made a good thing of it – but that stands for nothing still it satisfys me & always urges me on to the end when I fancy that – his monument is a little round free stone by the side of the alter it records no name or date its Latin & the substance of it is this 'At the day of resurrection I hope it will be known who I am' his sallary was £35 yearly & his charitys was great considering his income if he saw a bare footed beggar in the street he woud take him home & give him [h]is shoes very often the only pair he possesd waiting in the house till his shoemaker set him at liberty with new ones – & his last sixpence has often been thrust into the hands of a widow or orphan – his heart was so open to the miseries of mankind that his friends often deemd it nessesary to borrow the greater part of his sallerey when it was due – to keep it for his maintenance & let him have it as he wanted for that purpose – such as these shall never dye – if they must – 'the pillowd firmament is rotteness & earths base built on stubble' (To Hessey, 17 May 1821; *Letters*, pp. 190–1)

I have put on the black waiscoat you gave me for this last week & shoud have done so with the coat but it is too dandyish for this country – but its not to mourn for the injurd quean – I hated her while living & I have no inclination to regret her death – I hated her not as a woman or as a queen but as the vilest hypocrite that ever existed – common sense gives me her spectacles to look upon every thing Im of no party but I never saw such farcical humbug carried on in my life before & I never wish to see it agen for its lanched me head over ears in politics for this last twelvemonth & made me very violent when John Barleycorn inspird me – [*Three lines heavily deleted, which seem to read as follows:* who made me side for the king & a little true subject tho I was formerly as I was touchd with a stain of radicalism] every one has his share of humbug & I have mine (To Taylor, 18 Aug. 1821; *Letters*, pp. 208–9)

I may alter but I cannot mend grammer in learning is like Tyranny in government – confound the bitch Ill never be her slave & have a vast good mind not to alter the verse in question (To Taylor, 21 Feb. 1822; *Letters*, p. 231)

my mind is placid & contented & that is somthing for when I was first took god forgive me I had hard work to bare up with my malady & often had the thought of destroying myself & from this change in my feelings I satisfactorily prove that Religions foundation is truth & that the Mystery that envelopes it is a power above human nature to comprehend & thank god it is for if a many uneasy discontented minds knew of the bargain they shoud gain by being good they might still be discontented & I might be one of them besides there is little merit in undergoing a hardship for a prize when we know what it is – the labourer goes to work for his hire & is happy or sullen according to the wages alowd him – I agree with you that the religious hypocrite is the worst monster in human nature & some of these when they had grown so flagrant as to be discoverd behind the mask they had taken to shelter their wickedness led me at first to think lightly of religion & sure enough some of the lower classes of dissenters about us are very decietful & in fact dangerous characters especialy among the methodists with whom I have determind to assosiate but then there are a many sincere good ones to make up & why shoud the wicked deter us from taking care of ourselves when they ought to appear in our eyes as a warning to make us turn to the right way – my opinion Taylor of true Religion amounts to this if a man turns to god with real sincerity of heart not canting & creeping to the eyes of the world but satisfying his own conscience so that it shall not upbraid him in the last hours of life that touchstone of faith & practice carless of what the world may say either for him or against him that man in my opinion is as certain of heaven in the next world as he is of death in this – because we cannot do wrong without being conscious of it – & if no dread overweights us at that hour it is the surest proof of innosence ...

I have not answerd Hesseys last letter I delayd it to have some doubtfull passages in our dissenters creeds here explaind but I can see thro the vulgar errors that blinded them & correctly find their origional notions myself it was respecting their ignorant notions of tenets which they stile 'Free Grace' 'Election' & 'Predestination' things that are far better kept out of the way of the ignorant who interpret them to suit their own purposes & make religion grossly rediculous by such abuses (To Taylor, [after 3 April 1824]; *Letters*, pp. 292–3)

I have joind the Ranters that is I have enlisted in their society they are a set of simple sincere & communing christians with more zeal then knowledge earnest & happy in their devotions O that I coud feel as they do but I cannot their affection for each other their earnest tho simple extempore prayers puts my dark unsettld consience to shame this is how they keep the sabbath at 7 o clock they meet to pray at 9 they join the Class at half past 10 they hear preaching at half past 2 they meet agen to pray & at 7 in the evening preaching again thus passes the Sabbath with the Ranters making an heaven on earth there is a deal of enthusiasm in their prayers & preachings & manners but as it is real & not affected it is not to be found fault with but commended my feelings are so unstrung in their company that I can scarcly refrain from shedding tears & when I went church I coud scarcly refrain from sleep – I thank god that he has opend my eyes in time & let all scoffers remember this line of Young 'They may live fools but fools they cannot dye' – I shall never forget the horror that I felt in reading this line but enough – (To Hessey, 20 Apr. 1824; *Letters*, p. 294)

I do assure you that I live as near as ever I can & tho I did not tell you I have been out to hard labour most part of this summer on purpose to help out my matters but the price of labour is so low here that it is little better then parish relief to the poor man who where there is a large family is litterally pining I know not what will be the end of these times for half the Farmers here will be broken again this dry summer & I think that low rents & no taxes is the only way to recall a portion of their former prosperity but I am no Politician & know little or nothing about such matters (To Taylor, 15 July 1826; *Letters*, pp. 381–2)

I intend the first oppertunity that offers to take a cottage with as much land as will find me employment the year round for it is very irksome to be obliged to beg of people to get work of them which is actually the case for there is so many that they are forced to employ that those they are not forced to take not being paupers they will not have therefore if labour will not bring a man independance it is worse then nothing & he may as well sell himself for an india slave as belong to such places this is not without illustration for it was asserted in the Newspaper about a fortnight back that a man actually turned thief to get himself transported because he would not go home to his parish & that where he lived at would not employ him I need not add that his hopes were not dissapointed but how he feels himself in his new situation I cannot tell (To Hessey, 21 Jan. 1827; *Letters*, pp. 390–1)

I have a passionate fondness for Solitude & would much rather avoid then court the notice of my superiors when I say superiors I mean men of titles wealth & fashion with nothing or little of impartial feeling towards an inferior who wants all three of these grand matters to reccommend him to their notice the proudest feelings I posses in becoming known to the world arise from the lucky accidents that introduce me to men of genius these I consider the most fortunate incidents of my life & I would always as I have done strive to gain the notice & esteem of such men & under that feeling I indulge in the desire of becoming a regular correspondent with yourself & I hope you will not construe that desire into either flattery or compliment – for I am proud (& it is the only pride I possess) to think I have not that shallowness of feeling about me to possess neither the one or the other (To Henry Behnes, 23 July 1827; *Letters*, pp. 392–3)

I do not know how times are with you in the city but with us 'sales & bankrupts' form the general conversations among all classes & conditions of men how it will end I cannot imagine but it does not seem to be much felt in your loyal city as the newspapers give accounts as usual of your pulling d[own] [pa]llaces only as it would seem for the happiness of building them up again in spots where a husbandman would scarcely think it suitable to errect his cottage but taste now has nothing to do with such things where fashion is every thing & royal fashions too they must be excellent or it would evidently be considered radicalism to think otherwise (To H.F. Cary, 25 Jan. 1830; *Letters*, pp. 494–5)

What do you think by the bustle & bother of this country meeting mania when every village is metamorphosed into a Forum & every Giles into an Orator but the strangest metamorphose of all is these out-of-place tory folks becoming radicals & brawling in every corner of the country about reform

Are these the signs of better times I much fear it – yet it is strange to turn round for a moment & see these proteus assemblages – *self* being the only thing that sticks to its own colours ... (To William Robertson, 29 Jan. 1830; *Letters*, p. 497)

The times as you say are bad & the worst is that I fear all this bother about 'country meetings' & other rigmarole pretentions will not better them – tho there are many voices mixed up in the cry commonsense is seldom among them for self interests & individual prosperitys are the universal spirits that stir up these assemblages of reformers

The Farmer as usual is on the look out for 'high prices' & 'better markets' as he stiles them altho these markets are always known to be curses to the cottager the labourer & the poor mechanic

The Parson is now rather stirring up to radicalism (which some years ago he cryed down as infidelity) for a reduction of taxes merely because he sees that somthing must be done & as he wishes to keep his tythes & his immense livings untouched he throws the burthen on government

The Speculator is looking out for a new paper currency which placed a false value on every species of his trafic & thereby enabled the cunning to cheat the honest & the unprincipled to ruin those who had a principle for so long as country banks are alowed to accumulate their three farthing bits of paper on the public as money without any other check then a trust on their honesty – so long will a few build their prosperity on the ruin of thousands

Yet I cannot help thinking that a paper currency founded upon *just principles* would still be a very commodious way of traffic much better then gold – but I would have every bank issuing one pound notes (which is but a shadow of a promise for a substance which the promiser has pocketed) dependant as branch banks on the Bank of England (many of the other banks are not worth a capital letter) nay every bank issuing paper at all ought to have that check upon them as I think to prosper the general good of the community rather then to encourage the knavery of individuals – but you are a better politician then I am – yet I feel as common sense dictates & I think that a universal reduction of tythes – clerical livings – placemens pensions – & taxes – & all renovated & placed upon a reasonable equality suitable to the present decreased value of money & property is the only way to bring salvation to the country

I know such thoughts sometime back would have been considered as proceeding from a Leveller & a Radical – the meaning of the last word being indefinite like Wig & Tory I cannot say what it means tho I have often heard it bruted in ministerial papers – but I am sure I am no Leveller for I want not a farthing of that which belongs to another – all I want is to keep the little that fortune alowed me to call mine but if government goes on thus partially taking a little from those who have only a little & leaving the wealthy untouched I cannot help but think I shall quickly be what I have been – but times must change & they cannot right[ly] get worse – heavy burthens with proper assistance become light ones – & when there is so many idle lookers on who have no burthens to bear & immense strength to bear them they ought to assist with the rest wether they belong to church or state thats my political creed & if the ministry will for the first time attempt real good to the country this parliment I shall say 'God speed em' but I have no faith in believing impossibilitys becoming possible (To Taylor, 1 Feb. 1830; *Letters*, pp. 498–500)

How the times have altered the opinions & views of the people even here we have our villages mustering into parliments & our farmers puffing themselves up into orators & there is scarcley a clown in the village but what has the asumption to act the politician & I hope this general stir may produce general good but the farce of the thing is that our tory folks should be grown into radicals & be brawling after the reform which they alone have so long & so obstinately prevented – what is the reason – it is a known fact in natural history that foxes will do all they can to drive badgers out of their holes – that they may get in themselves[7] – & I think there is a parrarel in the matter true enough to alow the comparison – (To George Darley, [January-February ? 1830; *Letters*, pp. 501–2)

... however time makes changes among us all – from the throne to the cottage there is no difference he proves us all nothings at last – (To Taylor, 1 July 1830; *Letters*, p. 511)

I have made a few more enquir[i]es respecting those strangers whom the 'Hue & Cry' leads me to suspect are the creators of those horrid mysterys that darkness envelops & daylight discovers – The Gig was very light & apparently small for two men to occupy one was dressed in a light great coat & the other in a dark one they came in at a end of the town no strangers ever enters as it is a bye road leading no where but to bye places – they passed my father & another & asked the way for Spalding when near the public Hous 'Blue Bell' they met another man on horseback who either before or after stopt at the Bell & called for a glass of Gin – his appearance & manner waked the suspicions of Mrs Bradford who thought that these errands was of too much mystery to be honest – the day after this – Dr Johnsons stacks at spalding was destroyed

Last week a strange man on horseback in a shooting jack[e]t sort of coat galloped over Mr Sweetings Farm like a madman leaping a hedge & ditch & stopping at nothing in passing a labourer raking straw he hastily cried out 'Will[8] you are getting straw whose Farm is it' & on the mans telling him he said aye aye it will make a fine stack – & instantly galloped off & dissapeared 'Will' was the name of the labourer who declared that he had never seen the man on horseback in his life before & the ploughmen in the neighbouring grounds held their consultations on the matter of the mystery with the labourer & came to the consclusion that it must be the devil on horseback in fact it was a 'devils drive' neck or nothing – & on saturday night that horrid tragedy in deeping fen occured which chills my blood almost into water to think of – Is there no trace to track the tyger to his den whose ruinous actions are so legible & so heartrending – the above statement is partly my own observation & partly hearsay if you think them worth enquirey come over your self & do so – the people are both neighbours of mine & have the facts fresher on their memorys then I have & will tell you more particulars & better then I can – for I have so many other things [?missing] & knowing my memory that one impression quickly wears out another (To Frank Simpson, [late December 1830]; *Letters*, pp. 522–3)

I have been often astonished at the humbug of the {Sea} fashions of parlimentary pretentions & have since been alarmed at the upstir of fire & famine & such like currencys & under the influence of these ridicules I have scribbled a poem of 50 verses [*The Hue & Cry*] detailing the alarms & as it is just finished my vanitys fancy that it might as a trifle make me a trifle – (To Henry Behnes Burlowe, 28 Dec. 1830; *Letters*, p. 524)

I wish success heartily to my friends wether wigs torys or radicals but as to enemys in any of these matters I wish none for if I wished them success I should never wish they migh[t] get it neither do I wish them further harm than that they may meet so much dissapointment in me as to alter their opinions [*blank*] has been & [*blank*] but between such matter I am as a blank leaf between two pages of letter press ready to receive all impressions that coincide with my opinions or refute them & never caring to take any note of those that do not I cross them out as accounts with which I have nothing to do – I hate party feudes & can never become a party man but where I have friends on both sides there I am on both sides as far as my opinions can find it right but no further not an inch – the rest is nought but leather & prunella[9] (To Mrs Emmerson, [Dec. 1830–Jan. 1831; *Letters*, p. 527)

I have taken a large sheet on purpose to give you a specimen of the latest sins I have commited in ryhme & I also send you a Newspaper in which the Poem I spoke of in my last is inserted & which I have corrected as it should be read – they are neither of them political but as to myself I bear so poor an opinion of them & the unpublished one especially now that I feel almost as troubled at my vanity of disclosing it to you as if I had commited treason or arson or some other fashionable calamity – & as you ask me how I get on it gives me an oppertunity of explaining {my} the present resolutions of fanc[y]ing I had written somthing worthy of Cruikshanks Illustrations – God forgive me such a blasphemy for I have only been guilty of it a moment as I now see on copying it out that it is good for nothing so never show it to him at all – nessesity was the spur of the moment for I am at the worlds end Harry & if you could get Mr Hall to pay me ever so little of what he promised me I shall be set up & satisfied & the Hue & Cry may serve your maid for kindling the fire or you to light your pipe with – thus much for preface here comes the pretention (To Henry Behnes Burlowe, [after 4 Jan. 1831]; *Letters*, p. 528)

... & still I have many hopes of the present ministry for I think if they can find out the way to better the unbearable oppressions of the labouring classes they will do it – that Lord Althorp[10] is an excellent sample of honest intentions & if he ends his course as he begins it wether he looses or wins he will wear an honour that becomes the Gem of all nobil[i]tys & remains the most noble – ... we are quiet in our neighbourhood but as a spark dropt in gunpowder – the least impression either of oppression or imaginary oppression would burst into a flame – & yet the 'people' as they are called were a year or two back as harmless as flies – they did not seem even to be susceptible of injustice but when insult began to be tried upon them by the unreasonable & the proud their blood boiled into a volcano & the irruption is as certain as death if no remedy can be found to relieve them God forbid that I should

live to see a revolution it is bad enough to be under the appre-
hensions of such a matter but every day convinces us that a
hazardous change of calm or tempest is approaching (To Taylor,
24 Jan. 1831; *Letters*, p. 533)

O if the taste that once was when Chaucer & Spencer & Milton &
others of the glorious company of song was found lying in a
cottage window piled up with the bible & prayer book – if this taste
would survive we might hope for better days better tastes & better
dispositions of people but instead we have clamorous meetings of
reformers & anti reformers one swearing that black is white &
another that white is black – & of this there is no end (To [Taylor],
[May? 1831]; *Letters*, p. 540)

... & in the winter it was dangerous for any lone person to go even
a journey to Peterbro – such was the state of feeling among that
useful but ignorant class of people our peasantry that mischief
became so predominant & daring as to threaten the peacable even
in their cottages & I hope for the sake of my own feelings never to
see such another threatning winter again – for I fear there is even
in our day a class of desperadoes little or no better than the rabble
that made up the army of Jack Cade
   'a ragged multitude
   'Of hinds & peasants rude & merciless
     *   *   *   *   *

   'All scholars lawyers courtiers gentlemen
   'They call false caterpillars & intend their death'[11]
the universal wish of such ignorance is 'that henceforward all
things shall be in common' & surely when such a desperate flood
gathers into strength – the mind must feel terror at its threatning
destruction – their passions are not softened by reason or guided
by common sense – the mob impulse of the moment kindles their
minds into mischivous intentions & reflection never stays their
course for a moment brute strength is all they possess & it is as
dangerous a monopoly in the hands of a mob as it is in that of so
many savages & I may say I never saw so terrible a threatening of
rev[o]lutionary forbodings as there was in the maschine breaking

& grain destroying mania of last winter – & I am sorry to say they had too much apology for joining in such disturbances as their wants had been so long neglected as to be entirely forgotten untill it burst out into the terrible jepordays – (To Marianne Marsh, 6 July 1831; *Letters*, pp. 543–4)

I pretend to very little knowledge in men manners & things – I have only opinions & these are founded upon common sense as far as reason alows me to do so for common sense is the right use of reason among common people who have no advantages of education to come at by different ways so were I am wrong I like to correct it myself as I find it out & where I dont to be corrected by others I feel as a kindness – I should much like madam to know your & Miss M[ortlock]s opinion of the best part of Cobbets Gramer his party prejudices are fooleries which your good sense will look over as mere nothings (To Marianne Marsh, [1831–2]; *Letters*, p. 556)

I have to thank you very kindly for some little books which I read with {some} satisfaction & those which put together the 'ayes' & 'noes' of Mr Cobbet may be very useful to plain dealing people as to party they will not see
    I look upon Cobbett as one of the most powerful prose writers of the age[12] – with no principles to make those powers commendable to honest praise – the Letters to farmers contain some very sensible arguments & some things that appeared to be too much of party colouring – there is no medium in party matters {they are} where there is excess it is always on one side – & that is the worst of it – I am no politician but I think a reform is wanted – not the reform of mobs where the bettering of the many is only an apology for injuring the few – nor the reform of partys where the benefits of one is the destruction of the other but a reform that would do good & hurt none – I am sorry to see that the wild notions of public spouters always keep this reform out of sight – & as extreams must be {corrected} met by extreams – the good is always lost like a plentiful harvest in bad weather – {the} mobs never were remembered for a good action but I am sorry to see it now & then verging into

the middle classes of society whose knowledge ought to teach them commonsense & humanity for if they have it they never let it get into their speeches (To [Marianne Marsh], [early January 1832]; *Letters*, p. 560)

I am no leveller but I wish every mans security into his own pocket in preference to that of government security or friendly interference ... (To [?Taylor] [Jan.-Feb. 1832]; *Letters*, p. 570)

I have very little interest in the slavedealing arguments but I have a feeling on the broad principle of common humanity that slavery is not only impiety but disgracful to a country professing[13] religion – but then I have an idea that war is as excessive a wrong where mens attributes are founded on the basis of religious right – 'do unto others as we would be done unto' – & surely slavery & war must be two very great & very black contradictions to such principles – & yet people argue that blacks were made for bondage & that war was nessesary to keep peace – & so ones qualms are forced to be satisfied – (To [Thomas Pringle], [after 8 Feb. 1832]; *Letters*, p. 572)

... to have such men for Landlords is a satisfactory happiness – for so long as the Miltons & the Exeters have been a name in the neighbourhood – there is not one instance that I know of where they have treated willing industry with unkindness in either insulting dependants with oppression or treating poverty with cruelty – not one – & this is a proof to me that nobility is the chief support to industry & that their power is its strongest protection (To ?Elizabeth Gilchrist, [early 1832]; *Letters*, pp. 576–7)

My dear Wife

I have wrote some few times to enquire about yourself & the Family & thought about yourself & them a thousand othe[r] things that I use to think of the childern – Freddy when I led him by the hand in his childhood – I see him now in his little pink frock – sealskin cap – & gold band – with his little face as round as a apple & as red as a rose – & now a stout Man both strangers to each other the father a prisoner under a bad government so bad in fact that its no government at all but prison disapline where every body is forced to act contrary to their own wishes 'the mother against the daughter in law & the daughter against the mother in law' 'the father against the son & the son against the Father' – in fact I am in Prison because I wont leave my family & tell a falshood – this is the English Bastile a government Prison where harmless people are trapped & tortured till they die – English priestcraft & english bondage more severe then the slavery of Egypt & Affrica while the son is tyed up in his manhood from all the best thoughts of his childhood bye lying & falshood – not dareing to show love or remembrance for Home or home affections living in the world as a prison estranged from all his friends still Truth is the best companion for it levels all distinctions in pretentions Truth wether it enters the Ring or the Hall of Justice shows a plain Man that is not to be scared at shadows or big words full of fury & meaning nothing[14] when done & said with them truth is truth & no further & the rights of man – age of reason & common sense[15] are sentences full of meaning & the best comment of its truth is themselves – an honest man makes priestcraft an odious lyar & coward & a filthy disgrace to Christianity – that coward I hate & detest – the Revelations has a placard in capitals about 'The Whore of Babylon & the mother of Harlots' does it mean Priestcraft I think it must – this rubbish of cant must soon die – like all others – I began a letter & ended a Sermon – & the paper too

I am dear Wife yours ever John Clare
(To Patty Clare, [1849–50]; *Letters*, pp. 668–9)

Notes

1 Joshua White, *Memoirs of the Professional Life of the Right Honourable Horatio Lord Viscount Nelson* (1806; item 398 in Clare's library; Powell, p. 33).

2 The attempt by George IV to divorce his wife was more than a personal issue, since the queen's cause was taken up by radicals and other opponents of the government and 'gave rise to the last great wave of public demonstrations before the Reform crisis' (Eric J. Evans, *Britain Before the Reform Act: Politics and Society 1815–1832*

[London and New York: Longman, 1989], p. 28).

3   The prospect of mob violence was not imaginary. Captain Lambert, a tenant of Fitzwilliam's at Malton, had his house attacked by the mob when he refused to illuminate for the Queen's acquittal, and quit his tenancy as a result; while not condoning the mob's actions, the draft reply shows a certain sympathy with their motives (Mary Ann Lambert to Lord Fitzwilliam, 22 Nov. [1820], Lord Fitzwilliam or Lord Milton to Mary Ann Lambert, 28 Nov. 1820; Fitzwilliam correspondence, Northants. CRO, Box X1609, folder 2).

4   It is possible that Clare is using 'look' as a transitive verb.

5   The stranger was probably Lord Cardigan, who was referred to in a piece on 'Lordly Humanity' in *Drakard's Stamford News* on 9 Feb. 1821, reprinted 23 Feb. 1821.

6   Incorporated into 'The Parish' as lines 1596–1799.

7   See William Tyndale's introduction to his translation of the New Testament: 'Wherfore I beseche George Ioye, ye and all others to, for to translate the scripture for them selves, whether oute of Greke, Latyn or Hebrue. Or (if they wyll nedes) as the foxe when he hath pissed in the grayes hole chalengeth it for his awne, so let them take my translacions and laboures, and chaunge and alter, and correcte and corrupte at their pleasures, and call it their owne translations, and put to their awne names, and not to play boo pepe after George Ioys manner' (*The New Testament Translated by William Tyndale 1534*, ed. N. Hardy Wallis [Cambridge: Cambridge University Press, 1938], p. 18).

8   Storey erroneously reads this word as 'Well', which obscures the point that it was considered suspicious that the stranger should know the labourer's name.

9   Pope, *Essay on Man*, IV. 204: 'The rest is all but leather or prunella'.

10   A leading Whig politician, M.P. for Northamptonshire, and a close political colleague of Lord Milton.

11   *2 Henry VI*, IV. iv. 31–2 and 35–6.

12   For Clare's view of Cobbett see also pp. 299–300.

13   'a country professing' is written over 'humanity' which is deleted.

14   *Macbeth*, V. v. 26–8.

15   The titles of Paine's three most famous works; for Clare's view of Paine see pp. 294 and 304–5, note 54.

APPENDIX

The Cambridge Chronicle, 24 December 1830

On Sunday morning, about one o'clock, the premises occupied by Mr Clark, a Scotch farmer, situate in a place called Stowgate, about midway between Deeping St James and Crowland, Lincolnshire, were discovered to be on fire by the persons upon watch, and before assistance could arrive were enveloped in flames. Crowland, the Deepings, and their neighbourhood, poured out their population, to stop the progress of the devouring element, but with very little effect. A barn more than 70 feet long by 50 wide in which were 60 quarters of wheat and other valuable property, an adjoining building containing a fixed thrashing and dressing machine, a stack the produce of 70 acres of beans, 3 stacks of wheat, stalls large enough for feeding fifty beast, and the stables, were entirely consumed; and with them many valuable animals, including 12 fat beast 2 milch cows, 4 horses, and a number of pigs! The cries of the poor animals for relief were painful in the extreme, and the wreck when the sabbath daylight came, more horrible than can well be conceived. The loss sustained is estimated at from £2,000 to £3,000. A dwelling-house, about 50 yards from the barn was saved. Mr Clark is highly respected in the neighbourhood, employs many labourers, and is considered an excellent master. The labourers are fully employed and well paid, receiving from 12s. to 16s. a week. Mr C. is fortunately pretty well covered by insurance in the Sun Fire-office.

On Thursday morning, the 16th inst. about nine o'clock, a person of rather gentlemanly appearance, about 60 years of age, was seen passing through Stradishall, ten miles from Bury, in a decent gig, and was observed to drop some papers, which on being picked up were found to be of an inflammatory, but very incoherent nature, threatening 'to put the farmers in bodily fear, &c. if the labourers were not better paid,' and signed with the formidable name of 'Swing'. The gig was immediately followed by

Mr Brown, steward to Mr Rayner, of Stradishall, who succeeded in having the person apprehended at Stoke by Clare. Several torn papers, of a similar character, and exactly corresponding with the handwriting of those which he was seen to drop, were found in his boots and upon his person; and others were picked up in Stradishall and Hundon, of which the following are specimens:-
'England! Beware that you do not bring Vengeance down upon your Heads by Robbing the Poor.
  'Swing.'
'If you dont behave better and give the Poor Man his due I will visit you or my name is not
'Swing.'
  'You Clergy, ye Vipers, you love Tithes, Cummin, and Mint; ye are men-eaters and not soul-savers, but Blind leaders of the Blind, twice dead, plucked up by the Roots.'
On being conveyed before the magistrates, he stated that his name was Joseph Saville, that he came from a place near Ampthill, in Bedfordshire, a collector of straw plait. He had upon him no less a sum than five hundred and eighty pounds which he deposited in the Clare branch of the Bury and Suffolk bank; and from an order-book it appears he has travelled through almost every county in England – latterly in Yorkshire. He had upon his list the names of two tradesmen in Bury, where he is known to be a traveller in business. He has been committed to Bury gaol, where he has since confessed having sent a very extravagant but harmless letter to the post-master. Unless additional evidence can be brought, it is thought that the character of the offence with which he is charged does not exceed that of misdemeanour. In politics as well as plait, he appears to be a true and worthy disciple of Cobbett. He has expressed great satisfaction at the return of Hunt for Preston. The papers found upon him have been transmitted to the Home Secretary's Office, where a comparison of them with others will likely afford a further elucidation of Mr Saville's career. – On Monday evening his son arrived at Bury, and was admitted to him in gaol. – Mr S. formerly resided at Gamlingay, in this county, & regularly attended Cambridge market.

LYNN, Dec. 22

At a recent tithe audit of the Bishop of Peterborough, held at Terrington, the farmers present, required a reduction 20l. per cent. The following is a copy of a letter, addressed by the venerable prelate, on the subject in question:-

To the occupiers of Land in Terrington St Clement's and Terrington John's.

GENTLEMEN, – I have learnt with surprise that you required at the last audit a deduction of 20 per cent. from the composition for which you had agreed with Mr Brackenbury. As the price of wheat in the Lynn Market is higher than the price at which the composition was calculated, you cannot be losers by the bargain; the money which you pay under the name of composition is the purchase money of every tenth shock; and since you now obtain at the Lynn market a higher price than that at which your own payments are estimated, there can be no ground for an abatement. Property in tythe is no less sacred than property in land: both kinds of property are under the protection of the law, and the law will protect them both alike. If therefore a proprietor of tythe requires as in the present case, a payment for them less than the tythes themselves are worth, it is consistent neither with law, nor with equity, to require a deduction, nor would you yourselves be gainers in the end, if tythes were diminished one half, or even if they were totally abolished; your rents would be increased proportionally, and perhaps in a greater proportion. In most cases, where land has been exonerated from tythe, the additional rent of the land has been greater than the previous amount of composition. You must see, therefore, that it is no more for your own interest, than it is just to the Rector, to require a diminution of your present composition. I would cheerfully take into consideration any well grounded complaints; but the deduction which you require, is not founded on any complaint that the composition is too high. Indeed you well know that the composition for the rectorial tythes of Terrington is lower than any other in Marshland. No other complaint was alleged at the late audit, than that in the present disturbed state of the country, your property was insecure. Now if any of you had really lost his property by the hands of an incendiary, I would readily assist such an unfortunate sufferer in any way I could; but to require that the Rector should lose a fifth of his property because there is a probability that your own may suffer, is alike contrary to reason and to justice. Hitherto there have been no fires in Marshland, and the precautions which have been taken will probably prevent any: but if any such misfortune should happen, I should act as I have already declared. – As this is the first time I have been Rector of Terrington, (a period of more than twenty three years,) that such an extravagant and unnecessary demand has been made upon me, I fear that advantage has been taken of the disturbed state of the country, (now drawing however to a close) to demand abatements which would otherwise never have occurred to you. But I will certainly not yield to intimidation, though I am ready to do every thing which strict justice requires. I confide in the laws of my country which equally protect the property of the landlord, the property of the tenant, and the property of the tythe owner. There is one point however which I will notice before I conclude. I understand that in some parts of the parish, the late harvest was deficient. In consideration of this deficiency and in consideration of this deficiency *alone*, I consent that Mr Brackenbury shall for the present year deduct 10 per cent from the composition which you have agreed to pay him, and as the reduction will be made at my suggestion I shall of course indemnify him for the loss. In this manner I do more than strict justice requires from me, and full as much as you yourselves when you duly reflect on the circumstances of the case can possibly desire.

    I am Gentlemen,

      Your faithful humble servant,

        HERBERT PETERBOROUGH.

HASTINGS, 7 *December*, 1830

The Cambridge Chronicle, 7 January 1831

Mr Joseph Savill. – The following is a letter relative to the individual who was committed to Bury gaol, on a charge of dropping papers of an inflammatory nature, signed Swing:

'To shew the character of Mr Savill, although we regret his folly in dropping papers of the nature described, he was the author of a Sick Society, for the benefit of the poor of the parish of Gamlingay, also a Sunday School, both of many years standing. About Christmas he provides a good dinner for the poor widows; has given a large quantity of potatoes to the poor; has been the means of distributing some hundreds of bushels of coals in winter; has made a proposition for the poor to dig up the waste ground, (of which there are many acres in the said parish) for their benefit; has been one of the first to lower his tenants' rents; is a warm advocate and supporter of Bible and Missionary Societies, and for promoting Religious Knowledge among Sailors and Soldiers. He has resided here 30 years, and has always been much respect.

Signed,

WILLIAM PAINE,	Parish officers of
JOHN OSBORN NORMAN,	Gamlingay, where
JOHN DEW,	the said J. Savill
THOMAS ARNOLD.	resides

Gamlingay, Jan. 1, 1831.

Glossary

aby *v.*, abide, endure
aguise *v.*, disguise
albe *conj.*, although, albeit
all my eye & peggy Martin *comb.*, load of nonsense
amede *v.*, ameed, requite, reward
an' *adj.*, and
anker *v.*, hanker
arter *prep.*, after
'atins *n. pl.*, matins, morning break for a snack
awkward squad *n.*, military recruits not yet trained for the ranks
awthorn *n.*, hawthorn

bannock *n.*, round, flat home-made loaf or cake
banter *v.*, cheat, trick, bamboozle
bantum *n.*, bantam, cock
barrack shoes *n.*, clumsy, ill-fitting shoes issued to soldiers
batter *adv.*, better
bawk *n.*, narrow strip of grass between ploughed fields
beaver *n.*, hat, originally of beaver fur
bent *n.*, twig, grass-stalk
blea *adj.*, bleak, exposed
blealy *adv.*, coldly, bleakly
blob *v.*, blab
bluid *n.*, blood
bluther *n.*, blather, nonsense
boaking taggs *n. pl.*, vomiting rabble
bottle holder *n.*, one who gives moral but not material support
brawn *n.*, boar, swine
bred *n.*, bread
brod *n.*, brad, nail
brush *v.*, rush
bruzzer *n.*, bruiser
budget *n.*, bag, pack
burthend *adj.* loaded, burdened

carsey *n., adj.*, kersey (after the village of Kersey), coarse cloth
causey *n.*, footpath, pavement, causeway
caytive *adj.*, caitiff, base, worthless, mean
chelp *v.*, chirp, chatter, gossip

chet *v.*, cheated
childern *n. pl.*, children
chink *v.*, make the sound of coins striking each other
cit *n.*, citizen
clack *n.*, chatter, boastful talk
clane *v.*, clean
cloa'hs, cloaths *n. pl.*, clothes
clout *v.*, clog
clown *n.*, rustic
coat *n.*, cote
cocking *adj.*, cocky, conceited
cos *v.*, curse
cot *n.*, cottage
cotter *n.*, cottager
cowboy *n.*, boy who looks after cows
cowslap *n.*, cowslip
crack *v.*, boast
crim. con. *n.*, criminal conversation, adultery
crimp *v.*, wrinkle
crowflower *n.*, buttercup, crowfoot, *Ranunculus acris*
crumble *n.*, crumb
culturd *adj.*, cultivated
cumber grounds, *n. pl.* useless things (originally trees), dregs
cum-mull *n.*, common call for cows to come for milking

Dagon *n.*, national deity of the Philistines, half man, half fish
dapple *n.*, dapple-grey horse
dareing *v.*, threatening
dead *n.*, death
deffley *adv.*, deftly, nimbly
didapper *n.*, dive-dapper, dab-chick, also used for other diving wildfowl
di'el *n.*, devil
dizen *v.*, dress showily, adorn
dotterel *n.*, pollarded tree
doused *adj.*, deuced, damned
dyke *n.*, ditch

earnest *n.*, money paid as first instalment especially to confirm credit
edding *n.*, heading; grass left at the end of a ploughed field where the plough turns
efeth *inter.*, in faith
eke *v.*, stretch out, lengthen, increase
eldern *n.*, elder tree, elderberry, *Sambucus nigra*
ell *n.*, measure of length (45")
elting *adj.*, moist, damp (of soil newly ploughed)

ettled *v.*, nettled

fane *n.*, vane
fell upon the town *comb.*, dependant on the parish poor rate
fet *v.*, fetch
feth, fex *n.*, faith, a petty oath
flaggy *adj.*, rushy, reedy
fleerin', fleering *n.*, *adj.*, gibing, sneering
fob *n.*, pocket
foil *v.*, trample down, tread under foot
forked *adj.*, testy, crabby
furlong *n.*, originally the length of furrow in a common field
furze kidder, *n.*, one who cuts furze for fuel

gamely *adj.*, merry
gang *v.*, go, depart, walk
gaud *n.*, gaudy show
gaul *v.*, gall
gern *v.*, grin
getty *adj.*, jetty, jet-black
gi *v.*, give
gif *conj.*, if
goody *n.*, familiar name for an old woman
grain *n.*, large branch of a tree, bough
green sickness *n.*, anaemic disease mostly affecting young women, giving
    a pale or greenish tinge to the complexion
grub(ble) *v.*, dig up, uproot
gulld *adj.*, of a hole or rut washed out by water

hant *v.*, haven't
head ach *n.*, common poppy, *Papaver rhoeas*
heben *n.*, ebon, ebony
heir *v.*, inherit
higgle *v.*, haggle, buy and sell as a pedlar
hight *adj.*, called, named
hing, *v.*, hang
hipt *adj.*, corrupted
hod *v.*, had
horse blob *n.*, marsh-marigold, *Caltha palustris*
hurd *n.*, *v.*, hoard

janant, *n.*, giant
joul *n.*, jowl

kingcup, king cup *n.*, (1) summer buttercup, crowfoot , such as *Ranunculus*

acris (2) lesser celandine, *R. ficaria*
knappers *n. pl.*, knees

lawn *n.*, (1) greensward, open space, small pasture (2) fine linen
leman *n.*, lover, sweetheart
light *v.*, lighten
ling *n.*, (1) heath (2) heather, *Calluna vulgaris*
loath *adj.*, Clare's spelling of 'loth'
loo *v.*, love
loose *v.*, Clare's spelling of 'lose'
losel *n.*, profligate, rake, ne'er-do-well
lurcher *n.*, (1) dog used in hare coursing (2) swindler

macaroney *n.*, macaroni, eighteenth-century dandy imitating continental
    fashions
mak(e) gamely *comb. adj.*, making fun of, mocking, jeering
maul *v.*, labour, toil, drag along wearily
mavis *n.*, mistle thrush or storm cock, *Turdus viscivorus*
max *n.*, gin
millar thumb *n.*, small freshwater fish, *Cottus gobio*
mo *conj.*, more
moiler *n.*, labourer
mood *n.*, mud
mort *n.*, lot, large number
mun *v.*, must

nappy *n.*, strong ale
near *adv.*, Clare's spelling of 'ne'er'
netherd *n.*, neatherd, cowherd
nick *n.*, familiar name for the devil
no *adv., conj.*, now
nokt *v.*, knocked
nott *v.*, knot

od' rot him *comb.*, God rot him; oath common from about 1810
oratorial *adj.*, oratorical
outherod *v.*, outdo Herod (represented in medieval Mystery plays as a
    blustering tyrant)
overwartling *adj.*, contrary, cross-grained

pad *n.*, path
paridge *n.*, porridge
patronizer *n.*, patron
paviour *n.*, person who lays paving stones
peal *n.*, peel, baker's shovel, pole with a broad flat disk at the end for

thrusting loaves, pies, etc., into the oven and withdrawing them from it

pecker *n.*, hoe

pelf *n.*, money, ill-gotten gains

pepse *v.*, beat, pelt

pey'd *v.*, paid

pindard *n.*, pindar, person employed to impound strayed cattle

pine *v.*, starve

pish *inter.*, exclamation of contempt

plate *v.*, plait

pluther *n.*, blather

pooty *n.*, landsnail, *Capaea*, particularly *C. nemoralis*

printers devil *n.*, errand-boy in a printing office

puff *n.*, advertisement containing exaggerated or false praise

pye *n.*, magpie

quak *v.*, croak, squawk, caw

racket *n.*, gaiety, social excitement; *v.*, live a gay life

ramping *adj.*, coarse, luxuriant

reak *v.*, wreak

roast *n.*, roost

rotten *n.*, rotten wood

rotten borough *n.*, one of the boroughs which, before the Reform Bill in 1832, were found have no real constituency

rouge *n.*, rogue

rougish *adj.*, roguish

rout *n.*, party, social gathering

rowl *v.*, roll

runnel *n.*, stream, brook, rill

St Thomas tide *n.*, St Thomas eve, 20 Dec.

sap *v.*, undermine

schollard *n.*, an intentionally ignorant version of 'scholar'

scrany *adj.*, wild, distracted, crazy

scrat *v.*, scratch

sea roamer *n.*, (1) beachcomber (2) pirate

seely *adj.*, silly

sherk *n.*, shark

shoety *n.*, shoe-lace

shoffle *v.*, shuffle

shoon *n. pl.*, shoes

sich, sick *adj.*, such

sink *n.*, pool or pit formed in the ground for receiving waste water, sewage, etc; cesspool

slive *v.*, sneak
snailhorn *n.*, snail-shell, whether inhabited or not
snob *n.*, colloquialism for shoemaker
snubbled *adj.*, short and stumpy
spavin *n.*, disease of horse's hock joint, resulting in lameness
splawfoot *adj.*, splay-foot, clumsy
squash *v.*, splash
standards *n. pl.*, upright pieces of timber of standard measurement
strapper *n.*, possibly =understrapper, a subordinate
strouting *adj.*, strutting
struggle *n.* , variant of strag or straggle; thin-growing straggling crop
swaily *adj.* , shady, cool
swipes *n. pl.*, cheap, inferior beer
swop *v.*, swoop

teaze *v.*, irritate
then *conj.*, Clare's usual spelling of 'than'
thimble rig *n.*, a swindling game usually played with three thimbles and
    a peg which was ostensibly placed under one of them, an unfair game
    well known among the frequenters of races and fairs
thrum *v.*, twang
to'k *n.*, turk, sadist
tother *pron.*, the other
touk *n.*, talk
town *n.*, usually used by Clare in the sense of village
trepan *v.*, trap, ensnare, beguile
truckle *v.*, submit, cringe
turk *n.*, sadist, tyrant
twig *v.*, understand
twitch *n.*, couch grass, *Agropyron repens*
tyke *n.*, churl
tythe *n.*, tithe

unkend *adj.*, unrecognised
usuage *n.*, usage

vermint *n.*, vermin, any animal or bird injurious to game

wanting, *adj.*, needy
warp *v.*, entwine, weave, applied by Clare to the bending of the sticks
    which form the foundation of the covering for a gypsy's camp; also
    used of the building of a bird's nest
were *v.*, Clare's usual spelling of 'where'
whimsey *n.*, whim
whittler *n.*, 'provincial term of censure on any master who constantly

urges his servants to extra work like an overseer of slaves' (Clare, Pet.
  MS B1, p. 122)
wimper *v.*, ripple, meander
withouten *prep.*, without
witling *adj.*, talking aimlessly
wod *n.*, word
wok *n.*, work
wonty *n.*, warrant 'ee

yclypd *adj.*, called by the name of

Bibliography

The Early Poems of John Clare 1804–1822, ed. Eric Robinson and David Powell (Oxford: Clarendon Press, 1989)

John Clare, *Poems of the Middle Period 1822–1837*, vols. 1–2, ed. Eric Robinson, David Powell and P.M.S. Dawson (Clarendon Press: Oxford, 1996)

John Clare, *Poems of the Middle Period 1822–1837*, vols. 3–4, ed. Eric Robinson, David Powell and P.M.S. Dawson (Clarendon Press: Oxford, 1998)

The Later Poems of John Clare 1837–1864, ed. Eric Robinson and David Powell (2 vols., Clarendon Press: Oxford, 1984)

Oxford Authors *John Clare*, ed. Eric Robinson and David Powell (Oxford: Oxford University Press, 1984)

John Clare, *The Summons*, ed. by Eric Robinson (Market Drayton: Tern Press, 1989)

John Clare, *The Hue & Cry: A Tale of the Times*, ed. by Eric Robinson (Market Drayton: Tern Press, 1990)

The Letters of John Clare, ed. Mark Storey (Oxford: Clarendon Press, 1985)

John Clare By Himself, ed. Eric Robinson and David Powell (Ashington and Manchester: The Mid Northumberland Arts Group and Carcanet Press, 1996)

Selected Poems and Prose of John Clare, ed. Eric Robinson and Geoffrey Summerfield, (Oxford University Press, 1967)

John Clare: The Living Year 1841, ed. Tim Chilcott (Nottingham: Trent Editions, 1999)

John Barrell, *The Idea of Landscape and the Sense of Place 1730–1840, An Approach to the Poetry of John Clare* (Cambridge: Cambridge University Press, 1972).

[John Bridges] Peter Whalley, *The History and Antiquities of Northamptonshire. Compiled from the Manuscript Collections of the late Learned Antiquary John Bridges, Esq.* (2 vols., Oxford: Sold by T. Payne, London; D. Prince and J. Cooke, Oxford; and Mr. Lacy, Northampton, 1791)

William Cobbett, *Rural Rides*, ed. George Woodcock (London, Penguin, 1967)

Stephen Michael Colclough, *Voicing loss: versions of pastoral in the poetry of John Clare, 1817–1832* (Ph. D. thesis, Open University, 1996)

Charles Caleb Colton, *Lacon; or Many things in few words addressed to those who think* (19th ed., 2 vols., London: Longman, Hurst, Lees, Orme and Brown, 1823)

P.M.S. Dawson, 'John Clare – Radical?', *The John Clare Society Journal*, 11 (1992), 17–27

P.M.S. Dawson, 'Common Sense or Radicalism? Some Reflections on Clare's Politics', *Romanticism*, 2.1 (1996), 81–97

P.M.S. Dawson, 'Clare and the Ideology of "Common Sense"', *The John Clare Society Journal*, 16 (1997), 71–78

George Deacon, *John Clare and the Folk Tradition* (London: Sinclair Browne, 1983)

Ian Dyck, *William Cobbett and Rural Popular Culture* (Cambridge: Cambridge University Press, 1992)

Eric J. Evans, *Britain Before the Reform Act: Politics and Society 1815–1832* (London and New York: Longman, 1989)

C.V. Fletcher, *The Poetry of John Clare, with particular reference to poems written between 1837 and 1864* (M. Phil. thesis, University of Nottingham, 1973)

Kevin Gilmartin, *Print Politics: The press and radical opposition in early nineteenth-century England* (Cambridge: Cambridge University Press, 1996)

John Goodridge and Kelsey Thornton, 'John Clare: the trespasser', in Hugh Haughton, Adam Phillips and Geoffrey Summerfield (eds.), *John Clare in Context* (Cambridge: Cambridge University Press, 1994), pp. 87–129

N. Harte and R. Quinault, *Land and Society in Britain, 1700–1914* (Manchester, 1996)

Elizabeth K. Helsinger, *Rural Scenes and National Representation: Britain, 1815–1850* (Princeton: Princeton University Press, 1997)

Bob Heyes, 'John Clare and the Militia', *The John Clare Society Journal*, 4 (1985), 48–54

Christopher Hill, *Liberty Against the Law: Some Sevententh-Century Controversies* (London: Allen Lane, 1996)

Eric Hobsbawm and George Rudé, *Captain Swing* (1969: Harmondsworth: Penguin Books, 1973)

Harry Hopkins, *The Long Affray: The Poaching Wars in Britain* (London: Macmillan, 1986)

David Hume, *Enquiries concerning Human Understanding and concerning the Principles of Morals* (1777), ed. L.A. Selby-Bigge, third ed. with text revised and notes by P.H. Nidditch (Oxford: Clarendon Press, 1975)

Stephen Knight, *Robin Hood: A Complete Study of the English Outlaw* (Oxford: Blackwell, 1994)

Vicesimus Knox, *Essays Moral and Literary* (1786; 3 vols., London: G. Offer and T. Tagg, 1819)

J.M. Lee, *Stamford and the Cecils: A Study in Political Control 1700–1885* (B.Litt. thesis, Oxford, 1957)

John Lucas, *John Clare* (Plymouth: Northcote House, 1994)

John Lucas, 'Clare's Politics', in Hugh Haughton, Adam Phillips and Geoffrey Summerfield (eds.), *John Clare in Context* (Cambridge:

Cambridge University Press, 1994), pp. 148–177

James McKusick, 'William Cobbett, John Clare, and the Agrarian Politics of the English Revolution', in Timothy Martin and Nigel Smith (eds.), *British Literary Radicalism, 1650–1830: from Revolution to Revolution* (Cambridge: Cambridge University Press, forthcoming)

Rohan McWilliam, *Popular Politics in Nineteenth-Century England* (London: Routledge, 1998)

G.E. Mingay, *Land and Society in England 1750–1980* (London and New York: Longman, 1994)

Charles-Louis de Secondat Montesquieu, *The Spirit of Laws*, translated from the french by Thomas Nugent (2 vols., London: J. Collingwood, etc., 1823)

J.M. Neeson, *Commoners: common right, enclosure and social change in England, 1700–1820* (Cambridge: Cambridge University Press, 1993)

Roy Palmer, *A Ballad History of England* (London: Batsford, 1979)

Robert L. Patten, *George Cruikshank's Life, Times and Art* (New Brunswick, New Jersey: Rutgers University Press, 2 vols. 1992 and 1996)

Harold Perkin, *The Origins of Modern English Society 1780–1880* (London: Routledge and Kegan Paul, 1969)

The Correspondence of Alexander Pope, ed. George Sherburn (5 vols., Oxford: Clarendon Press, 1956)

[David Powell], *Catalogue of the John Clare Collection in the Northampton Public Library* (Northampton: County Borough of Northampton, 1964)

Edgell Rickword (ed.), *Radical Squibs & Loyal Ripostes: Satirical Pamphlets of the Regency Period, 1819–1821* (Bath: Adams & Dart, 1971)

[Joseph Ritson], *Robin Hood: A Collection Of all the Ancient Poems, Songs, and Ballads, Now Extant, Relative to that Celebrated English Outlaw: To which are prefixed Historical Anecdotes of His Life* (1795; London: C. Stocking, 1823) (Item 344 in Northampton Public Library)

Eric Robinson, 'John Clare (1793–1864) and James Plumptre (1771–1832), "A Methodistical Parson"', *Transactions of the Cambridge Bibliographical Society*, 11 (1996), 59–88

Edward Royle and James Walvin, *English Radicals and Reformers 1760–1848* (Brighton: The Harvester Press, 1982)

E.A Smith, *A Queen on Trial: The Affair of Queen Caroline* (Stroud: Alan Sutton, 1993)

Olivia Smith, *The Politics of Language 1791–1819* (Oxford: Clarendon Press, 1984)

Mark Storey (ed.), *Clare: The Critical Heritage* (London and Boston: Routledge & Kegan Paul, 1973)

E.P. Thompson, *Customs in Common* (London: The Merlin Press, 1991)

F.M.L. Thompson, *English Landed Society in the Nineteenth Century* (London: Routledge & Kegan Paul, 1963)

J.W. and Anne Tibble, *John Clare: A Life* (London: Cobden-Sanderson, 1932)

The New Testament Translated by William Tyndale 1534, ed. N. Hardy Wallis (Cambridge: Cambridge University Press, 1938)

Alan Vardy, 'Clare And Political Equivocation', *The John Clare Society Journal*, 18 (1999), 37–48

Marcus Wood, *Radical Satire and Print Culture 1790–1822* (Oxford: Clarendon Press, 1994)

Index of Titles and First Lines